THE ARCHITECTURE TRAVELER

A GUIDE TO 263 KEY AMERICAN BUILDINGS

Revised Edition

THE ARCHITECTURE TRAVELER

A GUIDE TO 263 KEY AMERICAN BUILDINGS

SYDNEY LeBLANC

Revised Edition

W.W. NORTON & COMPANY
New York • London

Copyright © 2005, 2000, 1996, 1993 by Sydney LeBlanc

Prior to 2000, editions were published as The Whitney Guide 20th CENTURY AMERICAN ARCHITECTURE

Manufacturing by Quebecor World Kingsport Press
Book design by Jay Anning; revisions by Ken Gross
Composition by Ken Gross
Production manager: Leeann Graham

Library of Congress Cataloging-in-Publication Data
LeBlanc, Sydney.
    The architecture traveler : a guide to 263 key American buildings / Sydney LeBlanc. – Revised edition.
        p.   cm.
    Includes bibliographical references and indexes.
    ISBN 0-393-73174-X (pbk.)
    1. Architecture—United States—20th century—Guidebooks. I. Title.

NA712 .L4 2005
720' .973'0904—dc22   2004065971

ISBN 0-393-73174-X (pbk.)

W. W. Norton & Company, Inc., 500 Fifth Avenue, New York, N.Y. 10110
www.wwnorton.com
W. W. Norton & Company Ltd., Castle House, 75/76 Wells St., London W1T 3QT

0 9 8 7 6 5 4 3 2 1

To my parents, Madge and Louis LeBlanc,
and to Michael Gianturco

CONTENTS

PREFACE TO THE REVISED EDITION

The world of architecture has experienced a sea change since I began writing the first edition of this book almost twenty years ago. Then, to most Americans, racing off with a camera and binoculars to see a building seemed like an obscure, almost eccentric pursuit. But these days, it's very different. Architecture has arrived as an exciting new pulse-point of popular culture, with its own set of superstars—celebrated personalities and buildings, too.

With its newfound popularity, architecture is creating quite a stir. Not long ago, I stood in a block-long line to see *My Architect*. This documentary on Louis Kahn was such a hit in art cinemas that it later crossed over to mainstream theaters and was nominated for an Academy Award. Trying to photograph Frank Gehry's new Walt Disney Concert Hall in Los Angeles recently, I found myself elbow to elbow with an excited crowd of fellow picture-takers that made it hard to get a clear shot.

Destination buildings like the Disney Concert Hall are certainly something to see. It's also fascinating to witness how they change the chemistry of their surroundings, shining a fresh light on nearby architectural treasures you might otherwise overlook. On a visit to see Gehry's Disney extravaganza, for example, you could easily take in Los Angeles City Hall, a Jazz Age masterpiece, and Arata Isozaki's Museum of Contemporary Art, among several others.

The new architectural fascination is also having the happy effect of encouraging the conservation of endangered buildings and making many of them accessible for the first time in decades. For example, Mies van der Rohe's 1950 Farnsworth House in Plano, Illinois, recently in danger of being carted off or demolished, is now open to the public on a regular basis, thanks to the National Trust for Historic Preservation and The Landmarks Preservation Council of Illinois, which joined forces to buy and save the mid-century masterpiece.

In our country, there are many great buildings to see and more opportunities than ever to see them. Walking tours offered in cities from coast to coast immerse visitors in important buildings and their neighborhoods. They often draw sell-out crowds.

Still, as you leaf through the book, there may be buildings that don't immediately entice you. Please bear in mind that buildings, like artists, writers, and film stars, tend to slip in and out of the spotlight. A structure that seems outdated today might seem like a classic tomorrow.

Wherever you go, I hope you will find many buildings in the book to make your trip more worthwhile, more interesting, and more fun. And whenever you go, I'm sure you'll find that architecture traveling offers its own reward: the only way to truly appreciate a building is to see it for yourself.

INTRODUCTION

The architecture traveler is an adventurous soul, willing to plan an entire trip to see a special building; to search for half a day to find it; to linger for hours on doorsteps in hopes of being invited inside. In part, this determination reflects a disconcerting reality. Architecture is all around us, and yet it is not always easy to see. Much of the most interesting work is hidden from view, which makes our visible and possibly accessible architecture all the more attractive.

This book examines 263 important American buildings and provides guidance and information to help you visit them: addresses, phone numbers, days and times the buildings are open, Web sites, regular tour schedules, and the prospects of arranging personal or group tours. Because the book is organized chronologically, it also provides a compact historical overview of American architecture since 1900 exemplified by the masterpieces still in existence.

How have I selected 263 buildings from among the thousands that deserve your attention? First, I have included the recognized masterpieces of twentieth-century architecture. These buildings, such as Frank Lloyd Wright's Robie House in Chicago and Ludwig Mies van der Rohe's Seagram Building in New York City, have profoundly affected the course of architectural history. For the remaining selections, the criteria are naturally more subjective and varied. I have tried to strike a balance encompassing diverse locations, building types, and architects, and between early and late representations of major architects' styles and careers.

In many cities, local landmarks like New York City's Chrysler Building or Seattle's Space Needle have become beloved civic symbols; they also give travelers a sense of the city shared. On the regional level, buildings like Irving Gill's La Jolla Woman's Club, John Staub's Bayou Bend in Houston, and Addison Mizner's work in Palm Beach so captured popular yearnings that they became the basis of styles that endure to this day. Alongside the older styles, new regional architectures continue to evolve, and works like Cameron Armstrong's metal houses in Houston offer contemporary responses to context and climate. Sometimes, an assemblage of buildings—rather than a single one—attracts our attention. The Art Deco District in Miami Beach and the Usonian community in Mount Pleasant, New York, are good examples.

Foreign architects have produced a number of America's outstanding buildings, and the book directs you to historic landmarks such as the Farnsworth House by Ludwig Mies van der Rohe and the Mount Angel Abbey Library by Alvar Aalto. In our present and much-heralded age of globalization, the "architects without borders" phenomenon continues to create new classic landmarks: Tadao Ando's Museum of Modern Art in Fort Worth, the Contemporary Arts Center by Zaha Hadid in Cincinnati, and the Seattle Central Library by Rem Koolhaas.

In my selection, I have favored buildings that are accessible or that can be seen from the street. Some of these buildings are well preserved and obviously cherished. Others, like Buckminster Fuller's Union Tank Car Dome in Baton Rouge, Louisiana, are rusting away in virtual abandonment.

Many of our revered monuments are sadly gone now, with the intentional destruction of the World Trade Center being the country's most tragic loss. But hope springs from the rebuilding effort at Ground Zero, and in other places as well. Important prototypes like Fuller's Dymaxion House and Albert Frey's Aluminaire House have been dismantled and reassembled in newly accessible locations.

Everyone who loves great buildings can also take heart at recent sensitive restorations of architectural classics like Richard Neutra's Kaufmann House in Palm Springs, Frank Lloyd Wright's Robie House in Chicago, and Rudolph Schindler's house and studio in Los Angeles. When renovations take place alongside sensitive new additions, as we find at the Los Angeles Central Library, the Palace of the Legion of Honor in San Francisco, and the Davis Museum at Wellesley College, among others, we have the pleasure of seeing buildings evolve across time, spanning decades and generations.

A provocative younger generation of architects has recently made a strong national mark. The "Solar Umbrella" house by Lawrence Scarpa and Angela Brooks in Venice, California; the Greenwich Street [Project] by Winka Dubbeldam; Dia:Beacon by OpenOffice Architects; and the Starlight Theatre by Studio Gang/O'Donnell are among the new works included here. These and others show a hopeful evolution toward an architecture that is both intellectually honest and widely appreciated. This evolution lays a remarkable groundwork for the twenty-first century: a passion for quality, a renewed dedication to materials and craftsmanship, and a desire to create a new American architecture that will capture the present and last over time.

ACKNOWLEDGMENTS

T he *Architecture Traveler* and I have benefited from the help of many people. I would like to thank the architects who provided information and photographs of their projects. The owners of many landmark structures have also generously provided pictures and information. I am grateful for their cooperation and, especially, for their crucial roles in maintaining our preserve of important buildings, often against considerable odds.

In the course of developing the early editions of the book, I was fortunate to have the attention of several superb professionals: Cornelia Guest, Roberto de Alba, and Micaela Porta. Stephen Fox provided a helpful overview of new Texas buildings. Lee Harris Pomeroy, FAIA, has unstintingly shared his thoughts about what makes architecture great.

My personal thanks go to my husband, Michael Gianturco. His impressive observations about American buildings have added a valued perspective to my work.

The present book has gained enormously from its exceptional editorial, production, and marketing team. I am grateful to Nancy Green, my editor at W. W. Norton, for her enthusiasm and support, as well as for her guiding intelligence throughout the process. Working with her, and with assistant editor Andrea Costella, has been a pleasure. I also admire Jay Anning's original design for the book and the striking new cover design by Michael Quanci. Leeann Graham, production manager, has assured that all the hopes and efforts poured into the book are finally and beautifully realized. Kevin Olsen, the marketing manager, has helped the book find its way into its readers' hands. Thank you all.

January 2005
New York City

How to Use This Guide

The main organization of the guidebook is chronological by date of completion (except for a small number of on-going projects, multiple entries, and works in progress). This order is supplemented by two practical cross-references in the back of the book: an alphabetical index of the architects included, and a geographical index, ordered by location. Web site addresses are included in the Location Index. With this triple approach, I hope to make the book more useful and your travels more enjoyable.

Taking advantage of the chronological listing of buildings, you may enjoy browsing through the decades of American architecture. If you are particularly interested in the work of an individual architect or firm, the Index of Architects lists those featured in the book and the locations of their buildings described here. When traveling to a specific city, refer to the Index of Locations to find all the buildings listed under that particular location and its surroundings.

Visitor information is contained in both the boxed heading (the address) and in the final paragraph of each listing: phone number, days and times the building is normally open and closed, the availability and times of regularly scheduled tours, and information on arranging special tours. Admission is charged at some buildings; however, I have not attempted to specify prices, which are always subject to change. I advise you to call ahead if admission charges are a concern.

Finally, while many of the buildings included in this guide are accessible all or some of the time, others are resolutely private. Please be mindful of the owners' right to privacy when you visit.

The "funny little house" Frank Lloyd Wright began at age twenty-two with money borrowed from his boss, Louis Sullivan, is a legendary monument and the architectural laboratory of his first golden age. This earliest of Wright's major works shows all his major influences: his love of nature, music, Japanese design, Froebel blocks, and his admiration of Louis Sullivan.

FRANK LLOYD WRIGHT HOME AND STUDIO, 1889-1909

951 Chicago Avenue
   at Forest Avenue
Oak Park, Illinois

Frank Lloyd Wright

Wright lived here for twenty years, and he built the house and studio in four main stages. Due to constant tinkering, it was really a work in progress, remarkable for the clarity and sophistication of his early ideas. The main house facing Forest Avenue is striking for its sharply pitched roof, brown-stained shingles, and olive trim. Its clear geometry refutes fussy Victorian ornament, and its coloring and cladding follow Wright's deep conviction that architecture should be in harmony with the natural landscape.

Inside, Wright is clearly on the way to the open floor plan, and firmly in control of the grand gesture. For example, the children's playroom features a magnificent barrel-vaulted ceiling that looks ecclesiastical but is said to have been perfect for bouncing balls. The colors have character, especially the earthy red walls and cream ceiling of the master bedroom—all the more beautiful for the evocative murals of Indians on the plains painted by artist Orlando Gianninni. Woodworking is extensive throughout the house and some of Wright's notoriously uncomfortable furniture is also in evidence.

A high point is Wright's famous studio and office, one of his great (and most personal) architectural spaces. The evolving Prairie style can be seen in the central rectangular entry, which is flanked by two octagonal drums. The taller clerestory-windowed structure houses the drafting room, a tiered structure where the eye seems to spiral up toward the light, anticipating by many decades the Guggenheim Museum plan.

The property fell into disrepair after Wright deserted his house and family in 1909. Now a National Historic Landmark, it is restored to its 1909 configuration and magically recaptures his spirit as well. The Frank Lloyd Wright Preservation Trust administers the property and offers tours at 11:00 AM, 1:00 PM, and 3:00 PM Monday through Friday and on weekends continuously from 11:00 AM to 3:30 PM. Closed Thanksgiving, Christmas, and New Year's Day. Self-guided walking tours of the Prairie School Historic District—the world's greatest concentration of Wright architecture, including more than twenty houses and Unity Temple—take place daily from 10:00 AM to 5:00 PM. For information on tours and special Preservation Trust programs, call (708) 848-1976.

ONE SOUTH CALVERT BUILDING, 1901

**201 East Baltimore Street
Baltimore, Maryland**

D.H. Burnham and Company

Only a few Chicago-style skyscrapers were built in the eastern United States, and even fewer are still in existence. One South Calvert—the only structure of its kind in Baltimore—represents the steel-framed skyscraper construction method developed in Chicago in the last two decades of the nineteenth century. Its design came from D.H. Burnham and Company, one of Chicago's pioneer skyscraper architects.

Originally the Continental Trust Building, this 16-story structure is clad primarily in stone, but brick and terra-cotta were also used. Besides the steel frame, the Chicago method of skyscraper construction is evidenced in the tall arches at the building's base and in the triple windows placed inside the arches. Ornamentation remains in the classical tradition, with Renaissance Revival pediments over some of the windows; at the top there is a row of columns under a decorated terra-cotta frieze and cornice.

The strength of the building was supremely tested in Baltimore's blistering fire of 1904 when the skyscraper flamed from top to bottom. Its "completely fireproof" interiors burned out entirely in the estimated 2,500-degree blaze, but the structure survived intact, so the fireproofing methods were considered successful on those grounds. In the ensuing restoration, the fire damage was repaired, although the ornamental cornice was not replaced.

Today, the building houses a bank on the ground floor and offices above. During office hours the lobby is accessible, and its marble walls and brass-railed grand staircases are essentially intact.

The bastion of culture that is the Metropolitan Museum of Art in Central Park—an expanse that runs from East 80th to East 84th Street—originated as a colorful Gothic structure designed by Calvert Vaux, erected between 1874 and 1880 and twice expanded unsatisfactorily by other architects. As the collections and influence grew, a larger building with a more cohesive appearance and plan was required. The dean of New York architects, Richard Morris Hunt, received the commission, and although he died before its completion, he knew that this would be his most enduring monument.

METROPOLITAN MUSEUM OF ART, 1902 (CENTRAL ENTRANCE PAVILION)

Fifth Avenue at 82nd Street New York, New York

Richard Morris Hunt

Hunt was the first American architect to study at the Ecole des Beaux Arts and his design recalls the grand public monuments of Paris. Hunt's scheme included a massive central entry section with wings enclosing courtyards. Only the main entrance was completed, in 1902, by his son, Richard Howland Hunt. The center still holds, despite repeated expansions since that time. It manages to assert tremendous authority and remains welcoming at the same time because of its broad front stairway and its magnificent arched entry flanked by columns. Medallion portraits of the old masters and personifications of Architecture, Sculpture, Painting, and Music humanize this towering façade.

In 1906, the next wave of expansion was occasioned by a large bequest from Jacob S. Rogers and the prospect of receiving the munificent collection of J. Pierpont Morgan, the museum's president. A new master plan, and the side wings along Fifth Avenue, were designed by McKim, Mead & White.

Contemporary expansions by Kevin Roche and John Dinkeloo in the 1970s and 1980s brought the gridded, reflective glass walls of modern architecture right up against the old classic structure. The light and airy new additions are striking in their own way, but Hunt's main hall has remained one of the truly awe-inspiring spaces in New York City.

The museum is open Tuesday through Thursday, 9:30 AM to 5:15 PM; Friday and Saturday, 9:30 AM to 8:45 PM; Sunday 9:30 AM to 5:15 PM. Closed on Monday (except national Monday holidays when it is open), and on Thanksgiving and Christmas. Tours take place daily (reservations are required for groups). For information, call (212) 535-7710.

4

The Flatiron Building owes its shape to the triangular slice of land on which it rests, where Broadway cuts a diagonal from East 22nd Street to Fifth Avenue; it owes its name to the common household appliance of the day.

This early New York skyscraper was designed by the famous Chicago architect, Daniel Burnham, a pioneer in the erection of tall buildings and a major force behind the Chicago World's Fair of 1893, which revived a preference for classical buildings at monumental scale.

With the design of the Flatiron Building, Burnham explored the creative possibilities for the skyscraper. Over 20 stories tall, the design employs skyscraper construction—a steel frame encased in masonry—with limestone blocks elaborately ornamented in alternating decorative bands from top to bottom. Its infamous waterpowered elevators have now been replaced with electric ones.

The Flatiron Building has become the centerpiece of a newly gentrified neighborhood filled with fashionable shops and upscale restaurants. It has also benefited from the delightful renovation of nearby Madison Park.

For general information, call (212) 477-0947.

With the ink barely dry on its design, the Rhode Island State Capitol building inspired a wave of statehouse construction across the country. Its 1892 publication in *American Architect* magazine revealed a streamlined version of the United States Capitol building in Washington, a classical white marble monument with symmetrical side wings, a central dome, and rotunda. Four domed tourelles frame the main dome, adding an extra flourish to the overall scheme.

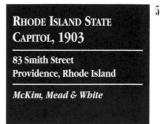

RHODE ISLAND STATE CAPITOL, 1903

**83 Smith Street
Providence, Rhode Island**

McKim, Mead & White

McKim, Mead & White's competition-winning entry pleased the Capitol Commission with its well-organized interior plan and authoritative appearance. Although the design was modified somewhat during construction, the finished building suits its City Beautiful setting atop Smith Hill; a grand, landscaped boulevard provides a ceremonial approach.

The Rhode Island State Capitol is open Monday to Friday 8:30 AM to 5:00 PM. Closed weekends and holidays. Tours are conducted in the mornings only. For information, call (401) 222-2357.

CARSON PIRIE SCOTT, 1904

**One South State Street
at Madison
Chicago, Illinois**

Louis H. Sullivan

A popular turn-of-the-century theme was the need to create a new architecture for the new century. In practice, the advance was more evolutionary than revolutionary. The Carson Pirie Scott store is virtually a freeze-frame of the transition, with one foot firmly planted in the nineteenth century and the other in the twentieth. Designed by Louis Sullivan in 1899 and constructed in two stages culminating in 1904, the building not only spans the two centuries in time but also in style—an extraordinary combination of the traditional and the modern.

Carson Pirie Scott is, in fact, virtually two buildings in one. The bold "Chicago-window" grid of the upper 10 stories is crisply modern. Yet it is superimposed above a two-story classical base embellished with cast-iron panels of wreaths and tendrils (which Sullivan also designed). Sullivan unified the ostensibly competing elements with a curved pavilion of tall colonettes at the corner. For practical purposes, the cornerpiece provides a gracious entry to the store, as well as an off-setting element of vertical energy in an otherwise strongly horizontal composition.

Sullivan's genius at successfully combining multiple stylistic possibilities was matched by his remarkable handling of the new load-bearing steel frame. He was able to free his masonry building from unnecessary mass, which in turn gave him the freedom to design the building in the most modern way.

At the time he designed Carson Pirie Scott, Sullivan was considered to be the master of tall commercial buildings—"skyscrapers" of the times—and the store is considered one of the first great examples of a modern style.

Carson Pirie Scott is a landmark fixture in downtown Chicago, and the store is open during regular retail hours. The store's telephone number is (312) 641-7000. The Chicago Architecture Foundation also includes the store in some of its tours. For information, call the foundation at (312) 922-3432.

Frank Lloyd Wright found a welcome early patron in Darwin Martin. President of the Larkin Company, a prosperous mail-order firm, Martin tried Wright out on a small house for his sister and brother-in-law (the Barton House at 118 Summit Avenue) in his family's compound-to-be. Wright's success led Martin to commission a series of homes, and his corporate offices, the famous Larkin Building (demolished in 1950), that considerably advanced Wright's architecture and his career.

DARWIN D. MARTIN HOUSE, 1904

125 Jewett Parkway
Buffalo, New York

Frank Lloyd Wright

Martin's family compound boasted a grand design on almost two acres near Frederick Law Olmsted's Delaware Park. The 10,000-square-foot main house, the largest of Wright's Prairie Style homes, is a multi-layered tawny brick residence in which Wright restates his simple prarie-home principles: long horizontal lines, interlocking planes, floating rooflines, bands of windows, integral decoration, and harmony with nature. Perhaps because this Prairie House is in the city, the gardens took on extraordinary importance. A pergola extended deep into the property, and there was a glass-roofed conservatory and birdhouse the size of a small house. Wright's original work also included a carriage house with chauffeur's apartment. A gardener's cottage and greenhouse came later.

In the unusually expansive and expensive main house, Wright advanced his quest of "breaking the box," obliterating the tightly compacted cubical room arrangements of Victorian design. Large rooms open easily into one another. Wright's genius for unified design ranged far and wide. Integral with the architecture, he designed oak furniture, stained-glass windows, carpets, fabrics, and lighting. In the main ground-floor rooms, Wright worked with his favorite golden colors, creating a soft golden glow which was sparked by the glint of gold-toned mortar cementing the Roman bricks.

The complex suffered terribly over the years. The Barton House, the gardener's cottage and greenhouse were sold off; the pergola, conservatory, and carriage house were demolished with apartments built in their place. In 1966 the State University of New York at Buffalo purchased the Martin and Barton houses. In 1994, SUNY and the nonprofit Martin House Restoration Corporation bought the rest of the property (except the Gardener's Cottage at 285 Woodward Avenue which is privately owned and impeccably restored) and began restoring and reconstructing the original complex. Completed buildings are open. In 2005, a new visitor's center by Harvard's Toshiko Mori brings an avant-garde addition. For information, call (716) 856-3858.

8

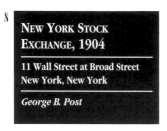
The New York Stock Exchange building captures a surprising turn-of-the-century contradiction: the longing for the richly ornamented classical architecture of the past in conjunction with the advances of modern technology. Following classical precedents, George Post designed the building as a classical Roman temple façade complete with arches, balustrades, massive columns, and a sculptured pediment filled with mythological figures. But behind the tall columns there is a glass "curtain wall," one of the first in New York City, that floods the cavernous interior trading floor with light.

The frenetic activity of Wall Street trading takes place in one of New York City's great architectural interiors. The exchange is open from 9:30 AM to 4:00 PM, Monday through Friday, except major holidays. Starting at 9:00 AM, the Visitors Center dispenses tickets for free, self-guided tours from the entrance at 20 Broad Street. A new computer-generated virtual trading floor by Asymptote opened in 1999. Advance reservations are required for groups of ten or more. For reservations or information, call (212) 656-5168.

N ew York's lively Soho district (*south of Houston* Street) offers a high concentration of turn-of-the-century cast-iron buildings and is probably the most intact such neighborhood in the United States. Nevertheless, the entire area was scheduled for demolition in the 1960s to make way for Robert Moses's urban dream of a Lower Manhattan Expressway. Soho is safe now, thanks to the Landmarks Preservation Commission founded in 1973.

SINGER LOFT BUILDING, 1904

561 Broadway
New York, New York

Ernest Flagg

The neighborhood manages to retain its gritty turn-of-the-century industrial air, even as the old buildings have become occupied with fashionable boutiques and art galleries.

The Singer Loft Building is an especially noteworthy—and beautiful—reminder of the time and the technology. An innovative composition of colored terra-cotta, glass, and steel, the building clearly foretells the coming of the glass curtain wall. Designed by New York architect Ernest Flagg for the Singer Sewing Machine Company, the 12-story L-shaped office and loft tower wraps the corner. The main façade on Broadway rises to a graceful arch below a cornice projecting one floor from the top. Using wrought iron rather than cast iron, Flagg created the delightfully curved balcony railing and tracery framing the great arch. This Broadway façade is echoed by a secondary façade around the corner on Prince Street, where the Singer name is still visible on the transom.

Ernest Flagg designed a number of important New York landmarks, including the venerable former Scribners' bookstore on Fifth Avenue. Lost now is his 47-story Singer Building and Tower at 149 Broadway, completed in 1908. The prominence of the newer Singer Building overshadowed the earlier and smaller structure in Soho, which came to be called "The Little Singer Building." Today it is the only one, and its loft floors contain homes and offices.

With the opening of Prada's Soho "Epicenter" store, on Broadway and Prince, the Singer Loft Building has gained a new visibility thanks to the stream of visitors who make their way to see Rem Koolhaas's signature interiors.

MINNESOTA STATE CAPITOL, 1905

75 Constitution Avenue
St. Paul, Minnesota

Cass Gilbert

The state of Minnesota was only thirty-seven years old when Cass Gilbert received the commission to design its capitol. Gilbert took as his model St. Peter's Basilica in Rome, and particularly Michaelangelo's famous dome for the Vatican. The dome is smaller here, but it is still the building's distinguishing feature, all the more so because of the gold-leaf ball that sits at its top. The gold ornamentation is further carried out in a robust gold-leaf sculpture group over the main entrance that shows a muscular charioteer marshalling four horses and riders, whose arms overflow with Minnesota products; a banner announces "Minnesota."

Up the grand front steps and through the tall archways, visitors enter into a massive rotunda that extends from the first floor to the dome. All four interior floors are lavishly fitted out with the more than twenty varieties of stone used in the halls, stairways, and chambers. Minnesota limestone from Mankato and Kasota is used on the walls throughout. Corridors feature vaulted ceilings decorated with hand-painted arabesques depicting Minnesota's agricultural abundance. Gilbert also commissioned the artwork that decorates the interiors.

The "grand floor" is the second floor, where the Senate, House of Representatives, and Supreme Court chambers are located. The Senate and House Chambers have been restored to their 1905 appearance with skylights, original colors, furnishings, and artwork.

Gilbert supervised construction and decoration of the Capitol. "In the old days," he said, "the architect, the painter, and the sculptor were frequently one and the same man. There is no reason they should not be so now."

While Gilbert was honored for his statehouse design, he is best known for the Woolworth Building in New York City, a then-startling Gothic skyscraper completed in 1913.

The Minnesota State Capitol is accessible from I-94 and I-35E in St. Paul. It is open 9:00 AM to 4:00 PM weekdays; 10:00 AM to 3:00 PM Saturday, and 1:00 to 4:00 PM on Sunday. Free guided tours offered by the Minnesota Historical Society begin on the hour until one hour before closing. The Capitol is closed Easter, Thanksgiving, Christmas, and New Year's Day. For recorded information call (651) 297-3521. Groups of ten or more must reserve two weeks in advance; the number to call for reservations is (651) 296-2881.

T his huge, white marble hotel fills a city block atop Nob Hill, where it is one of the city's most popular landmarks. Built by the daughter of a Comstock silver king, the original seven-story hotel was beset by disasters. The 1906 earthquake was frightening but not damaging. Shortly before the brand-new hotel opened, a terrible fire almost destroyed it. California's first woman architect, Julia Morgan, restored the structure and completed the interiors. In 1962, Mario Gaidano added a slender 24-story white and gold tower of modern design that offers spectacular views of San Francisco Bay.

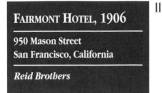

II

FAIRMONT HOTEL, 1906

950 Mason Street
San Francisco, California

Reid Brothers

The tradition of old-world elegance lives on in the hotel's public rooms, particularly the ornate lobby with its marble walls and columns and grand stairway. There is also a ballroom with clouds painted on the ceiling, and a rooftop garden. The Fairmont Hotel is known to television viewers as the setting of the series "Hotel." And on a historical note, the United Nations Charter was drafted in the hotel's Garden Room.

For visitor information, call (415) 772-5000.

UNITY TEMPLE, 1906

**875 Lake Street
at Kenilworth Avenue
Oak Park, Illinois**

Frank Lloyd Wright

Frank Lloyd Wright's design for Unity Temple, a church and Sunday School for his Unitarian clients, is the world's first modern church. There are no Gothic arches—the lines are straight and bold. Wright rejected the cross-shaped plan so common in church architecture, as well as in his own house designs. Instead he chose a plan based on squares and rectangles, and these elements are interwoven throughout the building. The long, low horizontal lines that had become Wright's residential trademark took a turn for the vertical, and with this change came an interesting new scale and proportion.

Unity Temple's monumental exterior encompasses both the church and the smaller Sunday School beyond, connected by a low entranceway. The building complex is anchored by four massive corner piers, with balconies between them. The walls are solid concrete that were surfaced in pebble aggregate, a new and prophetic breakthrough that helped to change this former "engineering" material into an architectural one. A band of windows is set high into the wall to block out noise from the street and admit to light to the interior.

The interior of Unity Temple is equally monumental. The central auditorium is a massive square with incut corners. There are double galleries on three sides and a pulpit platform on the fourth side with an organ behind it. Sand-finished plaster walls echo the theme of squares and rectangles with their graphic wood trim. The furniture and light fixtures are also by Wright.

Unity Temple offers guided tours on Saturday and Sunday at 1:00, 2:00, and 3:00 PM. Self-

guided tours are permitted Monday through Friday 1:00 to 4:00 PM (Memorial Day to Labor Day 10:00 AM to 5:00 PM). For information, call (708) 383-8873.

The Frank Lloyd Wright Home and Studio Foundation, 951 Chicago Avenue in Oak Park, also conducts tours of Unity Temple daily except on Thanksgiving and Christmas. For tour information, call (708) 848-1978.

J. Pierpont Morgan, then the world's richest man and one of the great American collectors, built this library for the rare books and manuscripts that were his passion. The well-traveled, cultivated financier revered Italian Renaissance architecture, which he felt expressed his collection's importance. He could have commissioned anyone, but America's premier neoclassical architects—McKim, Mead & White—happened to be based in the city. For Mr. Morgan, Charles McKim created his masterpiece.

PIERPONT MORGAN LIBRARY, 1907

29-33 East 36th Street
  at Madison Avenue
New York, New York

McKim, Mead & White

The Morgan Library opened to the public in 1924 and now fills a complex occupying half a city block. Still, "Mr. Morgan's Library" retains the aura of power and privilege—and the bounty of a worldwide collector—in its beautiful period rooms.

As large and opulent as an Italian palazzo, the library portrays the Renaissance idea of integrating all the arts. Architecturally, the Tennessee pink marble structure is classically simple: a broad rectangle with a central, recessed portico entry, accentuated with paired double Ionic columns. Bronze front doors are topped by a sculpted lunette and an angel-borne panel on the cornice. Construction was also classical: The marble blocks are joined by grinding rather than mortar, an ancient Greek technique.

The library contains three splendid main rooms and a rotunda filled with colorful marble surfaces and columns, mosaic panels, and columns of lapis lazuli. The East Room is the main repository for the library's collection of rare books, manuscripts, and drawings. Its walls are lined with three tiers of bookcases made of bronze and inlaid Circassian walnut. Zodiac signs decorate the spandrels; out of sequence, they reflect Morgan's personal reconfiguration of the constellations.

Morgan's private West Room study is artistically and historically fascinating. Here Morgan hosted an extraordinary "fund-raiser" in 1907, hitting up wealthy friends for personal contributions to help the nation avoid impending financial collapse. An artistic highlight is the coffered wooden ceiling from Italy.

In 2002, the library launched a twenty-first century transformation that adds a fresh new layer of classical architecture. A lucid design by Renzo Piano includes three steel-and-glass pavilions inserted between the existing buildings, with a glass-roofed courtyard as the central unifying space. Piano reoriented the entrance to Madison Avenue with a steel-framed glass wall that also exposes the McKim building's beautiful rear elevation for the first time. A finely wrought faceted steel cube, 20 feet to a side, hovers above one pavilion—an ultra-sleek new library vault that protects especially rare books. The museum is closed until early 2006. For information, call (212) 685-0610.

PLAZA HOTEL, 1907

**Fifth Avenue
    at Central Park South
New York, New York**

Henry Janeway Hardenbergh

The grand aristocrat of New York hotels, the Plaza commands its Central Park site as if it were the center of the city. It was certainly designed for the tastes of its fashionable guests—an oversized French chateau that was just like home, only larger.

Henry Janeway Hardenbergh, the Plaza's architect, was known for outstanding residences, including the Dakota Apartments on Central Park West, the city's first luxury apartments.

At the Plaza, Hardenbergh recognized the importance of the corner site; the two main façades would be equally impressive. The building is classically organized, with a distinct base, shaft, and top. The 18-story structure is clad with brick and marble and is capped by a massive cornice and mansard slate roof with gables and dormers and copper cresting. Hardenbergh relieved the massive blockiness of the building by recessing the central sections, and by rounding the corners on the north and south.

When it opened, the hotel had two floors of elegant public rooms with staircases and 800 guest rooms. The Palm Court featured a Tiffany domed glass ceiling, later covered up. A restoration by Lee Harris Pomeroy Architects in New York City revitalized the public and guest areas. The Tiffany ceiling was also returned to its former glory. In 2004, new owners announced plans to convert the hotel into a luxury condominium.

For information, call (212) 759-3000.

Around 1900, "modern" meant railroad, a symbol of progress as well as the most popular travel option. Yet despite the progress of machine technology, and in surprising contrast to the forward architectural thrust of fellow Chicagoans Louis Sullivan and Frank Lloyd Wright, Daniel Burnham looked to the past for his inspiration. In all fairness, he was not alone in this. A veritable frenzy of neoclassical sentiment was sweeping along the

UNION STATION, 1907

**Massachusetts Avenue
at North Capitol Street**
Washington, D.C.

D.H. Burnham and Company

east coast, and Burnham embraced it. His railroad gateway to the nation's capital recalls the glories of imperial Greece and Rome, monumental in scale and lavish in ornament.

Union Station fulfilled Burnham's vision of the "noble, dignified classical style." He designed the white marble terminal with a sense of pageantry and procession—the traveler is welcomed by enormous arched porticoes flanked by Ionic columns, surmounted by 25-ton larger-than-life sculptured figures, which represent fire, electricity, agriculture, and mechanics.

The largest structure in the country under a roof at the time it was built, the 97,500-square-foot terminal encompasses three halls: Main, East, and West. The Main Hall is the largest, measuring 220 x 120 feet, enclosed by a 96-foot-high barrel-vaulted and coffered ceiling that admits a flood of natural light through its skylights. The Main Hall is also the most elaborate, with white marble floors decorated with red diamond insets and a gold leaf ceiling. Standing guard from their posts along the ledge of Main Hall mezzanine are thirty-six plaster statues of Roman legionnaires. At its inception, the terminal was a mini-city, complete with hotel, police station, doctor's office, liquor store, swimming pool, Turkish baths, a butcher, a baker, and even a mortuary.

Burnham said, "Make no little plans. They have no magic to stir men's souls." He could not foresee the sad decline of rail travel in the 1950s that almost took his grandiose Union Station down with it. For almost thirty years the building languished in uncertainty. The 1964 landmark designation prevented demolition but failed to inspire any new life or purpose. A 1968 plan for a National Visitor Center failed miserably; opening in 1976, it closed in disgrace after only two years.

The station was finally saved by the Union Station Redevelopment Act of 1981, a public-private effort and massive renovation. Architects Benjamin Thompson & Associates, Inc., architectural preservationists Harry Weese and Associates of Chicago, and others worked to achieve an authentic restoration as well as a viable building. Union Station reopened in 1988.

The station is open twenty-four hours a day. For information, call (202) 289-1908.

Gamble House is the ultimate California bungalow. Built for David and Mary Gamble of the Procter & Gamble Company of Cincinnati, it is the standout in a neighborhood so rich with chalet-style Arts and Crafts architecture that the locals call it "Little Switzerland."

The house reveals the many sources Charles S. Greene and his brother, Henry M. Greene, combined in developing this unique California style: elements of the "Shingle Style" homes of the east, Frank Lloyd Wright's "Prairie Style" of the midwest, the Swiss chalet, and Japanese influences. But most of all, the transplanted easterners were inspired by the luxuriousness of nature in their new locale, and by a desire to put tradition behind them.

The Greenes' special skill was creating such a natural-looking house, despite its complicated and highly decorated design. Long and low, Gamble House has deep eaves extending over porches and balconies. Structural timbers were evident, clearly showing how the house was constructed. Large, brown shingles cover the outside walls, and the verandas and sleeping porches feature elaborate stickwork.

Craftsmanship, inside and out, is something to marvel over. The front door, for example, offers a fine piece of Tiffany art glass in the shape of a spreading oak tree. The interior woodworking is legendary, especially the handcrafted, hand-polished teak panels of the entry, living room, and dining room. Even the staircase is a woodwork of art. The Greenes designed the furniture as well.

Gamble House is near the intersection of the 134 and 210 freeways. (Frank Lloyd Wright's La Miniatura is a few blocks away.) Tours are offered Thursday through Sunday from noon until 3:00 PM, except holidays. Reservations for groups of ten must be arranged one month in advance. For information and reservations, call (626) 793-3334.

In the last years of his revolutionary career, his innovative Chicago skyscrapers of the 1890s sadly behind him, Louis Sullivan embarked on a series of bank buildings for tiny midwestern communities. These small but elegant structures are no less admirable than the skyscrapers; in fact the bank was honored with its own postage stamp in 1981.

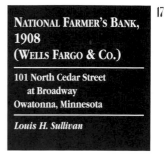

NATIONAL FARMER'S BANK, 1908 (WELLS FARGO & CO.)

101 North Cedar Street
at Broadway
Owatonna, Minnesota

Louis H. Sullivan

For his skyscrapers, Sullivan had devised a basic division of parts—the base, the midsection, and the top—and this formula also worked for the bank, despite its smaller cube-shaped structure. Here, the base consists of the first floor, which is clad in a beautiful but unornamented red sandstone. But it is the midsection that steals the show. Sullivan's love of ornamentation—and his special ability to combine the decorative with the plain—is evident in the green terra-cotta bands of leaves and acorns outlining the red masonry walls at the front and side of the building. These two main exposures also feature a dramatic center arch inset with windows of brilliant glass mosaic. The top is a simple masonry tier projecting slightly outward.

As a prelude to the richly ornamented interior, Sullivan designed a low main entrance that opens into the enormous central banking room. On the inside, the huge, arched stained-glass windows are detailed with gold leaf, and there are two large murals within the arches. The ornate clock over the vault is the work of Sullivan's partner, George Elmslie, who also assisted in the bank's design and ornamentation.

At the time the bank was built, Sullivan was virtually alone in championing progressive American architecture. He ferociously condemned the rampant neoclassicism brought on by the Chicago World's Fair of 1893, calling it "an appalling calamity." Sullivan predicted that "the damage . . . will last for half a century from its date, if not longer."

The bank suffered its own calamity and failed in 1926, and in 1929 the building was bought by Security State Bank. Later in that eventful financial year, Security was purchased by Northwest Bank Corporation, and merged with Wells Fargo in 1999.

Over the years, there have been two major restorations of the remarkable structure: by Harwell Hamilton Harris in 1958 and under the direction of David P. Bowers of Val Michelson & Associates in 1982.

Owatonna is a city of about 20,000 people, located sixty miles south of Minneapolis/St. Paul via Highway 35W. Bank hours are 8:00 AM to 5:30 PM Monday through Friday; 8:00 AM to noon Saturday. For visitor information, call (507) 451-5670.

ROBIE HOUSE, 1909

**5757 Woodlawn Avenue
Chicago, Illinois**

Frank Lloyd Wright

The evolving architectural genius of Frank Lloyd Wright reached full maturity with his three-dimensional design for Robie House, the largest and most monumental of his early works. Like the "Prairie Style" homes that preceded it, Robie House is long, low, and horizontally oriented. It also reveals a cohesive and streamlined layering that had not been seen before. Wright appears to have been influenced by the developments in modern machine technology, for Robie House resembles the airplane as well as the luxury ocean liner, both of which were objects of great fascination at the time.

Robie House is a Prairie Style house in a city setting, and there is a new tautness that is appropriate to its tight corner lot. Wright's design solution consists of large horizontal slabs, ingeniously stacked to create multiple interior levels, open balconies, and enclosed terraces. The strong horizontal lines of the balcony and the roof are complemented by the exterior bricks, which are also long and thin. Continuous bands of windows alternate with the solid exterior

walls of soft, red Roman brick, capped with limestone. The cross-shaped theme of many Wright designs of this period appears in Robie House in the extended overhang of the uppermost story.

As with all of Wright's works, the setting was the key to the design. On the outside, the house acts as a fortress to shield the residents from the traffic of the street, with the entrance hidden away to the right. Inside, Wright achieved privacy by inverting the traditional living arrangement: the living and dining rooms are located on the second floor, with the children's playroom and the billiard rooms below. The interior plan is remarkably long and open, with the living and dining rooms separated by a massive fireplace, the hearth that Wright believed to be the spiritual center of the modern home. The open interior ensures that each major area of the house has access to a porch or balcony, assuring the indoor/outdoor integration that Wright particularly favored.

Robie House is one of the most influential designs in the history of architecture, a demonstration of new ideas that changed the course of architecture and greatly enhanced the place of the architect in the building process.

The Frank Lloyd Wright Preservation Trust administers the property and is currently restoring it to its original appearance. Tours continue during construction (though with some limitations): weekdays 11:00 AM, 1:00, and 3:00 PM; weekends, every 20 minutes from 11:00 AM to 3:00 PM. For tour information, call (708) 848-1976.

First Church of Christ, Scientist is one of two great remaining landmarks of California Arts & Crafts architecture (Gamble House in Pasadena is the other). Like the famous California bungalows of the time, the church is eclectic, romantic, and sympathetic to nature. But it also exhibits a grand sprightliness that is peculiar to its eccentric architect, Bernard Maybeck.

FIRST CHURCH OF CHRIST, SCIENTIST, 1910

Dwight Way at Bowditch Street Berkeley, California

Bernard R. Maybeck

The church appears, pagoda-style, as a series of stepped rooftops with extended rough-hewn gables. Boughs of wisteria drape the ceremonial entrance portico with its freestanding gates, creating an entry that feels open and sheltering at the same time. It leads to a low ceilinged vestibule that gives on to the main church.

While the exterior seems soothing and practically residential, the interior is overwhelming and evocative. The church proper features the simple Greek cross plan, but above that almost anything goes. Colossal wooden beams carved in a Gothic style are mounted on columns and form an "X" across the ceiling. Delicately stenciled in ornamental tracery, these beams seem to float overhead, as walls of factory windows with tiny panes deny the structure's substance. Maybeck, the son of a German immigrant woodcarver, trained at the Beaux-Arts School in Paris. Berkeley's hills are dotted with his California Craftsman bungalows, but the church was his masterpiece. He kept photographs of it by his bedside until the day he died.

Guided tours are conducted the first Sunday of every month at 12:15 PM. Visitors are also welcome at weekly church services on Wednesday at 8:00 PM and Sunday at 11:00 AM. The building is closed at all other times. Groups of ten or more should make reservations. For information and reservations, call (510) 849-4347.

NEW YORK PUBLIC
LIBRARY, 1911
CENTRAL RESEARCH
LIBRARY

Fifth Avenue at 42nd Street
New York, New York

Carrère & Hastings

The New York Public Library is an august marble monument surrounded by the friendly buzz and hubbub of an Italian piazza. The broad marble steps facing Fifth Avenue become a terrace, while outdoor cafés on either side provide pleasant, Parisian-style places to eat and linger under the trees. Behind the building, the newly restored and beautifully planted Bryant Park is a breath of fresh air in midtown Manhattan.

A National Historic Landmark, the white Vermont marble palace is among the city's finest Beaux Arts monuments and one of the world's greatest research (noncirculating) libraries. The competition-winning design by Carrère & Hastings won out over their former employers, McKim, Mead & White, although both firms preferred the classic style—and classic materials—for grand public monuments.

In accordance with Beaux Arts ideals, the library's entry is elegant and formal. A pair of "literary lions" carved in stone stand guard on either side of the broad, central stairs. The stairs rise in two tiers to the entrance portico, defined by pairs of fluted columns, high arches, and massive, bronze front doors. It took three sculptors to create the statuary that graces the main façade of this colossal building that stretches two blocks long.

Just inside is Astor Hall, a vast field of marble with high, arched bays on all four sides rising to a segmental vault and a pair of significant marble staircases leading to the upper floors. The overwhelming marble classicism of Astor Hall prepares you properly for the upper two stories, where the circulation spaces of cross-axial plan are all clad with marble and lofty in feeling.

Fortunately, the almost overwhelming formality and monumental nature of the building is enlivened by the pleasant interior light emanating from the two courtyards and by the companionable presence of old wood furniture and trim. And despite the immense size of the building and the collections—housed on eighty-eight miles of shelves—the library functions miraculously well. Librarians pride themselves on being able to retrieve virtually any book in less than ten minutes.

The library's remarkable collection includes the Gutenberg Bible, located in the Rare Books and Manuscripts Room, and Thomas Jefferson's handwritten copy of the Declaration of Independence. Major exhibitions from the library's collection are mounted in Gottesman Exhibition Hall on the first floor, and the Art and Architecture Collection is on three.

The library is open Tuesday and Wednesday from 11:00 AM to 7:30 PM; Thursday through Saturday from 10:00 AM to 6:00 PM, closed Sunday and Monday. Tours are conducted Tuesday through Saturday at 11:00 AM and 2:00 PM and last approximately one hour. Sign up in advance at the Friends of the Library Desk, to the right of the Fifth Avenue entrance. For tour information, call the Volunteer Office at (212) 930-0501.

F rank Lloyd Wright was born just twenty miles from Spring Green, and he returned from Oak Park, Illinois, as a prodigal son in 1911. The land had been in his family for many years, and Wright planned to construct a cottage in the countryside to share with Mamah Borthwick Cheney, his paramour. The cottage expanded into a complex that would be Wright's primary home and studio for the rest of his life.

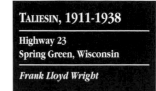

TALIESIN, 1911-1938

Highway 23
Spring Green, Wisconsin

Frank Lloyd Wright

Twice, in 1914 and in 1925, the house was almost destroyed by fire. The earlier disaster, ignited by a deranged servant, killed Mrs. Cheney and her two children. In rebuilding his beloved Taliesin, Wright used the remaining structure as a base for the new design. Now Taliesin is a 37,000-square-

foot self-sufficient complex, arrayed around courtyards and pools. It includes the multi-story main house, guest rooms, Wright's studio and office, a root cellar, a shop area, an ice house, farm buildings, gardens and terraces, and Taliesin dam, a beautiful form of cascading stone.

Wright's "house of the north" (contrasting with Taliesin West, his winter home in Arizona) derives its name from an ancient Welsh word meaning "shining brow"—the brow of the hill. For Wright it was vital that Taliesin become part of the landscape. Taliesin is built of yellow limestone from nearby quarries, laid to resemble natural stratifications. Parts of the main house are separated by function, giving the appearance of clustered pavilions. The multiple rooflines, with their deep overhangs, seem to overlap and provide further unification of the overall design. Stone walls and terraces link the pavilions and outbuildings, courtyards and pools.

A visit inside the main house provides a glimpse of one of Wright's most evocative rooms— the 28 x 36-foot living room that overlooks the valley and water gardens below. Off the living room, a 40-foot walkway cantilevers out into the treetops. Wright's studio is attached to the house by a covered breezeway.

The 600-acre Taliesin estate includes Hillside School (1902), now home to the Frank Lloyd Wright School of Architecture, Midway Farm (1940s), Tan-y-deri House (1906), and Romeo and Juliet Windmill (1897). The landscaped grounds, roads, and dam are vivid reminders of Wright's devotion to nature and its part in the overall architectural composition.

Taliesin is three miles south of Spring Green, Wisconsin, forty-five minutes from Madison. It is owned and operated by the Frank Lloyd Wright Foundation. Guided tours are given every day from May 1 to October 31: walking tours are held hourly from 10:30 AM to 4:30 PM; house tours are hourly from 10:00 AM to 4:00 PM. Estate and sunset tours are also available. Reservations required. For information, call (608) 588-7900.

GRAND CENTRAL TERMINAL, 1913

**Park Avenue at 42nd Street
New York, New York**

Warren & Wetmore

At the time Grand Central Station was built, train travel represented great progress, and a city's train station symbolized civic modernity. Ironically, the architecture of the past was thought to be the most modern expression of the station's importance.

The country's first fully electrified station, the "new" Grand Central Terminal was ten years in construction. The mammoth stone megastructure fills six city blocks above ground, with sixteen city blocks of tracks below grade and elevated streets wrapping the station on the second level.

The monumental 42nd Street façade, with its tall arched windows and massive columns, is crowned by a Mercury clock by Jules Coutan. Inside, the main lobby and grand concourse offers one of the most glorious enclosed spaces in New York City, and a perfectly positioned marble staircase from which to appreciate the spectacle in its entirety. Architects Warren & Wetmore designed a magnificent interior of stone and marble where light streams in from high semicircular windows on the north and south sides, and through large arched windows on the east and west. The vaulted ceiling presents a celestial scene, a blue dome embellished with the signs of the zodiac, as seen from above.

The station's city landmark status was endangered in the late 1960s when Penn Central sought to erect a tower above it. The case went all the way to the Supreme Court, which upheld the constitutionality of landmark law in general and the landmark status of Grand Central in particular. In 1991, however, the status was diminished in another way: Amtrak rerouted its long-distance trains to New York's Pennsylvania Station. Grand Central, the station designed as a gateway to a continent, is now "only" a commuter station, but a very grand one all the same.

A much needed revitalization, completed in 1999, added a new entrance, a new concourse, a new grand stairway at the eastern end, and several balcony-level restaurants. Perhaps best of all, a soap-and-water cleaning removed decades of grime that obscured the fantastic celestial ceiling. Once again, the sky is blue, the constellations glittering gold.

The Municipal Art Society conducts one-hour walking tours every Wednesday at 12:30 PM. For information, call MAS at (212) 935-3960. On Friday at 12:30 PM, weather permitting, the Grand Central Partnership offers ninety-minute walking tours of the area, including the Chrysler Building and other nearby landmarks. For information, call (212) 697-1245.

If Chicago launched the skyscraper, then New York propelled it to new heights. When it opened in 1913, the Woolworth Building ranked as the world's tallest, and as the undisputed trendsetter of the new skyscraper style.

With its breathtaking Gothic spire and medieval details, the Woolworth Building satisfactorily settled the issue of just what a skyscraper should look like. A Gothic cathedral, said Cass Gilbert, provided the proper historical precedent.

WOOLWORTH BUILDING, 1913

Broadway at Park Place
New York, New York

Cass Gilbert

According to the Beaux-Arts architect, nothing else captured so completely the modern skyscraper's heavenly aspirations. Irreverent New Yorkers quickly christened it the "Cathedral of Commerce."

A symbol of American capitalism at its most robust and powerful, the Woolworth Building's statistics were remarkable at the time: a 792-foot tower; 54 stories of office space for 14,000 workers; a 58th floor observation tower; and a cavernous, vaulted, marble-clad lobby with twenty-nine elevators, two of them express. The building cost $13.5 million, and was paid for in cash.

Even more remarkable today is Gilbert's skillful integration of the skyscraper elements into a unified composition. The 20-story U-shaped base yields gracefully to the rise of the square tower, which steps back twice before reaching the pinnacle, resplendent in all of its spires and gargoyles.

The Woolworth Building was not New York City's first skyscraper, but it was—and still is—one of the most magnificent masterpieces of an ornate, eclectic age. The company didn't fare as well. It closed in 1998. In 1999, a new owner, The Witkoff Group, converted the top 30 floors to luxury condominiums. New York University opened a satellite campus on the lower floors.

You can still visit the magnificent lobby, but the observation deck is no longer open to the public.

LA JOLLA WOMAN'S CLUB, 1914

715 Silverado Street
at Draper Avenue
La Jolla, California

Irving Gill

Irving Gill, an early and brilliant prophet of modern architecture in America, retained a love for the Spanish mission tradition of southern California. Through the patronage of Miss Ellen Browning Scripps, a remarkable philanthropist, Gill was commissioned to design the La Jolla Woman's Club; the project cost $40,000 in 1914.

The La Jolla Woman's Club building shows Gill's modern side, as well as his romantic inclination. The beige concrete walls are smooth and unornamented and the roof is flat. Large, graceful arches frame the wraparound porch and the leafy columned pergola extends to the street. It is surprising to learn that in this building Gill pioneered tilt-wall construction, pouring concrete onto a huge table tilted fifteen degrees. The forms were lifted into place, with four-inch steel bars providing structural reinforcement. Windows were integrated into the forms.

Inside the main front doors, a pair of arched wood frames inset with glass and decorative ironwork, the interiors are simple but serene. Walls are flush with their casings. Gill used no moldings for pictures, no baseboards or wainscoting that would catch and hold the dust. Light enters through stained-glass windows placed high on the walls and through large windows opening to the gardens.

Gill was born in New York, the son of a contractor. With only a high school education, he was building "modern" structures while his European contemporaries were just formulating theories for them. His acknowledged masterpiece, the Walter Dodge house in Los Angeles, built for a famous patent medicine mogul, was unconscionably demolished in 1970.

Gill's architecture might have been internationally influential—voracious copying of his style gives San Diego its appealing and cohesive appearance—but his career was stunted by the return to full-fledged traditionalism that swept the country from about 1916 to the mid-1930s.

The La Jolla Woman's Club is open to visitors Saturday from 9:00 AM to noon. The Bed and Breakfast Inn, also by Gill, is next door. For club reservations or information, call (858) 454-2354.

Even though it was built in 1914, this 42-story skyscraper looks surprisingly modern, with clean lines, large windows, and restrained ornamentation. Its pyramid tower even resembles the pencil-point spires that so often capped skyscrapers built in the 1980s. But the Smith Tower is not a frigid corporate tower; its bronze windows set in solid brass frames give it an overall golden cast. For decades this was the tallest and grandest building west of the Mississippi River, and to this day many Seattle residents consider it a favorite landmark.

L.C. SMITH TOWER, 1914

Second Avenue at Yesler Way
Seattle, Washington

Gaggin & Gaggin

Smith Tower's octagonal shape results from its irregular city site, and its design was intentionally dramatic. The original owner, L.C. Smith (as in Smith-Corona), observed the favorable publicity attending the Eiffel Tower's opening in 1889, and he reasoned that superior architecture and engineering would create the same kind of success for his building and his business. It is hard to say that the building alone put Smith-Corona on the map, but Smith Tower certainly has won its place in history as a National Historic Landmark.

Smith went all the way to Syracuse, New York, to hire his architects, Gaggin & Gaggin, who had built nothing taller than a few stories. They designed a building with "no artistic sacrifices," and to the highest technical standards. The interior fireproofing, for example, required 700,000 pounds of metal. The 1,400 doors, 2,000 windows, and 40,000 feet of molding were all hand-painted with eight coats of baked-on enamel resembling mahogany.

In the lobby, Gaggin & Gaggin did not have to utilize faux techniques. Walls are paneled in Alaskan marble and Mexican onyx. Eight copper and brass elevators were installed, and they are still operating today. Every office has windows that open.

An extensive renovation in 1986 brought back the building's authentic luster and restored the small, translucent glass blocks in the sidewalk that illuminate the building from below.

Smith Tower is open during regular business hours. There is a small museum inside with artifacts from Seattle's past. For visitor information, call (206) 622-4004.

GHIRARDELLI CHOCOLATE COMPANY, 1860-1915 (GHIRARDELLI SQUARE)

Bounded by Polk, Larkin, Beach, and North Point Streets
San Francisco, California

Various architects

In a miracle of inspired renovation, this four-story, red-brick chocolate factory was combined with neighboring structures to create a spirited multi-level shopping and dining complex with eighty shops and restaurants. San Francisco developer Matson Roth recognized the potential of transforming the vast, loft-style floors of these industrial buildings near Fisherman's Wharf into active, usable commercial space. One new building was added to the mix, and now the entire complex is abuzz with activity throughout the day and night.

Ghirardelli Square originated the "festival marketplace" trend. Open seven days a week, it has become one of the most popular tourist attractions in this most popular American tourist city.

At a time when public expositions offered exceptional opportunities for architects to show off, Bernard Maybeck created a magnificently eclectic group of structures for the Panama-Pacific International Exposition of 1915, celebrating the opening of the Panama Canal. The "palace" is a three-part construction: an arc-shaped gallery, a colonnade, and a rotunda. Maybeck's Beaux-Arts training in classical architecture is revealed in the overall design, which he embellished with urns, columns, and statues at monumental scale.

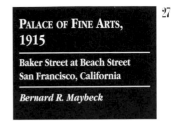

PALACE OF FINE ARTS, 1915

Baker Street at Beach Street San Francisco, California

Bernard R. Maybeck

A temporary exhibit never meant to last, the Palace was constructed of plaster of paris mixed with hemp fiber over a wood frame. As it deteriorated, however, it became increasingly dear to the people of San Francisco. In 1959, through the generosity and efforts of Walter S. Johnson, the Palace of Fine Arts was rebuilt in concrete so that this delightful bit of the city's past could be properly preserved.

The Palace of Fine Arts is the only exhibit that remains from the fair; it has been reincarnated into the Exploratorium, a lively museum of science past, present, and future. In 1981, the Palace of Fine Arts was featured on a postage stamp in the series on Architecture.

The Palace of Fine Arts' outdoor structure is always open. The Exploratorium is open daily from 10:00 AM until 6:00 PM, Wednesday until 9:00 PM. Closed major holidays. For general information, call (415) 561-0360.

CALIFORNIA PALACE OF THE LEGION OF HONOR, 1916

Lincoln Park
San Francisco, California

George A. Applegarth

San Francisco's beloved neoclassical museum owns 87,000 artworks and one magnificent setting on a wooded bluff overlooking San Francisco Bay near the Golden Gate bridge. The structure reproduces almost exactly an 18th-century Parisian palace, with a triumphal arch flanked by colonnades framing a central courtyard. A three-year expansion completed in 1995 added 35,000 square feet (a 42% increase) while keeping the familiar exterior virtually intact.

The renovation, by Edward Larrabee Barnes in New York City and Mark Cavagnero of San Francisco, continues the French theme with a glass pyramid like I. M. Pei's at the Louvre but much smaller. This pyramid becomes the skylight for the central court of a whole new layer of galleries carved out beneath the existing building. These new galleries add 9,500 square feet of exhibition space surrounding this sunny central court. The lower level has also gained a large new cafe. The structure has also been strengthened against earthquakes.

Artistically, the museum is strongest in French painting, drawings, and furniture. But the collection is growing rapidly and spans about 4,000 years. The Achenbach Foundation has donated its superb Graphic Arts collection, which includes Old Master prints and drawings, Japanese prints, and 19th-century photography. Although the museum is San Francisco's most traditional in terms of its art collection, its facilities are up to the minute: the museum has digitized its entire collection.

The Palace of the Legion of Honor Museum is open Tuesday through Sunday from 9:30 AM to 5:00 PM; closed Monday. It is located in Lincoln Park, 34th Avenue and Clement, one block north of Geary. For information and directions by car or on public transportation, call (415) 863-3330.

Vizcaya is one of the American great houses, a neoclassical palace overlooking Biscayne Bay. The European past of the last four centuries is conjured up in the architecture—Renaissance, Baroque, and Rococo—and its thirty-four rooms are filled with priceless furnishings from the sixteenth to the eighteenth centuries. The estate's gardens alone are worth the trip.

VIZCAYA, 1916
(THE DEERING ESTATE)

3251 South Miami Avenue
Miami, Florida

Francis Burrall Hoffman

The estate was constructed as a winter retreat for wealthy industrialist James Deering of International Harvester; he called it Vizcaya, a Basque word meaning "elevated place." Vizcaya evolved into a personal treasure house of European decorative arts. Relics of half a dozen grand European villas are incorporated into its structure, everything from massive doorways to painted ceilings.

The pale pink stucco mansion with its central courtyard was designed by Francis Burrall Hoffman, a New York City architect who left the prominent office of Carrère & Hastings to start his own firm in 1910. The house is surrounded with twenty acres of formal Italian gardens, and an elaborately decorated private casino is included in the complex. Deering's estate captures so perfectly the opulence of wealth before income tax that it was used as the setting for the motion picture *Citizen Kane*. Vizcaya is also said to have inspired its sister in extravagance, Hearst Castle at San Simeon, the home of the real-life Citizen Kane, William Randolph Hearst.

Vizcaya is open to the public every day except Christmas from 9:30 AM to 5:00 PM (the ticket booth closes at 4:30). Special group tours (including foreign language tours) are available by appointment. Reservations are required for groups of twenty or more, and should be made six weeks in advance during the peak months of November through May. For group reservations, call (305) 250-9133. For general information, call (305) 250-9133.

The Hallidie Building is famous for having the first true glass curtain wall in America, but it is fascinating also for its incongruous juxtaposition of trail-blazing technology with remnants from the romantic past, like the delicate, Victorian cast-iron ornamentation that decorates the transparent glass panes.

The grid-paned glass wall is also noteworthy for the way it is mounted. Rather than hanging from the frame, the glass is mounted on projecting brackets three feet in front of it. The glass is so clear that it is virtually invisible and allows the structural frame to show right through. Windows pivot sideways to allow for ventilation and washing. Semicircular wrought-iron fire escapes and diagonal stairs manage to look both practical and whimsical.

Offices (including the San Francisco Chapter of the AIA) fill the eight-story building, which is named for the inventor of the cable car, Andrew S. Hallidie. The office floors have been remodeled many times and little, if any, of the original details have survived.

The Hallidie Building is open during regular business hours. For the best view of the façade, walk across the street to the Galleria shopping complex, where there is a four-story Palladian window overlooking the building.

The Woodbury County Courthouse stands out as a model of progressive architecture at a time when most prominent American designers sought inspiration in the past. This courthouse is no neoclassical fantasy. Its brick walls are broad and the lines are clean. Ornamentation has not been forsaken, but the design is restrained and refined. The larger-than-life statues positioned atop flat, brick columns flanking the entry add just the right accent of monumental elegance and a hint of streamlining.

WOODBURY COUNTY COURTHOUSE, 1918

620 Douglas at Seventh Street
Sioux City, Iowa

*William L. Steel
and Purcell & Elmslie*

A great deal of care was given to the building's internal ornamentation. There are brick columns, flat and square like those at the entrance, but here they are capped with vines carved in stone. These columns support a ceiling that is bordered with decorated stone, and in some places the ceiling is given over to the decoration entirely. A large, glass dome set off by terra-cotta ornament illuminates (artificially) the central interior. The original murals are intact.

The trio of architects—William Steel, George Elmslie, and William Purcell—were former associates of Louis Sullivan, whose Chicago firm was instrumental in developing the appearance and technology of the modern skyscraper. It is fitting, then, that they concentrated on the here and now, although most of their colleagues were rummaging around in ancient history.

And now the courthouse has a long history of its own. Its seventy-fifth anniversary occurred in 1993, and to honor this event and to preserve the building, the county embarked on a large-scale restoration by Weatherall Erickson of Des Moines.

The courthouse is located off I-29 at the Business District exit, north or south. It is open from 8:00 AM to 4:30 PM Monday through Friday. Groups of ten or more should make reservations. For reservations and information, call (712) 279-6459.

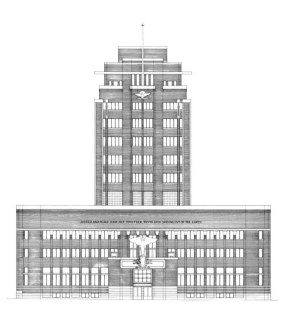

ST. BARTHOLOMEW'S CHURCH, 1919

Park Avenue at East 51st Street
New York, New York

Bertram Grosvenor Goodhue

The Byzantine splendor of St. Bartholomew's Church provides landmark architecture and a cherished garden spot on Park Avenue's last non-commercial site. This picturesque complex is dominated by the church, an elaborately carved and articulated edifice made of salmon-colored brick and Indiana limestone; it is characterized by a flattened dome and a pinnacle that soars to 570 feet. The main entry incorporates a portal designed by McKim, Mead & White in 1902, which served as the entrance to the old St. Bartholomew's Church on Madison Avenue. After Bertram Goodhue's death, a community house was built in a compatible style. Also in the spirit of compatibility, the tower next door is surfaced in the same warm-colored brick as the Church.

Goodhue's intricate design and lavish ornamentation is a startling contrast to his West Coast work. At the San Diego Exhibition of 1915, he single-handedly revived the Spanish Colonial style still popular today.

In the 1980s, St. Bartholomew's Church ignited a storm of controversy. The church planned to demolish the community house and part of the garden to make way for a large, commercial office tower on the valuable Park Avenue site. New York City's Landmarks Preservation Society denied the request; the church and gardens became designated landmarks to be preserved intact.

The church is open 365 days a year from 8:00 AM to 6:00 PM, Thursdays until 7:30, and Sunday until 8:30 PM. The number to call for visitor information is (212) 378-0200.

Within just a few blocks of the church are a number of twentieth-century architectural monuments, including Grand Central Station, the Pepsi-Cola Building (now Walt Disney headquarters), the Seagram Building, and Lever House.

For Frank Lloyd Wright, the commission for Barnsdall House was the beginning of an idyllic "California Romanza," but for the Chicago oil heiress and art patron Aline Barnsdall, the dream turned out otherwise. Barnsdall's initial request was fairly modest: a home for herself and her young daughter, Sugartop, and a small theater on the property to bring Chicago-style culture to town. With Wright's encouragement, the project mushroomed into a full-blown cultural complex, but only the main residence and two guest cottages were completed.

BARNSDALL HOUSE, 1921 (HOLLYHOCK HOUSE)

4808 Hollywood Boulevard
Los Angeles, California

Frank Lloyd Wright

The two-story main house is situated on top of Olive Hill, contradicting Wright's usual conviction that a building should be of the landscape, not on it. But because the house was to be the center of the 36-acre cultural compound, Wright let it command the hill.

Wright's fascination with ancient Mayan forms is evident. The plain, beige, concrete walls angle slightly inward to imply a subtle pyramid. Cast concrete bands featuring stylized hollyhocks (Barnsdall's favorite flower) provide the ornamentation, both inside and out.

Wright used his favorite cross-shaped plan, which allowed him to juxtapose inside and outside "rooms." To enter the house, you'll walk through an outdoor pergola, and through a low, dark foyer. From here, the enormous living room opens up. Its soft gold walls and pale, watercolor ceiling practically glow. The living room fireplace is virtually mythologized. A reflecting pool is sunk into the floor around it, and a cubist-inspired concrete mural above the mantle depicts Aline Barnsdall's life. Wright also designed much of the furniture, including dining room chairs with the hollyhock motif running up the back.

Aline Barnsdall hated Hollyhock House. The roof leaked, and the cultural complex failed to materialize. After only six years, she donated the property to the city. The house is now part of Barnsdall Art Park, but it is closed for renovation until 2005. Exterior tours continue Wednesday through Friday by appointment only, and Saturday and Sunday without appointments, hourly from 12:30 to 3:30 PM on those days. For information, call (323) 644-6269.

FORD GLASS PLANT, 1922

**3001 Miller Road
Dearborn, Michigan**

Albert Kahn Associates

In America, as in Europe, factory buildings were important architectural laboratories in the early twentieth century. Detroit architect Albert Kahn was a poet of industrial design, and the Ford Glass Plant is his most famous work. Responding to Henry Ford's demand for cheap, fast construction to meet the company's astonishing growth, Kahn arrived at several important design innovations.

The plant manufactured the first shatter-proof glass for car windshields. The process required four glass-making furnaces 125 feet high, running at 2,500 degrees Fahrenheit. Kahn's design (much altered over the years) let light and air in, and heat out—a great boon for workers before air conditioning. He rejected the conventional "sawtooth" roof, with north-oriented windows aligned with the production lines. Instead, Kahn designed butterfly skylights and glass walls that offered production managers new freedom for layouts on the factory floor. Heat was vented through retractable steel roof monitors 25 feet high.

Kahn almost designed the curtain wall here. Multistory factory buildings were typically built of brick, with steel-framed windows set into the masonry walls. For the 200-foot south façade, Kahn ran brick to just 14 feet high, with a wall of corrugated steel, steel sash, and glass above it. The windows were sheathed over the building's structural columns—rather than abutted between them—a design so ingenious that Walter Gropius paid a visit.

In 2005, an extensive, sensitive renovation by Arcadis converted the facility into a training center for advanced automobile manufacturing. Arcadis restored Kahn's south glass wall using the original blueprints, but with insulated glass. The original colors—red-orange brick, black frames, and warm gray trim—were replicated as well. In place of the four, long-vanished smokestacks, the architects planted trees to commemorate those industrial relics that Kahn had instilled with distinction in his design.

The Glass Plant is a highlight of Ford's Rouge Factory Historic Driving Tour (exterior only; no other visits are permitted). Buses depart from the Henry Ford Museum's Greenfield Village, at Village Road and Oakwood Boulevard in Dearborn. Daily, except Christmas Day and Thanksgiving, tours start every half hour from 9:30 AM to 2:30 PM. Reservations and early arrival are recommended. The tours also present Ford's far-sighted acceptance of sustainable design, which is being implemented in stages throughout the huge Rouge facility. The 10.4-acre "living roof" by William McDonough can be viewed from an observation deck during this tour. As you pass the Ford Glass Plant, you may see sparks flying—arc-welding robots are located behind the new glass façade. For information, call (313) 982-6001.

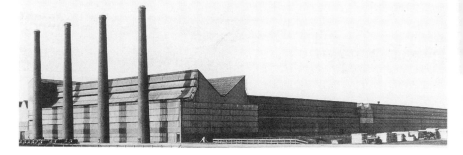

The classic ideal of the Greek Doric temple inspired the Lincoln Memorial, one of Washington's most revered public monuments. There is an eternal stillness about this structure, with its perfect proportions, pure white marble, and statue of Abraham Lincoln in profound contemplation, as if for all people and for all time.

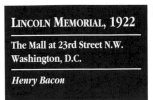

LINCOLN MEMORIAL, 1922

The Mall at 23rd Street N.W. Washington, D.C.

Henry Bacon

Classically minded Henry Bacon designed the 100-foot-tall monument, which rises to approximately nine stories. Following ancient Greek rules for temple construction, Bacon's columns taper toward the top and are slightly convex to correct for visual distortions. Inside the monument, two rows of Ionic columns frame the famous statue of Lincoln by David Chester French, which is considered one of the world's great sculptures.

In some ways, the temple commemorates the Union as much as its hero. The Lincoln Memorial occupies a place of honor at one end of the Mall's reflecting pool, opposite the Washington Monument, and each of its Doric columns represents one of the thirty-six states in the Union at Lincoln's death. When the memorial was completed, there were forty-eight states and their names are inscribed on the parapet above the columns. Murals by Jules Guerin render the freeing of the slaves and the unity of North and South, Lincoln's major achievements.

SCHINDLER HOUSE, 1922

**833 North Kings Road
West Hollywood, California**

R.M. Schindler

The vision of southern California as a tropical Eden inspired the creation of R.M. Schindler's innovative house and studio, one of the first International Style houses in America. A native of Austria who had apprenticed with Frank Lloyd Wright, Schindler thought it was possible to live outdoors in California year-round, and he devised a brilliant design combining outside "rooms" with the inside ones to take advantage of the warm, sunny climate. A social visionary as well, Schindler joined with a friend, the engineer Clyde Chase, in building a house for both their families to share.

Before long, Schindler learned that he was wrong about the weather—winter finally came, and sometimes it rained. The social experiment also proved unworkable and the friends departed after two years. But the accomplishment of his design remains.

The gray concrete house is just one story with a flat roof, and it is set well back in the landscape of its city lot. The open, pinwheel shape of the plan is a result of the two-family program, which called for a studio and adjacent yard for each couple. The families were to share a common kitchen, an outdoor living room with a fireplace, and a rooftop sleeping porch outfitted with special "sleeping baskets."

Schindler intended the house to be inexpensive (wrong again). For "economy," he and Chase devised an early form of tilt-wall construction by pouring concrete into rectangular forms; the interstices were then filled with glass to create tall, narrow windows. Large, redwood-framed sliding doors, now glass but initially covered in canvas, must have given the house the feeling of a sophisticated tent.

Schindler lived and worked here until his death in 1953. The Neutras shared the house in the late 1920s, when it was the center of Los Angeles's avant garde. By the 1970s, the house had become a modern ruin. Now restored, it is home to the MAK Center for Art and Architecture LA, and is open Wednesday through Sunday from 11:00 AM to 6:00 PM. Tours are held on Saturday and Sunday from 11:00 AM to 6:00 PM. For information, call (323) 651-1510.

I n the 1920s, Frank Lloyd Wright designed a series of
houses in the Los Angeles area that represented a change
in direction from his previous residential work.

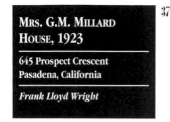

**MRS. G.M. MILLARD
HOUSE, 1923**

645 Prospect Crescent
Pasadena, California

Frank Lloyd Wright

These new houses, of which the Millard House is the
masterpiece, were constructed of an ingenious concrete
block cast with geometric patterns. With a single stroke,
Wright had invented a new method of construction with
built-in decorative possibilities; the pierced concrete blocks
introduced an element of openness, light, and airiness to the overall composition. The concrete
blocks were cast in molds three or four inches thick, with channels through which steel reinforcing rods were run vertically and horizontally to "knit" the building together on the site. This
method came to be known as the "knit block," although the actual process of weaving the blocks
together turned out to be more of a nightmare than an improvement.

Besides the differences in construction technique and materials, the Millard house differs radically from the Prairie Houses in its overall orientation. Where the Prairie House was long, low,
horizontal, and ground-hugging, the Millard house stands tall and vertical. Compact in plan, the
three-story house is vertically organized, with the entrance, living room, guest room, and garage
located at the center level, the dining room and kitchen on the floor below, and the master bedroom on the floor above. The two-story living room opens onto a balcony at the front of the
house and overlooks the luxurious garden terrace and pool at ground level. The architect's eldest
son, Lloyd Wright, supervised the construction and designed both the landscaping and a 1926
studio addition. The compact Millard house is also known as La Miniatura.

The house is a private residence, located just a few blocks from Gamble House.

STORER HOUSE, 1923

8161 Hollywood Boulevard
West Hollywood, California

Frank Lloyd Wright

Rambling up its Hollywood hill, the Storer house shows the results of Frank Lloyd Wright's second experiment with textile block construction and Mayan imagery, which characterized his work in Los Angeles in the early 1920s. Wright's concrete blocks are naturally not ordinary ones, but are custom blocks of plain and patterned designs, some with geometric cutouts to allow the passage of light and air.

Wright's ability to generate excitement and repose simultaneously is seen in this structure. Here he works this magic almost exclusively with the textile blocks, a natural material with a lively pattern. Double-faced, the blocks provide finished surfaces on interior as well as exterior walls.

The block pattern starts at the street, with a 10-foot retaining wall at the foot of the hill that also forms a railing for the terrace on the other side. Behind this wall, the house consists of two wings: a single-story dining and service floor at ground level, and the main entry and two-story living room to the rear of the site. It is this lofty living room, with its Mayan-inspired columns and tall, narrow windows, that constitutes the main façade on the street side; the room opens to a garden court toward the hill.

Wright would soon turn away from the textile block experiment, but at Storer house the construction technique captures Wright's dream of the California Romanza, a house "just haunting enough in a whole so organic as to lose all evidence of how it was made."

The house is a private residence.

When the American Radiator Building was designed, automobile radiators were black boxes often capped with bright header tanks and fittings crafted of polished brass. One of the country's first skyscrapers, the building appears to have been inspired by its namesake, as it is black and gold. In fact, Raymond Hood was an industrial designer as well as an architect, and he had designed radiator covers for the company that would commission him to design the building.

There was more to it than this, of course. Hood seems to have chosen black brick to counteract the effect he noticed in light-colored buildings where windows seem to become rows of black rectangles. Hood's black brick was meant to de-emphasize the windows and make the skyscraper appear more monolithic.

To break up the rather somber black-on-blackness of the original tower, Hood embellished the top with gold terra-cotta. The original window shades were red, a gesture that implied burning embers.

A New York City landmark, the building is an artistic icon as well. A famous Georgia O'Keeffe painting portrays the looming black tower at night, awash in glittering lights cast by its beacons placed on all the terraces.

After a long period of neglect, the building finally staged a strong comeback as a swank hotel. Opening in 2001, The Bryant Park Hotel offers interiors designed by prominent British architect David Chipperfield.

The hotel faces Bryant Park behind the New York Public Library on Fifth Avenue. Within walking distance are two other famous Hood works, Rockefeller Center at Fifth Avenue and 55th Street and the Daily News Building at 42nd Street between Second and First Avenues. For hotel information, call (212) 869-0100.

AMERICAN RADIATOR BUILDING, 1924 (THE BRYANT PARK HOTEL)

40 West 40th Street, between Fifth and Sixth Avenues
New York, New York

Raymond Hood

ENNIS HOUSE, 1924

2607 Glendower Avenue
Los Angeles, California

Frank Lloyd Wright

Even from a distance of several miles, the appearance of Ennis House silhouetted against the sky commands attention. A virtual Mayan fortress high on a hill in Griffith Park, overlooking Los Angeles, the house appears to be the master of all it surveys. A favorite location of Hollywood studio executives, the house has starred in many movies, including the infamous *Blade Runner.*

Ennis House is the largest of Frank Lloyd Wright's Los Angeles "knit-block" designs. With these specially constructed concrete blocks, Wright hoped to achieve a simplified construction method as well as an integral ornamentation for his designs. At Ennis House, the 16-inch blocks feature a geometric motif based on the square. Solid blocks form bands of decoration on the long, low garden walls, while open fretwork blocks are used to cover great expanses of the exterior walls.

The geometrically patterned blocks are also used inside the house, where they contribute to the atmosphere of ancient secrets. Changes in ceiling heights and lighting add to the drama. A long, low entrance hall leads to a stairway with a roof abruptly soaring to 22 feet. Wright's art glass windows and doors are beautifully preserved—especially the wisteria mosaic above the living room fireplace.

In 1980, the house was donated by its owner, Augustus Oliver Brown, to the Trust for Preservation of Cultural Heritage. Reservation only tours are held Tuesday, Thursday, and Saturday at 11:00 AM and 1:30 PM; other times by special request. For information and reservations, call (323) 660-0607.

Courtyard housing is a Los Angeles specialty, a civilized response to the balmy climate and mission tradition. One of the earliest, and still among the most charming, examples of courtyard architecture is the Andalucia. This idyllic little compound, built by Arthur Zwebell along with his interior decorator wife, Nina, helped establish the model for the many garden apartments that would be built in Los Angeles and other parts of the country.

ANDALUCIA APARTMENTS, 1926

**1471-75 Havenhurst Drive
West Hollywood, California**

Arthur and Nina Zwebell

The Andalucia is a symmetrical two-story structure that resonates with mission-style features: the plastered, arched entry; a red-tiled roof shading a second-story balcony with hand-turned balustrades; and, in the main courtyard, the Spanish-inspired fountain tiled in a bright and colorful mosaic. As for its courtyard, the Andalucia actually has a series of three, all luxuriously landscaped: an entry court, a central patio with the fountain as centerpiece, and a pool and patio area to the rear.

The Zwebells were self-taught architects who would soon turn their talents to stage-set design, but in the Andalucia they created a magical place that over the years became home to movie stars including Clara Bow and Marlon Brando.

Mr. Zwebell signed his name with a flourish in the fresh cement of the sidewalk—an artist personalizing his work—and the signature remains there today. Respecting the Andalucia's personal quality, the new owners who bought it in 1990—Craig Wright, with Don and Alice Willfong—restored the apartments and re-landscaped the courtyards to their original sunny, tropical elegance. Because the apartments are small, they combined them to make larger units; now there are eight apartments in the complex. The only other structural changes involved removing a raised

swimming pool (not original) and walling in the rear courtyard, where the owners display garden ornaments from their Melrose Place antiques shop, Quatrain. The apartments are rented furnished, as they were originally, and some apartments come with copies of Nina Zwebell's own upholstered pieces, which Wright has reproduced in local workrooms.

LOS ANGELES CENTRAL LIBRARY, 1926

630 West Fifth Street
Los Angeles, California

*Bertram Grosvenor Goodhue
and Carleton Winslow, Sr.*

The Los Angeles Central Library lost 375,000 books and much of the building in a devastating 1986 fire—but it gained a consensus. Leaving the downtown landmark for the suburbs, a popular idea in some circles, seemed out of the question after the famous torch-topped monument's brush with destruction. Instead, the library opted to repair and expand the building (using a complicated air rights transfer), upgrading technical and information systems in the process. The ambitious program, masterminded by Hardy Holtzman Pfeiffer, doubled the size to 540,000 square feet and restored and expanded the library's park into a delightful urban oasis. The library reopened to great applause in 1993.

When it was built, the library set new standards for eclecticism. Its blending of Byzantine, Egyptian, Roman, and Art Deco themes in a modern structure was considered quite a breakthrough, and it provided a model for such major civic buildings as the Los Angeles City Hall of 1928 and Goodhue's renowned Nebraska State Capitol. The library design was all the more remarkable considering the architects' recent past. At the San Diego Exposition of 1915, their Spanish Colonial design literally stopped the clock and initiated a national enthusiasm for the mission style. With the library, they were changing architectural directions for the nation once again.

Goodhue and Winslow designed the library as a massive rectangular building, with a chunky central tower that rises to a colorful, tiled pyramid at the top. As befitted a building of such civic importance, the architects set off the structure with a public park. The building and the lawn are different on every side, but the most impressive approach displays fascinating sculptured plinths by Lee Laurie that personify the ideals of Science, Art, Statecraft, Philosophy, Letters, and History.

This combination public spirit and architectural magnificence continues in the artful interiors, now meticulously restored. Among these treasures are enormous murals by Dean Cornwell depicting the history of California, the beautiful stenciled ceilings, and the vaulted central rotunda.

From the front, the library looks much the same now, for about two-thirds of Hardy Holzman Pfeiffer's new wing is underground. The many useful new facilities include a 235-seat auditorium and a childrens' theater. A glass atrium illuminates the floors below ground with the bright Los Angeles light.

Tours are held daily. For information and schedules, call (213) 228-7168.

One of the great monuments of modern architecture, Lovell Beach House was the first major International Style house in America. Built for a progressive Los Angeles physician, the house represents R.M. Schindler's breakthrough into the realm of advanced design.

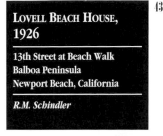

LOVELL BEACH HOUSE, 1926

13th Street at Beach Walk
Balboa Peninsula
Newport Beach, California

R.M. Schindler

Lovell Beach House displays the pure "machined" characteristics of the International Style: the appearance of weightlessness, white stucco walls, long horizontal lines, and ribbon windows set almost flush with the exterior walls. But on close inspection—for example, the geometric window designs that look a little like Mondrian, and a little like Wright—Schindler's modernism looks both personal and artistic.

The beach house combines grace, lightness, and strength. Schindler brings enormous buoyancy to this fascinating and complex design. The house is lifted above the beach on five concrete cradles that allow light and sand beneath the structure. From near the center of the ground level, a pair of graceful staircases leads up to the main living floor of the two-story house. This main floor is a long, lofty living room open to the ocean, with service rooms to the rear. Upstairs, four bedrooms with sleeping porches are recessed toward the rear of the house.

A private residence, the beach house precedes Dr. Lovell's equally famous residence by Richard Neutra in the Los Feliz section of Los Angeles, which was built a few years later (see page 52).

44

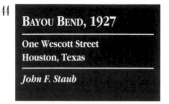

BAYOU BEND, 1927

One Wescott Street
Houston, Texas

John F. Staub

In Houston, a house by John Staub is in the same category as an Addison Mizner house in Palm Beach. It is architecture that succeeds in capturing the dreams, myths, and history of a place so thoroughly that it becomes preferred style—the local classic. The most beloved Staub house, Bayou Bend, is also the most accessible. This gracious southern mansion, with its stunning gardens, is now a museum featuring a premier collection of American furniture, paintings, metals, ceramics, glass, and textiles.

Just five minutes from the downtown skyscrapers, Bayou Bend seems to be in another world entirely. Set within fourteen acres of leafy woods and eight distinctive gardens, the mansion is the centerpiece. John Staub called it "Latin Colonial," a pale-pink stucco house that is classic in design and proportion but festive with cast-iron balconies and trim reminiscent of the New Orleans French Quarter. Staub designed Bayou Bend for a famous Houston philanthropist, Ima Hogg. The only daughter of a former Texas governor, "Miss Ima" was beginning to assemble the collection that would grow to almost 5,000 pieces and prompt her to turn the mansion into a museum. During her long and active life (she died in 1975 at age 93), friendships with Henry Francis DuPont of Winterthur and Joseph Downs, curator of the Metropolitan Museum's American Wing, were among the influences on her selections.

The gardens of Bayou Bend, designed by Ellen Shipman of New York, were carved out of the "dense thicket." Like the collection, the gardens also evolved gradually and today there are eight—White, Butterfly, East, Diana, Clio, Euterpe, Carla, and Topiary—plus the areas of native woods.

Bayou Bend, the museum, opened in 1966 and is owned by the Museum of Fine Arts, comprising the museum's Decorative Arts Wing. The house and gardens are open to the public Tuesday to Saturday, 10:00 AM to 5:00 PM, Sunday 1:00 to 5:00 PM, closed Monday. For tour information, call (713) 639-7750.

The skyscraper was born in Chicago, where fascination with tall buildings reached fever pitch in 1922. In that year, the *Chicago Tribune* announced a design competition for the newspaper's new home, symbolizing the power of the press through advanced architecture. The opportunity to design a structure of such high visibility, along with the prospect of a $50,000 prize, drew 260 entries—100 of them from Europe. Architectural critic Paul Goldberger described the competition as "something of a world's fair of skyscraper design."

CHICAGO TRIBUNE TOWER, 1927

435 North Michigan Avenue Chicago, Illinois

Howells and Hood

The winning entry, by John Mead Howells and Raymond Hood, reflected the accepted model for skyscraper design in America—the Gothic cathedral—right up to the circle of buttresses surrounding its crown. It was a lavishly detailed historical design, but a solid and well-portioned one.

It triumphed over submissions of the most advanced European modernists, who had yet to build any skyscrapers of their own.

If the American winner was traditional, the European entries presented bold skyscraper innovations. The most highly acclaimed design, a stepped-back tower by Eliel Saarinen of Finland, won second prize, and prompted Saarinen to move to Chicago. Walter Gropius and Adolph Meyer submitted a Bauhaus-style skyscraper, and Adolph Loos' envisioned an 11-story square base surmounted by a gigantic Doric column. The Europeans lost the competition but won the war. Their entries marked the official transition to modern skyscraper design.

Within the last decades of the twentieth century, historical styles regained some measure of respect. The Chicago Tribune Tower has become a venerable landmark in downtown Chicago. Its lobby is open from 8:00 AM to 5:00 PM Monday through Friday. For visitor information, call (312) 222-3232. Also, the building exterior is included in tours conducted by the Chicago Architecture Foundation, 224 South Michigan Avenue, (312) 922-3432.

GRAUMANN'S CHINESE THEATRE, 1927 (MANN'S CHINESE THEATRE)

6925 Hollywood Boulevard
Los Angeles, California

Meyer and Holler

A flamboyant picture palace from the grand old days of Hollywood, Mann's Chinese Theatre now draws thousands of tourists each year who are eager to match their handprints and footprints with those of the stars.

The theater was the last one built by showman Sid Graumann, who invented the Hollywood premiere as a public relations event. Graumann's grasp of the spectacular is exhibited in his last movie house, designed by Meyer and Holler. Graumann reputedly imported pillars from a real Chinese temple for the forecourt. But whatever the Chinese theme is lacking in total authenticity, it more than makes up for in sheer audacity.

The entire ensemble clamors for attention. The pagoda-style copper roof on a central tower is the high point, and is flanked by two masonry wings 40-feet tall that extend from the tower to form an elliptical forecourt. The walls facing the street feature full-height pylons on either end of the façade; the pylons are embellished with decorative bands and topped by tall, copper obelisks shooting flames. The walls are green, the doors are Chinese lacquer red.

Most visitors, however, come not for the movies, but to see the signatures—handprints and footprints of the stars—encased in the forecourt's concrete. Local legends credit Douglas Fairbanks and Mary Pickford with starting the tradition by stepping accidentally into the wet cement; others insist it was Norma Talmadge.

Movies are still shown here, and there are neon dragons calling attention to the current marquee. For schedules, call (323) 464-6266.

The exuberant spirit of Los Angeles in the 1920s is captured in its symbol of civic pride, City Hall. A consortium of local architects produced this eclectic but memorable design—an Italian-style arched entry and courtyard at the street, a jazzy, stepped-back tower 28 stories tall, and a pyramid topping the roof. Inside, the central rotunda combines the classic marble grandeur of a cathedral with Hollywood "show biz" in more or less peaceful coexistence.

Los Angeles City Hall, 1928

200 North Spring Street
Los Angeles, California

John C. Austin, John and Donald Parkinson, Albert C. Martin, Sr.

This civic monument became known to millions of Americans in the 1950s, when its image served to identify the setting of the hit television series "Dragnet." But while gaining fame across the country during that decade, City Hall lost some of its prominence at home. A change of building code revoked the former height limitations that had ensured the prominence of City Hall. Now, of course, the 28-story City Hall has been far outstripped in size, but it nevertheless continues to outshine many of its soaring sisters. An observation deck on the 27th floor provides breathtaking views of the sprawling city, including the new Walt Disney Concert Hall a few blocks away.

Said to have starred in more movies and television shows than most actors, City Hall has reopened following an extensive renovation. Public tours are held Monday to Friday, from 9:00 AM to noon. Reservations advised. For information, call (213) 978-0642. The L.A. Conservancy also hosts tours the first Saturday of the month at 11:00 AM, reservations required. Call the L.A. Conservancy at (213) 623-2489.

PHILADELPHIA MUSEUM OF ART, 1928

Benjamin Franklin Parkway
at 26th Street
Philadelphia, Pennsylvania

Borie, Trumbauer & Zantzinge

The Philadelphia Museum of Art is called the "Philadelphia Acropolis," and it is in fact one of the largest Greek-temple-style buildings in the world. As a civic event, the museum and the Benjamin Franklin Parkway complement one another in a mixture of City Beautiful planning and Beaux Arts classicism. The stately boulevard provides a properly awesome approach to this obviously important monument. Given the building's size, its classical grandeur, and the art and treasures inside, visiting the museum is a little like visiting Versailles.

The parkway entrance presents the museum's most imposing face: a central portico flanked by symmetrical porticoed wings that form an honor courtyard with a fountain. A wide, ceremonial stairway (famous as the place where the movie hero Rocky "goes the distance") ushers visitors from the street to the courtyard, but the main entrance is on the opposite side, overlooking the Schuylkill River. A walk around the building conveys its full size and the intricacy of such classical detailing as colorful friezes, terra-cotta ornamentation, and griffins on the roof. The building itself is strongly colored the intense natural yellow of its main materials, Mankota and Kasota stone (500,000 tons of it).

The vast museum was built for a city that owned very little art. But the museum's collection of artwork and period rooms now ranks as one of the best in the country. Permanent and temporary exhibits are installed primarily on the two palatial upper floors, E-shaped in plan. The heart of this building is a great, marble stairway flanked with Ionic columns and covered with a barrel-vaulted ceiling. In the dim inner light, this enormous central well, with its marble walls and floors, seems ancient and austere.

The museum's architects—especially Horace Trumbauer—were socially prominent civic boosters. The firm won the museum design by competition, although the design changed radically and frequently in the twenty years between the commission and the completion.

The Philadelphia Museum of Art is open Tuesday to Sunday 10:00 AM to 5:00 PM, Friday until 8:45 PM. Closed Monday and legal holidays. Gallery tours are offered on the hour from 10:00 AM to 3:00 PM. For general information, call (215) 763-8100.

T he rich and seductive tropical style of old Palm Beach is largely the vision of one man, the self-taught Addison Mizner. A well-traveled society architect and bon vivant, Mizner arrived in Florida from his practice in New York. Almost immediately he began transforming this southern jungle land into an elegant winter resort for the wealthy. His clients' dreams, and the architecture of Spain, the French

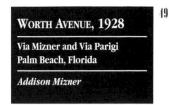

WORTH AVENUE, 1928

**Via Mizner and Via Parigi
Palm Beach, Florida**

Addison Mizner

Riviera, and Central America, inspired Mizner's basic formula: light stucco walls in pastel tints, topped with tile roofs and weathered cypress woodwork, and the inevitable coconut tree with its decorative tufted shape and play of light and shade.

The small, upscale shopping enclave off Worth Avenue dates to the early 1920s, when Mizner purchased Joe's Alligator Farm using money from his patron Paris Singer, heir to the sewing machine fortune. Mizner carved out four blocks between the Atlantic Ocean and Lake Worth. The cluster of shops, restaurants, and apartments was built in the same style as Mizner's fabulous villas,

with cloistered arcades, Cuban barrel-tile roofs, stucco walls, Venetian arched windows, decorative railings, tiled stairways, and patios with fountains.

Worth Avenue's architecture has remained virtually unchanged. Exclusive boutiques can be found on two shopping levels, connected by steps, bridges, and passageways. Mizner's Mediterranean-style interiors provide instant antiquity via knotty cypress beams, coral keystone, *saultillo* tile floors and stencil painting. If you're "just looking," Mizner's creation of an intimate scale animated by constantly changing details is still a pleasure.

Mizner's office occupied a four-story tower on Worth Avenue. His practice resembled a one-man band: designing; building; manufacturing both clay roof tiles in his own kilns and ironwork with his own blacksmith; and reproducing furniture, which he sold by catalog. Mizner's contribution here is immortalized in the street name, Via Mizner (Via Parigi honors Paris Singer), and in the approximately thirty-six private homes still in Palm Beach. Several more villas incorrectly claim Mizner's cachet, but there is no doubt about the authenticity of Worth Avenue and the Everglades Club that anchors the west end of the avenue.

The Worth Avenue shops are open during regular retail hours. For information, call the Worth Avenue Association at (561) 659-6909.

ARIZONA BILTMORE HOTEL, 1929

24th Street and Missouri
Phoenix, Arizona

*Albert Chase McArthur and
Frank Lloyd Wright*

Writing to the widow of Albert Chase McArthur, architect of record for the Arizona Biltmore, Frank Lloyd Wright confessed, "I have always given Albert's name as architect . . . and always will. But I know better and so should you." As McArthur's "collaborator," Wright clearly played the dominant role in the hotel's design. His signature shines in the stretched proportions of the main entry with its oriental roof; the long, low spans of the guest wings; and the way the building reverberates with the textures and colors of the desert.

The notion of Frank Lloyd Wright working "incognito and behind the scenes," as he did here, contradicts all evidence of his ferocious ego. But in 1927, during a particularly low point in his on-again, off-again career, Wright came to Phoenix to assist his former apprentice.

There is no doubt that Wright created the hotel's most visible component: the distinctive combination of plain and patterned, pre-cast concrete blocks. Wright invented the molded block technique for La Miniatura in Hollywood in 1920 (the Millard House, see page 37), and he was taken with the fact that the patterned blocks contained their own "decoration." For the Biltmore, rectangular, gray, steel-reinforced blocks were molded on site from Arizona earth and sand. The decorative blocks feature a bas-relief resembling an abstract palm leaf, and recall ancient Aztec and Mayan motifs. Hollow in the center, the blocks are erected back to back, an ingenious method that provides effective insulation and allows both inner and outer walls to be constructed simultaneously.

Fire destroyed the fourth floor and the beautiful copper roof in 1973. Since then, the Biltmore has been rebuilt and remodeled six times under the supervision of Taliesen Associates Architects and Wright's widow, Olgivanna. But still the hotel went into decline. In 1992 Phoenix developer Sam Grossman and his wife Peggy bought the property. Their fresh and elegant restoration, by Vernon Swaback Associates of Phoenix (whose principals once worked for the Frank Lloyd Wright Foundation), was completed in 1995.

Wright's officially uncredited influence is mitigated by his famous *Biltmore Sprites*—elongated concrete female figures recast from the 1914 original Midway Gardens sculptures and moved here in 1982—that stand guard at the entrance.

For information, call the Biltmore at (602) 955-6600.

G reta Garbo bought her trousers in the men's department, Clark Gable ordered paisley wool ski suits, and William Randolph Hearst picked up swimsuits for San Simeon's house guests. While catering to a select clientele, this Art Deco masterpiece also represented retailing at its most radical.

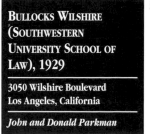

BULLOCKS WILSHIRE (SOUTHWESTERN UNIVERSITY SCHOOL OF LAW), 1929

3050 Wilshire Boulevard
Los Angeles, California

John and Donald Parkman

Its suburban location was essentially shocking—people shopped downtown, but automobiles were changing the old ways, and Los Angeles was already a car town. The main entrance faced the parking lot rather than the street, another shocking departure. The forward-thinking owners, John Bullock and P.G. Winnett, envisioned the store as a cluster of individual boutiques. Prominent Los Angeles architects John Parkman and his son Donald first designed the store with a flat roof and multi-windowed façade. Then, Winnett and the younger Parkman discovered Art Deco and Bauhaus designs at the Exposition des Arts Decoratifs in Paris in 1925. This changed everything. Tearing up the original plans, they started over.

In its new incarnation, the store was shaped like an asymmetrical pyramid, stepping up from a five-story base to the ten-story tower, illuminated at night as a beacon to shoppers. Glazed terra-cotta covers much of the exterior, and a thin veneer of black granite surrounds the base. "Zigzag moderne" motifs provide much of the ornament. Copper spandrels embossed in a snowflake pattern border the windows, which rise up the building in vertical rows. Display windows at street level are framed like pictures, with cast brass and bronze overhangs embellished with flowers. Overall, the various metals and sculptural motifs make the building appear luminous.

The extraordinary interiors showed the work of thirteen artists and designers, famous and unheralded. They collaborated with the architects to turn the structural elements into works of

art. Copper, nickel, bronze, and brass were combined with masonry, marble, cork, glass, and wood. Woven artworks were commissioned for the walls and floors, including seven carpets by Sonia Delauney.

In March, 1993, the store was closed by its corporate owner, Macy's. In 1996, the Southwestern University School of Law moved to the building, following an extensive renovation that preserved as much as possible of the existing architecture. One-third of the building is now a law library. Limited tours may be possible. For information, call (213) 738-8240.

PHILIP LOVELL HOUSE, 1929

4616 Dundee Drive
Los Angeles, California

Richard Neutra

It was not until 1932 that the International Style got its name, but outstanding examples of progressive European architecture began to crop up in America in the 1920s. One of the most accomplished of these was the Philip Lovell House, a "health house" designed by Richard Neutra for a Los Angeles physician and health faddist.

A native of Vienna, Neutra worked with Eric Mendelsohn, Otto Wagner, and Adolf Loos before moving to the United States in 1923. After a brief association with Frank Lloyd Wright, Neutra migrated to the West Coast, where Wright had several houses underway.

Here at Lovell House, only the broad, horizontal, cantilevered spans are reminiscent of Wright's work. Otherwise, the "modern" elements prevail: the boxy white modules, the flat walls and roof, the steel frame hung with panels of prefabricated concrete walls, and the standard steel windows. And then there is the architectural purity of the all-white exterior, and the overall sense that the interior volumes are weightlessly enclosed by the exterior elements. In effect, the Lovell House seems about to take off from its landing spot in the Hollywood Hills.

Neutra's breakthrough design of Lovell House became an instant landmark. The house was widely published and highly acclaimed, and it proved that architects and clients in America could be just as progressive as their European counterparts.

The house is a private residence.

A 32-foot-tall aluminum statue of Ceres, the Roman goddess of grain, tops the pyramidal roof of this Chicago landmark. Designed by sculptor John H. Stoors, Ceres is emblematic of what goes on inside: the vigorous daily exchange of contracts on commodities futures, including contracts on grains like corn and wheat. The building is simply a marketplace, but it takes on large symbolic importance. After all, fortunes are made and lost with incredible rapidity in this building's commodity trading "pits."

CHICAGO BOARD OF TRADE BUILDING, 1930

141 West Jackson Boulevard
Chicago, Illinois

Holabird & Root

The Board of Trade building has a landmark-quality location at the end of a city canyon formed by LaSalle Street. Its great vertical windows ascending from the third-floor level reveal the location of the enormous trading room, which is six stories high. The windows are capped, at about the level of the ninth floor, by a monstrous inset clock, flanked and attended by two tall, sculpted figures (representing Risk and Reward, one may freely surmise). The clock marks the passage of the trading day. It also makes a metaphoric nod at the passage of time into the risky, unknowable regions of the future, while inside the traders try to control risk, as of a crop failure, through the artful purchase and sale of grain futures contracts. From the clock upward, the shaft of this skyscraper rises 45 stories to tower over the neighborhood.

The architects, Holabird and Root, took pains to emphasize the vertical. The horizontal lines are carefully understated. The spandrels of the towers, for example, are recessed and discontinuous.

The firm, originally formed as Holabird and Roche, has roots in the Chicago architectural tradition that extend back to the late nineteenth century. After a change in partners in 1928, the firm produced an extraordinary series of skyscrapers of the modernistic type, including an addition to the Chicago Board of Trade and the especially notable Palmolive (now Playboy) building.

In the 1930s, the firm was strongly associated with the Art Deco style and the interiors show it. Inside the Board of Trade, at ground level, low corridors lined with shops lead to a lofty three-story lobby, which is regarded as a classic of Art Deco design. Notice the polished glass, nickel, and marble of these interiors, and how beautifully they affect the quality of the light. Then visit the trading room and hearken to the shouting in the pits. The 1982 addition by Helmut Jahn, an 11-story steel-and-glass atrium, is quite a contrast to the original building.

The Board's Visitor's Center, in response to security concerns, has fluctuating access and schedules. For information, call (312) 435-3590. The exterior is featured on Chicago Architecture Foundation tours; for information, call (312) 922-3432.

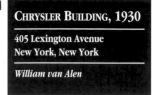

CHRYSLER BUILDING, 1930

405 Lexington Avenue
New York, New York

William van Alen

For a brief moment, the Chrysler Building won the "world's tallest building" contest going on among skyscraper developers. But the hubcap-studded landmark has endured as one of New York City's most beloved buildings. This Art Deco masterpiece has a liveliness and humor that lifts the spirits, whether viewed from up close, from a distance, or only in photographs (especially the one that shows William van Alen wearing a model of the Chrysler Building as a Halloween costume).

The 77-story Chrysler Building rises 1,048 feet to the top, where most of the action is. Van Alen realized that tall buildings were primarily defined by their pinnacles, and he created an extravaganza of Art Deco detail: five rows of stainless steel arches, diminishing in size toward the top of the building, with each row inset with triangular windows set in a zigzag pattern. A needle-like spire surmounts the entire creation. Curves and zigzags are combined imaginatively, reflecting

the Art Deco style of the day as well as Mayan and Egyptian patterns of ancient times. The main shaft of the building receives a fantastic flourish—at each corner van Alen mounted stainless steel gargoyles representing the hood ornament of the 1929 Chrysler automobile. At night, the creation presents a lively show of lights.

The lobby of the Chrysler Building provides some of the best Art Deco detailing in New York City. Rich, red African marble sets the tone for the lobby, where the elevator doors are inlaid with wood and brass in masterful Art Deco patterns.

The Chrysler Building is open during regular business hours and you can walk in and see the spectacular lobby. On Friday at 12:30 PM, weather permitting, the Grand Central Partnership conducts tours of the Grand Central Station area, including the Chrysler Building. Groups meet in the Sculpture Court of the Whitney Museum at Altria, 42nd Street and Park Avenue. For information, call (212) 883-2476.

It is fitting that the early Superman movies were set at the Daily News Building. While the comic strip hero leaped tall buildings in a single bound, the Daily News architect, Raymond Hood, spanned their styles in a smooth career arc. In 1927, Hood gained fame for taking the Gothic Revival skyscraper to awesome heights (see the Chicago Tribune Tower, page 45). But just a few years later his Daily News Building offered a clean new vision of skyscraper design.

DAILY NEWS BUILDING, 1930

220 East 42nd Street
at Second Avenue
New York, New York

Raymond Hood

Here Hood captured the soaring quality of the skyscraper —with tall, vertical rows of white brick piers rising crisply toward the sky and culminating in a new, flat top. Although to many the building looked like newspapers laid end to end, the appearance resulted from practical considerations. The piers provide the cover for the structural system of steel beams, which alternate with rows of utility conduits to establish the exterior rhythm. New York City's setback requirements influenced the overall shape, in conjunction with Hood's own shape-making skill.

In these last days before air-conditioning, the Daily News Building was built with operable windows. In fact, the windows were a crucial design issue. Hood based the interior modules on windows four-and-a-half-feet wide, the largest size a stenographer could open without assistance.

Hood moved from revival to modern design, but he did not eliminate tradition altogether. The building's piers, which appear ramrod straight, actually curve slightly inward, like Greek columns. There is also subtle decoration; the spandrels feature a progressive geometric pattern of red and black brick, which enlivens the severity of the white brick piers. A 1960 annex by Harrison & Abramowitz continued Hood's original theme.

The newspaper *The Daily News* occupied the Daily News building from 1930 until 1995. In early 1996, its name was still chiseled into the Art Deco facade, but the paper had moved away.

The building is open during business hours. Be sure to see the giant globe suspended in a cutout of the lobby floor; radiating from the sphere are brass strips set into the terrazzo that show the distance from New York to all the world's major cities.

The Grand Central Partnership conducts neighborhood walking tours which often include the Daily News. Groups meet at 12:30 PM on Friday in the Sculpture Court of the Whitney Museum at Altria, 42nd Street and Park Avenue. For information, call (212) 883-2476.

MIAMI BEACH "ART DECO DISTRICT," 1930-1939

Ocean Drive and Collins Avenue from 5th to 16th Streets
Miami Beach, Florida

Various architects

The renaissance of Miami Beach as a fantasy playground coincides with a renewed appreciation of its unique and colorful architectural heritage. Within the square-mile Architectural Historic District, there are over 650 significant structures, the largest concentration in the country. A light-hearted tropical style incorporating flowers, flamingos, and ocean liners was created by a small number of local architects who often lacked formal training but were wise in the ways of popular appeal.

Miami Beach architecture gained a huge new audience through its starring role as the stylish background of the television series, "Miami Vice." In real life, three different architectural styles can be distinguished, although the design elements are often intertwined.

The "classic" Art Deco buildings (1926–1936) are geometric but elegant, and richly ornamented with tropical themes. Later Art Deco buildings in the streamlined style known as "art moderne" mimicked the machines of motion: planes, trains, cars, and steamships. These are the buildings with rounded walls, eyebrow windows, and futuristic towers; colorful bands of painted racing stripes provide most of the decoration. In the Mediterranean revival buildings, arched windows, clay-tile barrel roofs, stucco walls, wrought iron gates, and courtyards evoke an old world mystique that could be set in Spain, Italy, France, or Morocco.

The Miami Design Preservation League conducts ninety-minute walking tours of the area Wednesday, Saturday, and Sunday at 10:30 AM and Thursday at 6:30 PM. The group meets at the League's Welcome Center, Ocean Drive at 10th Avenue; Sunday reservations required. In January, the League hosts its big annual event, the Art Deco Weekend Festival. For free-form touring, the League has also published a 192-page paperback entitled *Miami Beach Art Deco Guide*, which you can pick up at the Welcome Center. For information, call (305) 672-2014.

Aluminaire House—"A House for Contemporary Life"—first appeared as an exhibit at the Allied Arts and Building Products Exhibition held in New York in 1931. Designed in one week, constructed in ten days, costing 25 cents each cubic foot, this metal-kit prototype was meant to light the way toward progressive, affordable housing.

ALUMINAIRE HOUSE, 1931

**New York Institute of
Technology Campus
Carlton Avenue
Central Islip, Long Island,
New York**

*Albert Frey with Lawrence
Kocher*

The first steel and metal house in America, Aluminaire House reflected the fashionable European fascination with machines, together with the American reality of new materials, such as metal and glass, and new technology for using them. Innovations were many. The three-story rectangle was framed with light aluminum beams and sheathed in narrow-ribbed aluminum joined by washers and screws of the same material. All the window frames and doors were framed with steel. The walls were backed with paper-covered insulation board, a composition three inches thick that was said to provide more insulation than 13 inches of masonry.

Of the three interior levels, the only full floor is the middle one, which contains the main living spaces, including a living room two stories tall. The ground level is given over to a porch, a garage, and utility space; the upper floor provides a library, a shower room that cantilevers over the living room below, and a roof terrace covered by its own patch of lawn. With a completeness almost unimaginable on such a short schedule and budget, Aluminaire featured built-in furniture—including inflatable chairs—and ultraviolet lighting for indoor tanning.

Aluminaire House was designed by Albert Frey, a Swiss émigré and crusading modernist who had worked with Le Corbusier and had been in the United States for only one year. His partner, Lawrence Kocher, was an American architect and magazine writer who promoted the progressive spirit of machine-age architecture. The partnership was short-lived; Kocher remained in the east, but in 1934 Frey set up a practice in Palm Springs, California, where he continued to advance his modern ideas until he died at 98 in 1995.

Only one Aluminaire House was ever built, but it made history as one of the few American buildings in the 1932 International Style exhibit at New York's Museum of Modern Art. After several rebuildings, Aluminaire House has a new home at the New York Institute of Technology campus on Long Island. Architecture students are reconstructing the metal-kit house. When complete, the house will become a museum, open to the public. Aluminaire House archives will be housed there, along with research materials on affordable housing. For information, call J. Michael Schwarting at (631) 348-3363.

EMPIRE STATE BUILDING, 1931

Fifth Avenue at 34th Street
New York, New York

Shreve, Lamb, and Harmon

The Empire State Building debuted as the tallest building in New York City, and in the world. With 102 stories—almost a quarter mile high—it reigned over the skyline for decades, until the World Trade Center overshadowed it. Once again the city's tallest tower (at least until the WTC rebuilding occurs), it is a beacon on the skyline, especially at night, when its lighted crown glows red, white, and blue in the dark.

Workers labored twenty-four hours a day to construct this mammoth tower in just eight months. This feat was possible by the first "fast tracking" orchestration of design and construction of a major building. From the design standpoint, the vast size is relieved by both the massing and the materials. The firm of Shreve, Lamb, and Harmon created a finely pro-

portioned tower—with a five-story base, an H-shaped plan, and a series of setbacks that helps the building blend in with its surroundings.

In many ways, the Empire State Building is remarkably reserved. Its monochromatic color scheme—gray Indiana limestone brightened by bands of aluminum and nickel—is extremely low key.

The Empire State Building and its famous 86th-floor observatory is open daily, including weekends and holidays, from 9:30 AM to midnight. The last elevators go up at 11:15 PM. Evening views are spectacular. In 2005, entertaining new exhibits were added to depict the building's construction and its celebrated history, which includes prominent movie appearances in *King Kong* and *Sleepless in Seattle*. For information, call (212) 736-3100.

The founding of Cranbrook Academy in 1924 by publisher George G. Booth had the intended effect of providing a rare enclave of artistic instruction, and the fortuitous result of capturing the talents of Eliel Saarinen. The great Finnish architect planned to return to his homeland after two years teaching at the University of Michigan. However, Saarinen was commissioned to masterplan the campus, design the buildings and supervise their construction, and to teach architecture as well. It was a commission that would last for twenty-five years and produce one of the modern masterpieces of academic architecture and Saarinen's most comprehensive work.

KINGSWOOD SCHOOL FOR GIRLS, 1931 (CRANBROOK KINGSWOOD SCHOOL)

Cranbrook Academy of Art
1221 Woodward Avenue
Bloomfield Hills, Michigan

Eliel Saarinen

Kingswood School for Girls, with its warm, tan brick, and copper roof, was designed by Saarinen in 1929, constructed in 1930, and completed in 1931. Judging from the overall massing of the school, the ideas of Frank Lloyd Wright were influential—the stretched proportion of the main section, with its high horizontal windows tucked beneath a hipped roof and overhanging eaves, and by the adjacent wing, which also shows horizontal bands of windows and overhanging eaves. Internally, the changing levels of floors and ceilings and the interior openness are somewhat in the Wrightian style as well. Saarinen, however, imparts his own convictions to all his treatments. Especially noticeable are the telescoping chimneys, a motif that recurs throughout the building.

Over the years, Cranbrook Academy has been a most prominent force in the training of artists and designers, fulfilling Booth's early vision of an institution on the order of the American Academy in Rome. The 125-acre campus is open and you can drive around and see the Girls' School and many other fine Saarinen buildings. The Saarinen-designed art museum is open to the public from 1:00 to 5:00 PM Wednesday through Sunday. Saarinen's own home has also been restored to reflect the way it appeared in 1938, when he last lived there, and it is also open to the public.

Steven Holl's Institute of Science addition is filled with terrific child-friendly exhibits. Other new buildings include Rafael Moneo's studio addition and a swimming facility by Tod Williams Billie Tsien. For information and tour requests, call (248) 645-3200.

McGraw-Hill Building, 1931

330 West 42nd Street
New York, New York

Raymond Hood

When the Museum of Modern Art in New York organized its first exhibition of architecture in 1932, it celebrated those buildings designed in accordance with the principles of the European avant-garde. The term "International Style" was coined to describe these buildings, which were simultaneously lionized and institutionalized by the exhibition. Only one New York skyscraper was deemed worthy of admission into this elite group—the McGraw-Hill Building designed by Raymond Hood, whose work had evolved in the preceding decade from the neo-Gothic Chicago Tribune Tower to the heights of modernism.

"The McGraw-Hill Building comes nearest to achieving aesthetically the expression of the enclosed steel cage," proclaimed the exhibition catalog, intending a compliment. Indeed, the 60-story building's industrial toughness and ribbon windows are all modern, while the color and finishes are more "moderne" or Art Deco, the latest style. Colorful and catchy, the McGraw-Hill Building is clad in a vivid greenish-blue terra-cotta that belies the severity of the structure. The office floors step in three stages, capped by an enormous signboard, creating a shape and an impression that Vincent Skully describes as "proto jukebox."

The McGraw-Hill Company moved to new offices in the 1970s, and now the building is occupied by other tenants. But the McGraw-Hill name, in its original Art Deco style, is still displayed on the main façades.

The building is open during regular business hours.

S unset Towers was designed by Leland A. Bryant to bring Art Deco elegance from Europe to the United States, and especially to Hollywood's movie star clientele. Errol Flynn, Jean Harlow, Clark Gable, Howard Hughes, and Marilyn Monroe were early residents.

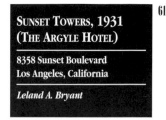

**SUNSET TOWERS, 1931
(THE ARGYLE HOTEL)**

8358 Sunset Boulevard
Los Angeles, California

Leland A. Bryant

The luxurious apartment house consisted of forty-six apartments on fourteen floors. It was set high up in the Hollywood Hills and offered a spectacular view of the city. When it opened, its size and distinctive Art Deco style were rivaled only by the unprecedented technology employed in its construction. Other buildings have their foundations cast into solid bedrock, but Sunset Towers was built on "rockers" to make it one of the first earthquake-proof buildings in Los Angeles. Its greatest technical distinction, however, was as the first all-electric apartment building in California, and its electric shaving plugs, set beside etched-glass plaques in bathrooms with special moldings, became famous throughout Hollywood.

One of the finest examples of Art Deco architecture in Los Angeles, the building's exterior is pale gray with silver highlights featuring intricate molding. The Los Angeles architect apparently

loved machines and movement as much as any European architect of the time, for over the entry he mounted a concrete frieze entitled, "The Age of Travel," depicting U-boats, airplanes, and a zeppelin.

After a long, sad period of neglect, Sunset Towers was massively renovated. Classic Art Deco furnishings were reproduced by Italian craftsmen according to the original specifications, including gondola beds by Emile-Jacques Ruhlmann, ebony desks by Pierre Chareau, and serpentine armchairs by Eileen Gray.

Sunset Towers began its new life as a grand hotel in 1988. It is now known as The Argyle Hotel. For information, call (323) 654-7100.

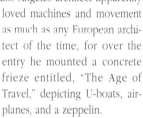

FOLGER SHAKESPEARE LIBRARY, 1932

201 East Capitol Street S.E.
Washington, D.C.

Paul Philippe Cret

Paul Philippe Cret was an eclectic architect in the best sense of the word, a French-born, Ecole des Beaux Arts graduate who respected traditional forms but understood that buildings can only be constructed in the present. The Folger Shakespeare Library is wonderfully eclectic too, its stripped-down classic exterior enclosing interiors of Elizabethan grandeur.

The cool, white marble exterior is enlivened by nine bas-reliefs by John Gregory depicting scenes from Shakespeare plays, fluted column-like piers between the tall, narrow, leaded-glass windows, and a frieze of chiseled inscriptions honoring the great playwright. A statue of Puck is prominently placed.

The Folger Library contains an almost unimaginable wealth of material for scholars. The Great Hall and the theater, however, are the main public spaces. A showcase for special exhibitions highlighting the collection, the Great Hall resembles an Elizabethan manor house, with its paneled walls and plastered ceiling impressed with Shakespeare's coat of arms and fleurs-de-lis, and hung with heraldic flags. The theater is meant to suggest an Elizabethan inn courtyard, the setting in which Shakespeare's plays were actually performed at the time he wrote them. Concerts, readings, performances, and other events are held here throughout the year. Outdoors, an Elizabethan garden is filled with herbs and plants from Shakespeare's time.

The Folger Shakespeare Library is open from 10:00 AM to 4:00 PM, Monday to Saturday, and closed on federal holidays. Walk-in tours are given daily at 11:00 AM. Entrance to the museum is free, but admission is charged for ticketed events, such as the plays and concerts. For information about the free exhibits or ticketed events, call (202) 544-4600.

The Nebraska State Capitol shows American architecture striving to be modern. This "Tower on the Plains" rises like a Manhattan skyscraper in sleek setbacks from a two-story base. Its overall appearance is smoothly vertical, its ornament subdued, flattened, and geometrical.

NEBRASKA STATE CAPITOL, 1932

1445 K Street
Lincoln, Nebraska

Bertram Grosvenor Goodhue

These machine-age motifs were blended with the traditional formula for monumental civic architecture. The approach to the building is properly ceremonial, and the plan is symmetrical: a cross within a square forming four interior courtyards. The 400-foot tower culminates in a dome, symbolically ornamented with a 32-foot, 8-ton bronze sculpture, "The Sower," by Lee Lawrie. There was no stinting on tradition when it came to the selection of cladding materials; inside and out, more than forty varieties of marble, granite, slate, and limestone are in evidence.

Homage is paid to local traditions as well. The doors to the Senate are highly carved to represent the "Red Man's Tree of Life." Over on the House side, tooled and inlaid leather-covered doors depict the "White Man's Tree of Life."

Bertram Goodhue was an innovative and influential architect who practiced with Ralph Adams Cram in Boston before opening his own office in New York City in 1914. Originally working in a Gothic Revival style like almost everyone else at the time, he soon progressed from medieval to Mediterranean. Goodhue was working his way into a thoroughly modern architecture when his career was cut short by his early death in 1924.

Free tours are conducted year-round, except for Christmas, New Year's Day, and Thursday and Friday of the Thanksgiving holiday. From Memorial Day to Labor Day, tours are conducted every half hour from 9:00 AM to 4:00 PM; the rest of the year, tours are every hour from 10:00 AM to 4:00 PM. Sunday tours are 1:00 to 4:00 PM. For information or group reservations, call (402) 471-0448.

At the time of its construction, the Philadelphia Savings Fund Society Building (PSFS) was the most innovative skyscraper in the world. Its location in Philadelphia comes as something of a surprise, however, given its status as the first skyscraper built to the specifications of the European avant-garde. And in light of the depression of the late 1920s, the wonder is that this icon of modernism was built at all.

The design team consisted of George Howe, a prominent traditional Philadelphia architect-turned-modernist, and a young Swiss architect, William Lescaze. Together they produced a striking new kind of skyscraper, stripped of the historical allusions of the past.

Howe and Lescaze's design solution, often imitated in the intervening years, consisted of a T-shaped tower set on a podium-style base. The success of this arrangement follows from the way it seems to anchor the building visually to the ground while providing a sort of launchpad from which the tower can rise. The strong vertical lines of the skyscraper are balanced by the promi-

nent horizontally banded windows, which wrap the building at its corners. Retail stores occupy the podium base, with the central banking hall on the second level.

In true International Style, the design expresses both the structural frame of the building as well as its volume. The materials are varied, but remain pure and precise: a gray, polished granite base, buff limestone for the banking office façade and for the vertical columns; and gray brick for the spandrels. Ornamentation, a big modernist taboo, is virtually eliminated, unless you count as decoration the enormous PSFS sign that dominates the top of the tower. The architects designed all the furniture, hardware, and fixtures, because the necessary modern elements did not exist.

Following a conversion by Bower Lewis Thrower, the bank building re-emerged as the Loews Phildelphia Hotel in mid-2000. For information, call Loews reservations at (800) 235-6397.

On one hand, the Cincinnati Union Terminal was a miracle of fortunate timing. The $41 million needed to build it was raised early in 1929; on Wall Street "the window was wide open." After the crash, the easily obtained financing went a long way given deflated construction pricing. The railway station was dedicated in 1933, a wonder of elegance in the pit of the depression.

CINCINNATI UNION TERMINAL, 1933 (THE MUSEUM CENTER)

1301 Western Avenue
Cincinnati, Ohio

Fellheimer & Wagner
with Paul Cret

In the longer view, however, the timing was not so good. The great era of American passenger trains had peaked in 1912, long before the Cincinnati Union Terminal was even designed. So when the terminal opened, its Art Deco façade designed by Paul Cret harked to the future, but the future was already behind it—the station was born a relic.

The building survived because of its own inherent mass and strength—the reinforced concrete semi-dome roof could bounce a wrecking ball. It was too expensive to tear it down.

The interior space is 500,000 square feet, the area of fourteen football fields. The plan conforms to the natural sequence of traffic densities: the maximum space is provided in the vast semi-circular

concourse, from which the streams of passengers flowed out, by means of a long covered gallery, to ramps and then to the train platforms. Floor areas diminish in proportion as the foot traffic thinned out toward the train platforms. All this sophisticated space planning lost its logic when the last train left.

In the 1980s, E. Verner Johnson, a Boston architect who specializes in museum design, conceived the terminal anew as a double museum for the Cincinnati Museum

of Natural History and the Cincinnati Historical Society. The building—and its surreal and colorful rotunda with the double-life-size murals depicting Cincinnati's history—was spectacularly refurbished in 1986. The vast spaces now house large exhibits (a recreation of the early Cincinnati waterfront, a depiction of the Ice Age replete with gigantic dinosaurs, a free-living bat colony in the building's basement).

Now it has a purpose that can never be made obsolete: history. And the trains (Amtrak) are back, too. Known as the Museum Center, the terminal building is open from 9:00 AM to 8:00 PM. Museum of Natural History hours are 10:00 AM to 5:00 PM Monday through Saturday and holidays (except Christmas and Thanksgiving). For general information, call (513) 287-7000.

RCA BUILDING, 1934 (GE BUILDING)

**30 Rockefeller Plaza
New York, New York**

Hood & Fouilhoux; Reinhard & Hofmeister; Corbett, Harrison & MacMurray

The RCA/GE Building is the centerpiece of Rockefeller Center, a mini-city located in the heart of midtown Manhattan. This complex of skyscrapers, shops, theaters, and plazas encompasses Radio City Music Hall, the Rainbow Room, an ice rink, and the famous Christmas tree that is lighted the first week in December.

John D. Rockefeller, Jr. envisioned the multi-building complex in 1928, at a time when most builders were thinking in terms of single structures. Mr. Rockefeller hoped to build a home for the Metropolitan Opera Company as part of a larger commercial venture, but the depression intervened. The opera company dropped out, and he was left with three full city blocks on his hands.

The RCA/GE Building emerged as a result of the reprogramming, and it is the dominant architectural creation. Clad in gray Indiana limestone, with recessed spandrels of gray metal in a darker tone, the 70-story tower is tall and slender, composed as a slab outlined by a series of slender setbacks. The building had to be designed to fit New York City's restrictive zoning ordinances, but the design team managed to instill great dignity and a sense of repose in the gigantic tower.

The Art Deco bas-reliefs that decorate the exterior are spectacular artworks. Inside the lobby, there is a famous mural, "American Progress," by José Maria Sert.

Perhaps the most influential achievement of Rockefeller Center was not this single building, but the concept of strength in numbers—that skyscrapers were no longer to be isolated structures, but part of a larger whole. This fundamental shift of vantage point would change the course of skyscraper development forever.

In the early 1990s, Hardy Holzman Pfeiffer renovated the "crown jewel" of 30 Rockefeller Center, the Rainbow Room. This ultimate penthouse nightclub brings back a worldly, glamorous past. The renovation also opens up truly breathtaking views of the city, starting with the one that flabbergasts visitors stepping off the elevator after a seventy-story ascent.

Tours of Rockefeller Center—and of NBC's Studios there—depart daily, except Thanksgiving and Christmas, from the NBC Experience Store. Reservations recommended. For information, call (212) 664-3700.

Fallingwater, the most acclaimed of Frank Lloyd Wright's private residences, perfectly dramatizes the architect's conviction that a building should be an integral part of its natural setting. A remarkable interweaving of house and landscape is accomplished with just a few simple elements— native stone, reinforced concrete, glass, and steel—but they are used with a vision and a mastery of technical processes to create Wright's most powerful piece of structural wizardry.

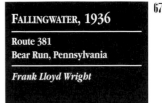

FALLINGWATER, 1936

Route 381
Bear Run, Pennsylvania

Frank Lloyd Wright

Wright believed that no one else noticed the particular beauty of a site until he built on it, and at Fallingwater, as with many of his designs, he found his inspiration in the setting. At first glance, the boldness of the broad cantilevered beams would seem at odds with the gentle wood-ed site, but Wright's artistic integration of house and nature is total. Suspended above the waterfall, with the stream flowing alongside its stone side walls, the multi-tiered house is so tied to the rock that it appears to be part of the actual formation.

While the house merges with the rock on one side, it opens out into the landscape on the other. There is a corresponding openness within. Walls are kept to a minimum, and almost every room has a terrace extending it to the outdoors. Continuity of materials, such as stone flooring for both the interiors and terraces, unites indoors and out into a single whole. Wright also designed the furniture and lighting.

Fallingwater was built for J. Edgar Kaufman, a wealthy Pittsburgh merchant. In 1962, the house was donated to the Western Pennsylvania Conservancy, which operates the house and hosts public tours. Today, among Wright's major houses, Fallingwater is the only one with its setting, original furnishings, and artwork still intact.

Fallingwater's rural location is between the towns of Mill Run and Ohio Pyle, about 2½ hours southeast of Pittsburgh. It is open from mid-March through Thanksgiving, Tuesday to Sunday from 10:00 AM to 4:00 PM, with tours every half hour; closed Mondays (except major holidays), and in January and February, with limited openings in December. Advance reservations are required (allow one month for groups of twenty or more). For information, call (724) 329-8501.

**SAN SIMEON, 1937
(HEARST'S CASTLE)**

750 Hearst Castle Road
San Simeon, California

Julia Morgan

In 1919, William Randolph Hearst decided to build a simple bungalow for himself and his movie-star girlfriend, Marion Davies. The site was spectacular—250,000 acres in the Santa Lucia Mountains overlooking the Pacific Ocean—and Hearst was among the world's wealthiest men. Nevertheless, he told Julia Morgan to design something elegant but spartan, something "Jappo-Swisso," whatever that might be.

The exotic fantasy castle shows what happens when a simple idea is attacked with unlimited amounts of time, money, architectural talent, and enthusiasm for empire building. After almost twenty years and $8 million, La Cuesta Encantada ("The Enchanted Hill") had evolved into one of the world's most astonishing private residences, rivaling Versailles in scale and grandeur. In *Citizen Kane,* the motion picture based on Hearst's life, San Simeon becomes the fabled golden mansion, Xanadu.

Everything has a name. La Casa Grande, the main house with its twin towers, commands the high point of the site. Three guest bungalows surround the main house: Casa del Mar, Casa del Monte, and Casa del Sol. For outdoor swimming, there was the monumental 104-foot Neptune

Pool of green and white marble, Italian temple façade, and classical colonnade; indoors, guests swam in the mystical blue and gold Murano-tiled Roman Pool.

The architecture is eclectic in the extreme. Spanish Renaissance cathedrals provided the main theme, but Gothic, Classical, and Italian influences abound. An indefatigable collector, Hearst scavenged Europe for treasures to fill the mansion's 100-plus rooms. He thought nothing of dismantling entire suites from Spanish palaces and reconstructing them at San Simeon. The main dining hall, for example, is furnished with 500-year-old choir stalls from Catalonia, seventeenth-century refectory tables, Siennese Palio banners, and a sixteenth-century Flemish tapestry.

Julia Morgan supervised construction of this frustrating project, where completed portions were ripped out and replaced again and again. The first female engineering graduate of the University of California at Berkeley, and the first woman certified at L'Ecole des Beaux Arts in Paris, Morgan was certainly up to the task. Construction probably would have gone on forever, but Hearst finally ran out of money in 1937.

San Simeon is open daily (except Thanksgiving, Christmas, and New Year's Day), with four tours from 8:20 AM to 3:00 PM in winter, later in summer, each lasting almost two hours. For information and reservations, call (800) 444-4445.

A dramatic changing of the architectural guard occurred in 1937 when the famous German architect Walter Gropius came to America. The founder of the Bauhaus accepted a position at Harvard's Graduate School of Design, and almost immediately began to revolutionize architecture in this country, starting with his family home in Lincoln. Although Americans had glimpsed modern European architecture in houses designed by Rudolph Schindler and Richard Neutra on the West Coast, Gropius provided a vital "oomph" that turned the tide. Boston became a crucible for the new buildings on the East Coast, described by the writer Ada Louise Huxtable as "the architectural shot heard 'round the world."

WALTER GROPIUS HOUSE, 1938

68 Baker Bridge Road
Lincoln, Massachusetts

Walter Gropius

The house that Gropius built is modest in scale. On first sight, it appears as a compact white rectangle atop a gentle hill, with its entry projecting forward at an angle in counterpoint to a spiral staircase. Key elements of International Style stand out: the flat roof, the ribbon windows, the second-story roof terrace, the lack of ornamentation, and the impression of volume rather than mass. On the inside, modernist ideals are expressed in the asymmetrical massing, in the open floor plan, and in the use of industrial materials such as steel columns, glass block, and cork floors. Gropius's collaborator, Marcel Breuer, another prominent Bauhaus émigré, built his own house next door and designed much of the furniture in the Gropius House.

Gropius's ideals of architectural purity did not stop him from appropriating classic elements of the local Yankee tradition: white clapboard walls (which he ran vertically rather than horizontally), a brick chimney, and a screened porch. A fieldstone foundation and retaining walls and a vine-covered trellis integrated the house into the landscape.

Gropius lived here for almost three decades, until his death in 1969. The Society for the Preservation of New England Antiquities (SPNEA), which now owns the house, recently completed a challenging four-year renovation, tracking down long-outdated original components, both custom- and mass-produced. The chrome banisters, glass blocks, and strip windows are shining again; the orchard and meadow were replanted to Gropius's design. The house is also a treasure trove of Breuer furniture, family memorabilia, and artwork by Laszlo Moholy-Nagy, Joseph Albers, Henry Moore, and other artist friends of the architect.

The house is about 30 miles from Boston. In season—June 1 to October 15—it is open Wednesday through Sunday; otherwise, open weekends only. SPNEA conducts tours on the hour from 11:00 AM to 4:00 PM. Groups require reservations. For information, call (781) 259-8089.

Marcel Breuer's 1938 residence is located next door, but it is not open to the public.

OHIO STEEL FOUNDRY, 1938 (WHEMCO)

1600 McClain Road
Lima, Ohio

Albert Kahn and Associates

Albert Kahn viewed a factory as a machine, and part of the industrial process, not just the housing for it. He is best remembered for his industrial architecture, a path he embarked on in 1917 at the request of Henry Ford. The auto magnate was searching for a better factory design, one that did not require conventional—meaning painstaking—construction. Ford urged Kahn to develop steel-framed structures with whole walls of glass and lightweight metal that could be quickly and simply built. Kahn's structures became elegant and intelligent prototypes for modern, steel industrial buildings.

Kahn's early work had produced the icons of mass production—the "smokestack industries" and factories still commonly represented as cartoon caricatures. But the Ohio Steel Foundry Roll and Heavy Machine Shop, completed in 1937, suggests how his thinking matured into a spare, fully realized design style. For all the scowling, no-nonsense insistence on utility and function, the foundry turned out to be beautiful. For good working light, it is virtually a glass house.

The raised central section of the roof is a thruway for an overhead mobile crane. Additional glass, canted to the sun, stands on either side of the crane's rails. Interior columns are not there simply to hold up the roof, but also to hold up the crane. Great structural integrity is contributed by trusses under the flat roof. These trusses are kept open, rather than massively webbed, allowing free passage of light and accommodating the need to manipulate and position, with the crane, colossal masses of metal. The tension between great masses and stresses on the one hand, and the high, airy, wide-open feel on the other gives the plant the quality of a well made bridge.

For information, call (419) 222-2111.

W hen architects build for themselves, the result often becomes a work in progress. Frank Lloyd Wright designed Taliesin West, his desert home and studio, in 1934, and built it soon after. However, he continued to modify it until he died there in 1959 at the age of 92. This counterweight to his summer home in Spring Green, Wisconsin (also rebuilt several times), superbly shows Wright's genius in marrying site with structure.

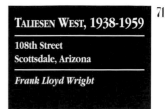

TALIESEN WEST, 1938-1959

108th Street
Scottsdale, Arizona

Frank Lloyd Wright

"Taliesin West had to be absolutely according to the desert," Wright proclaimed. Its spectacular site, which he selected through a series of overnight campouts, rests on the edge of a plain and the base of McDowell Peak, fifteen miles from Scottsdale. Here, Wright maintained, he "gathered his family and apprentices about him like some Apache chief." The remarkable complex contains living quarters for Wright's family and houses the Frank Lloyd Wright Foundation, the Archives, a School of Architecture, and the Taliesin Fellowship.

Inspired by the "nature masonry" of the surrounding mountains, Wright built Taliesin West with sloping walls of indigenous rock captured in poured concrete—a man-made extravaganza of sub-

lime desert colors in rusty reds, subdued oranges, tawny taupes, and steely gray. Massive redwood beams define the angled roof, which was originally covered with white canvas stretched between the trusses, although the canvas was later replaced with panels of translucent plastic. The buildings are interwoven with terraces, gardens, pools, and pergola in a way that underscores Wright's belief that inside and out should be united always. Wright's stunning collection of oriental art and sculpture also provides a unifying link between the house and the grounds.

Today, Taliesin West is a National Historic Landmark and headquarters of the Frank Lloyd Wright Foundation, which operates the Frank Lloyd Wright School of Architecture and Archives. Taliesin West is also home to Taliesin Associates Architects, Wright's successor firm.

Taliesen West is open daily, from 9:00 AM to 4:00 PM, closed Christmas, New Year's Day, Easter, and Thanksgiving; in July and August, the house is also closed Tuesday and Wednesday. The Foundation offers "Panorama" tours every half hour that take in the Kiva Theater, Music Pavilion, Cabaret Cinema, and Wright's private office (reservations not required). More extensive tours—some going out into the desert—are scheduled according to the season and require reservations.

For recorded tour information, call (480) 860-8810. For reservations and information about special programs, call (480) 860-2700.

MUSEUM OF MODERN ART, 1939

11 West 53rd Street/24 West 54th Street
New York, New York

Edward Durell Stone and Philip Goodwin
Redesign, Yoshio Taniguchi, 2004

It's an old story, but still interesting, that the Museum of Modern Art first championed modern architecture from a staid Beaux-Arts townhouse on ritzy Fifth Avenue. In 1932, renegade curators Philip Johnson and Henry-Russell Hitchcock shocked polite society with the legendary exhibit, International Style. Taken with modernism's white walls, flat roofs, and minimal decoration, MoMA trustees soon constructed America's first public International Style building as their home.

Edward Durell Stone and Philip Goodwin created a geometric box with quirky touches. The façade—a white marble frame inset with gridded translucent panels topped by twin horizontal strip windows—sported a saucy, curved entrance canopy and a metal rooftop canopy with circular cutouts. In time, several mismatched additions swallowed it up.

In 2004, MoMA debuted a total redesign and expansion by Japanese architect Yoshio Taniguchi that brought modernism full circle. With a restrained geometric design and simple but elegant materials, Taniguchi doubled the museum's size (to 630,000 square feet), while drawing attention to the world-class art, not the architect.

On 53rd Street, familiar elements remain: Stone and Goodwin's original façade was restored, as was Philip Johnson's 1965 façade. On 54th Street, however, MoMA's new magnitude becomes clear. Two glass-walled buildings on mammoth black granite bases abut the sidewalk, flanking

Philip Johnson's 1953 sculpture garden. Taniguchi lightened the effect by opening the garden to outside view through grills inset in the corrugated aluminum garden wall. Above this wall, museum exhibits are now visible through glass walls. These new views also connect the museum to the city as never before.

Inside, MoMA is a cavernous hive of art and activity. The lobby is a pedestrian through street open to all. With its green slate floors and wall-mounted, flat screen video monitors, it's a piazza for the digital age. Upstairs, an atrium, grounded by Barnett Newman's Broken Obelisk, rises five levels to the roof. Taniguchi stacked and interconnected these six above-ground levels with a variety of cutouts and openings to frame fetching interior and exterior views. In the snow-white interiors, the architect used various levels of transparency—clear, etched, dark, and screened glass—to vary the mood from place to place. The greatly expanded Architecture and Design Department's preeminent collection fills the third floor.

The museum is open Saturday through Thursday from 10:30 am to 5:30 pm; Friday until 8:00 PM; closed Tuesday, Thanksgiving, and Christmas. Groups require at least two-weeks notice. Enter or 53rd or 54th Streets, between Fifth and Sixth Avenues. For information, call (212) 708-9400.

Union Station captures the Spanish mission influence of southern California, with touches of Streamline Moderne thrown in for good measure. The massive Spanish Colonial Revival façade is enlivened by tall but slender Mexican fan palms that give it a festive and tropical air, which the colorful tilework at the giant arched entry intensifies.

UNION STATION, 1939

800 North Alameda Street
Los Angeles, California

John and Donald B. Parkinson;
J.H. Christie, H.L. Gilman,
R.J. Wirth

This last great passenger terminal was jointly built by the Southern Pacific, Union Pacific, and Santa Fe Railroads as the major termination for the entire continent. To handle a continent's worth of passengers, the architects designed an enormous main concourse and a lofty waiting room 52-feet high, set with marble floors. In the inside-outside tradition of California architecture, the waiting room is flanked by open courtyards, lush with landscaping.

No longer the continental transportation hub of its early days, Union Station now buzzes mostly with commuters—on Metrolink, Amtrak, and Metro Rail's Red and Blue Lines—who can daily enjoy the original furnishings, Art Deco signs, and the tropical paradise of the courtyard gardens.

For Amtrak schedule and ticket information, call (800) USA-RAIL; for Metro information, call (800) 266-6883. The L.A. Conservancy hosts tours on the third Saturday of the month, reservations required. Call the L.A. Conservancy at (213) 623-2489.

**KLEINHANS MUSIC HALL,
1940**
SYMPHONY CIRCLE

Porter North
  at Pennsylvania Street
Buffalo, New York

Eliel and Eero Saarinen

From his home base at Cranbrook Academy in Bloomfield Hills, Michigan, Eliel Saarinen collaborated with his son, Eero, to design a concert hall that would express orchestral music to the fullest. And when the concert hall was complete, connoisseurs hailed it as the most acoustically perfect music hall in the world. Today, it remains one of the finest concert-going experiences.

Seen from the air, Kleinhans Music Hall is shaped like a cello. These rounded shapes reflect the organization of the interiors: a large 2,938-seat auditorium, the smaller Mary Seaton Room, and the glass-walled lobby that connects them. The main auditorium has a zigzag roof line, which shows the location of the interior stairs and plays against the curves of the outer walls. As designed, the east end of the building was reflected in graceful pools, but these have now been filled in.

For the exterior finishes, the architects selected familiar materials the elder Saarinen had utilized at Cranbrook Academy: golden-hued Wyandotte brick and Mankato stone, which has a pattern resembling zebra wood. On the inside, the Saarinens sought open shapes that would allow sound vibrations to fill the spaces; rounded ceilings and flaring, wood-paneled walls in the larger hall also helped to achieve this goal. Recent investigations show that Charles Eames, a Saarinen associate at Cranbrook who would emerge as one of the most notable architects and furniture designers of the 1950s, was responsible for the furniture in the music hall's administrative offices and dressing rooms.

The collaboration here between Eliel and Eero Saarinen yields an interesting blend of old and new architectural approaches—a freeze-frame catching both the European ideals and devotion to craftsmanship of the elder Saarinen and the expressive curving shapes that would characterize the work of Eero Saarinen on his own.

Kleinhans Music Hall is home to the Buffalo Philharmonic Orchestra, which performs in the main hall; the Buffalo Chamber Music Society holds concerts in the Mary Seaton Room. Tickets for these and other events held at Kleinhans must be obtained from the individual sponsoring organizations. Architectural tourists are welcome, and tours may be arranged by calling Kleinhans Music Hall at (716) 883-3560.

A merica's art collection is a relatively new one, but it is contained and celebrated in a pink marble monument that rivals the grand old art palaces of Europe. An extraordinarily generous gift to the nation, the museum owes its existence to Andrew W. Mellon, who donated the $15 million building (in 1941) as well as his exceptional art collection. The respectful design reflects the preference of Mellon and his chosen architect, John Russell Pope, who believed that democratic ideals were best expressed through classical architecture for buildings of such national significance.

NATIONAL GALLERY OF ART, WEST BUILDING, 1941

Fourth Street
    at Constitution Avenue N.W.
Washington, D.C.

John Russell Pope

While it seems that Pope was oblivious to the outbreak of modern architecture in America, the Beaux-Arts trained designer actually created a very modern building within the classical framework. Here, at monumental scale, Pope's classicism is stripped down to essentials, clean and coherent: an enormous elongated H, with a domed rotunda and columned entry at the center, large halls on either side, and projecting wings with garden courts at both ends. The 522,500 square-foot building is clad in 310,000 cubic feet of Phantasia Rose Tennessee marble; it is one of the largest marble buildings in the world.

Even while working at monumental scale, Pope never lost sight of the art and the people who would view it. He created a progression of spaces from the ceremonial to the personal. Through bronze doors on the Mall, visitors enter the central rotunda, 100 feet across and 103 feet high, set with twenty-four Ionic columns of dark-green vert imperial Italian marble; the walls and entablature are covered in Alabama rockwood limestone, with dark green Vermont marble on the floor. The exhibition galleries feel more like rooms, with decorative treatments designed to suggest the backgrounds used during periods in which the art was executed. The paintings are primarily illuminated with natural daylight, diffused through glass skylights, along with the occasional use of electric lighting.

In 1978, the museum expanded into the East Building, designed by I.M. Pei (see page 153). The collection has become particularly impressive in nineteenth-century European paintings and Italian Renaissance works, and includes the only Leonardo da Vinci painting found outside of Europe.

The museum is open Monday to Saturday from 10:00 AM to 5:00 PM, on Sunday from 11:00 AM to 6:00 PM, except Christmas and New Year's Day. West Building tours are conducted throughout the day. For information, call (202) 737-4215.

FIRST CHRISTIAN CHURCH, 1942

531 Fifth Street
Columbus, Indiana

Eliel Saarinen

Eliel Saarinen, when initially offered the commission to design Columbus' First Christian Church, refused to take on the project. Saarinen had to be convinced that this church was meant to welcome equally the rich and the poor, small children and the elderly. Traditional Gothic and Georgian designs would not work, Saarinen wrote, because "the last drop of expressiveness has been squeezed out of these once so expressive styles." To create the kind of church he had in mind, the Finnish-born architect invented a new, contemporary form—and one of the first contemporary churches in the United States was the result.

Unlike traditional religious buildings, First Christian Church is geometric in design, simple and direct, its grid clearly visible. The sanctuary is housed in the massive rectangular flat-roofed building, with the 166-foot-tall flat-topped bell tower at its side. Built mainly of buff-colored brick and limestone, the church is marked by a large stone cross in the limestone façade.

Serene on the inside, the 144-foot-long sanctuary has a wide center aisle. The outside cross reappears on the inside, on the south wall of the chancel. The chancel area is elevated, and it holds the communion table. A double wooden gateway opens to reveal the baptistery pool. On the west wall hangs a tapestry, "The Sermon on the Mount," designed by Saarinen and his wife, Loja. Saarinen was also joined on the project by his son Eero, who in the early 1960s designed another famous Columbus church, the North Christian Church on Tipton Lane.

A three-story school is connected to the First Christian Church by a two-story bridge set on massive columns. This arrangement forms a lower level arcade flanked by terraces on either side. Charles Eames, who was associated with Saarinen at the Cranbrook Academy in Bloomfield Hills, Michigan, designed the children's furniture.

First Christian Church was the first contemporary building in Columbus, Indiana, a city famed for its architectural wealth. In number of buildings designed by noted architects, Columbus ranks fourth in the United States after New York City, Chicago, and Los Angeles. The church is among the city's most beloved classics.

The Columbus Visitors Center, 506 Fifth Street, provides comprehensive information. Open daily (except Sundays from December to February), the center hosts guided architectural bus tours Monday through Friday at 10:00 AM, Saturday at 10:00 AM and 2:00 PM, and Sunday at 11:00 AM (except December to February). Reservations are recommended. For more information, call (800) 468-6564.

W ho else but Buckminster Fuller could have given us Dymaxion House? This jaunty little flying saucer with the fin on top seems as unconventional and irrepressible as its illustrious inventor.

DYMAXION HOUSE, 1947

Henry Ford Museum/Greenfield
  Village
20900 Oakwood Boulevard
Dearborn, Michigan

R. Buckminster Fuller

But Fuller was perfectly serious. Dymaxion House was his dream house, and the dream was portability—a house designed to be dismantled, packed into a tube, and taken along when the family moved. The structure is circular, because Fuller saw this as the most efficient shape and, therefore, the most economical to build. The tiny 1,075-square-foot house weighed only 6,000 pounds, not much more than some automobiles. Although the house was designed in 1927, it was not produced until after World War II, when a special aluminum alloy developed for aircraft made construction possible.

Only two prototypes were ever built. Fuller intended to mass produce the houses, but he was unable to secure funding. Rumor also has it that the metal house was leaky and cold.

William L. Graham, an entrepreneur from Wichita, Kansas, bought both Dymaxion prototypes and lived in one of them from 1946 until 1972. The other was never assembled. In 1992, Graham donated the prototypes to the Henry Ford Museum and Greenfield Village in Dearborn, Michigan. The museum has reassembled the house and its handy carrying case.

Greenfield Village is open every day, except Thanksgiving and Christmas, from 9:30 AM to 5:00 PM; Friday and Saturday until 9:00 PM (June 13 to August 21 only). For information, call (313) 271-1620.

When Richard Neutra designed this futuristic dream-house for Edgar Kaufmann, the mountains made a perfect background for his vision of dramatic simplicity. By the 1990s, decades of development had devastated the pristine beauty and integral quality of the site as Neutra found it. (Kaufmann's eastern architectural icon, Fallingwater, has fared much better in this regard.) The 3,200-square-foot house itself suffered much interference. After Kaufmann died in 1955 there followed a period of virtual abandonment. Then, a succession of owners, including Barry Manilow, remodeled it almost completely beyond recognition.

But Julius Shulman's exquisitely lighted 1947 photo for *Life* magazine shows the purity of Neutra's original intentions, its total lightness of being. Open and airy, the Kaufmann House seems simply a series of floating planes: the pool, the entry canopy, the roof, and the elevated rooftop terrace, which has a stout stone chimney serving as anchor. Great glass walls enclose the house like a see-through shell. To protect this exposed shell, Neutra designed a system of mechanical louvers to create outdoor rooms and mitigate the strong desert winds.

In contrast with Neutra's Lovell house, which stairsteps up the Hollywood Hills, the Kaufmann house is as flat as a pancake in the desert. Its one-story design has a pinwheel plan that wraps around an enclosed garden; a rectangular guest wing extends in one direction, and an L-shaped garage and walkway branch off the other side. This elegant simplicity of structure and plan came at an astronomically high $300,000 in 1947, but Kaufmann clearly relished watching his wealth turned into architectural triumphs.

After all its hard times, the Kaufmann House looks meticulously new again. New owners, inspired by Shulman's early photograph, purchased the structure and hired Santa Monica architects Lee Marmola and Ron Radziner to turn it back into a beauty. The architects also restored the house next door, another modernist icon, which was designed by Albert Frey for Raymond Loewy and built in tandem with Kaufmann House. Both homes are private residences.

T he small community of Mount Pleasant in Westchester County offers a rare opportunity to see Usonian homes as Frank Lloyd Wright saw them, in a Broadacre City setting of his own design. Some fifty Usonian-style houses show Wright's ideal of unity with variety.

Wright personally designed three of the houses: Friedman House, Serlin House, and Reisley House; the others are constructed according to his principles. The homes are clustered on circular one-acre lots, laid out to Wright's 1947 masterplan, and are remarkably intact. The 97-acre community is structured as a cooperative. Residents share woodlands, a swimming pool, playgrounds, and a community center, and have a voice in all matters affecting the community. At the time, this arrangement, which seemed truly democratic to Wright, was wildly radical. Bankers found it all but unimaginable.

But the world changed drastically between 1940, when Wright began planning Usonia Homes with David Henken, and the time the first houses went up in 1947. After World War II, demand for housing soared and lifestyles became more relaxed and informal. The Usonian house was an ideal and relatively inexpensive solution. Small but spacious, the houses feature open plans and a compact "work center" kitchen at the heart of the

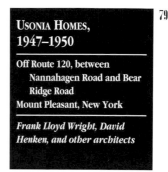

house. Patios replace porches, carports replace garages, furniture and ornamentation are built in, and maintenance items were reduced to the minimum.

Starting with Jacobs House in Madison, Wisconsin (1937), Wright devised a kit-of-parts approach to simplify design and construction of the Usonian houses. These devices include board and batten walls that form both interior and exterior finishes, the 2 x 4-foot planning grid, and concrete floors with in-floor heating. Wright being Wright, standardization did not hinder creativity. With Friedman House he continued to explore the circular theme that culminated in the monumental Guggenheim spiral.

Usonia Homes is located in Mount Pleasant, an unincorporated area adjacent to Pleasantville, New York, about thirty miles north of Manhattan. The Wright houses are Friedman House (1948), 11 Orchard Drive; Serlin House (1949), altered beyond recognition of the original design, 12 Laurel Hill Drive; and Reisley House (1950), still in exceptional condition, 44 Usonia Road. All the houses are private residences.

BAKER HOUSE, 1948

Massachusetts Institute of Technology
Cambridge, Massachusetts

Alvar Aalto

In the 1940s, the great Finnish architect Alvar Aalto left his homeland to escape the perils of war in Europe. He arrived in the United States to take up a six-year teaching position at the Massachusetts Institute of Technology (MIT), which placed him in close proximity to two giants of European modernism, Walter Gropius and Marcel Breuer, and turned the Boston-Cambridge area into a showplace of new architecture. Aalto's major contribution to architecture in America was Baker House, a dormitory and dining hall for senior-year students overlooking the Charles River.

Baker House breaks out of the box in a dramatic way—a building made into an undulating wave. The design is based on Aalto's theory that the most beautiful scenes are best viewed at an angle. Therefore, no room directly confronts the river view. On the campus side of the building, however, the curves give way to walls that are angular and squared off. The most prominent feature here is an enormous V-shape that results from Aalto's diagonal cantilevering of an outside stairway along one wall, paired with a cantilevered portion of the building on the opposing wall.

The building's interiors show an evolution of Aalto's understanding of how people live in and use a building. Rather than impose the separation of functions that modernism demands—living spaces here, service functions there—Aalto juxtaposes functions. Student rooms take up most of the curvaceous spine, with study rooms, lounges, and lavatories interspersed throughout the building.

In terms of Aalto's career, Baker House marks a new maturity of design, as well as a concern for the timelessness of his buildings. When Baker House opened, many people viewed the sinuous wall of rough dark brick with great alarm. The intervening years, and a superb 1999 restoration, have proven Aalto right. Baker House is one of those buildings that only seems to look better with age.

For information, call (617) 253-1000.

The new look of America's postwar commercial buildings first appeared in Pietro Belluschi's Equitable Savings and Loan Building in Portland, Oregon. An immediate critical success—in 1948, *Architectural Forum* magazine praised it as "a long overdue crystal and metal tower that catches the lightness of the multi-story cage"—the Equitable Building was soon overshadowed by more prominent structures in larger cities. Nevertheless, its technical and aesthetic accomplishments remain astonishing. It was the first aluminum clad building in America, the first to use double-glazed windows, and the first completely air-conditioned commercial building in the country. At the time it was built, this was the most progressive commercial structure in the world.

EQUITABLE SAVINGS AND LOAN, 1948 (THE COMMONWEALTH BUILDING)

421 S.W. Sixth Avenue
Portland, Oregon

Pietro Belluschi

A compact "skyscraper" in the International Style, the Equitable Building presents a lively exterior—a shimmering frame of light- and dark-colored aluminum inset with large expanses of luminous, sea-green glass. The pieces are assembled with the precision of fine furniture, and the greatest projection on the façade is confined to seven-eights of an inch. Originally 12 stories, later expanded to 13, the building houses retail shops at street level, where the tall ground floor features a row of brick columns. It was a point of pride that no masonry was used on the upper floors, which indicated a lightness of construction that was greatly admired. To counteract the pristine coolness of the exterior, Belluschi thought the interior should be bright and colorful, and he turned to the artist Alexander Calder for ideas.

Despite its International Style inspiration, Equitable maintained its local connections. Pietro Belluschi was a Portland resident known for his refined residential and church designs. The city

was also becoming a center for aluminum production. Belluschi's reputation soon grew to national and international proportions, and he would eventually leave Portland to become Dean of Architecture at the Massachusetts Institute of Technology. In recognition of the building's distinguished status as a prototype of postwar commercial architecture, Equitable (now The Commonwealth Building) received the American Institute of Architects Twenty-Five Year Award in 1982.

The building is open during regular business hours, and you can walk around and see the newly restored public areas. For information, call the building manager, American Property Management, at (503) 284-2147.

CHRIST CHURCH LUTHERAN, 1949

3244 34th Avenue South
Minneapolis, Minnesota

Eliel and Eero Saarinen

In this "honest" church resembling those of his native Scandinavia, Eliel Saarinen utilized the principles of contemporary design in the traditional realm of ecclesiastical architecture. And the impression of solemnity and spirituality became heightened rather than diminished by the new approach.

Starting with an extremely simple basic structure—a steel frame wrapped by walls of light beige brick and stone—Saarinen created a building that responds in a very sophisticated way to variations in sound and light. The church and its 88-foot tower are separated by a glass passage. Natural light from this passage softly illuminates the church interior. There are no parallel walls in the nave, which accounts for the exceptional acoustics.

The church is asymmetrical in plan, and at the same time it is serenely proportioned and balanced. One long wall includes splayed panels of open-jointed brick, which add texture while they help absorb sound. Saarinen used aluminum in new ways. He formed tall, slender crosses (atop the tower and behind the altar) into sleekly evocative sculptures.

This is Eliel Saarinen's last completed work, and a recipient of the American Institute of Architects Twenty-Five Year Award in 1977. His son Eero Saarinen later added an educational wing to the original church structure.

Visitors are welcome. The church is open from 9:00 AM to 3:00 PM Monday through Thursday, and on Friday until noon. Sunday services are held at 8:15 and 10:45 AM from Labor Day through Memorial Day and at 9:30 AM in the summer. Church members conduct tours of the building upon request. It's best to call in advance. For reservations and information, call (612) 721-6611.

I n hopes of sparking design innovations for a war-weary world, *Arts & Architecture* magazine in 1945 sponsored the Case Study House Program on property it purchased for that purpose on the California coast. Charles Eames and his Cranbrook Academy colleague Eero Saarinen were selected to build Case Study House #8, a house and studio. Eames, together with his wife and collaborator, Ray, would live here for the rest of their lives.

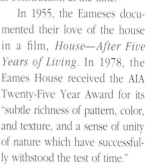

EAMES HOUSE, 1949
(CASE STUDY HOUSE #8)

Chatauque Boulevard,
   south of Corona del Mar
Pacific Palisades, California

Charles and Ray Eames

Eames actually designed two houses for his site. With the steel framing for his initial plan already delivered to the site, he redesigned the house and studio using the same materials, but in a different way. As finally constructed, the house consists of two rectangular box-like components, a 1,500-square-foot house and a 1,000-square-foot studio, wedged into the side of a hill that is anchored by a concrete retaining wall. An open court lies between them.

Eames sought a house that was light and open, with its structural components clearly visible wherever possible. He set out to meet these objectives using standard interchangeable, off-the-shelf materials and a building block approach. The basic module measures $7\frac{1}{2}$ x 20 feet. Eight of these modules make the house, with five modules comprising the studio. The result is not static, however, for there is great variety within this modular concept. The exterior is clad with stucco, cement, asbestos, and plywood panels, which appear as color blocks of white, blue, red, black, and gray. Three types of glass—transparent, translucent, and wired—are used for the windows.

Inside, Eames contrasted large vertical spaces, such as the 17-foot-high living room, with small and intimate enclosures. A spiral staircase illuminated with a wired-glass skylight leads to the second story. Upstairs, the master bedroom overlooks the two-story living room, but it can be closed for privacy with a sliding screen of translucent glass cloth laminate. Exposed Truscon open-webbed joists and Ferroboard steel decking, painted dark gray, form the ceiling in both the house and studio, a novel use of industrial materials for residential construction at the time.

In 1955, the Eameses documented their love of the house in a film, *House—After Five Years of Living*. In 1978, the Eames House received the AIA Twenty-Five Year Award for its "subtle richness of pattern, color, and texture, and a sense of unity of nature which have successfully withstood the test of time."

The Eames Office occupies the house and offers exterior visits weekdays from 10:00 AM to 4:00 PM by appointment only. (They have also opened a gallery and shop in Santa Monica.) For information, call (310) 459-9663.

GLASS HOUSE, 1949

New Canaan, Connecticut
Ponus Ridge Road between
Wahackme and Frogtown

Philip Johnson

The see-through house that Philip Johnson designed for himself takes the idea of home and turns it inside out. Walls become windows, and private life is opened up to the outdoors, rather than shielded from it. As a living space, the Glass House worked for Johnson because of its protected wooded setting. As architecture, the house is almost unequaled in the clarity of its design, apparently willed into existence almost out of thin air.

The Glass House consists of a single room, 32 x 56 feet, which seems to be nothing more than a chimney of dark red brick, arising from a floor of the same material, encased by a cage of steel and a skin of glass. The slenderest detail—a "chair rail" of steel on all sides—provides the tension that visually holds the house together. Opposite walls are identically symmetrical, and each is broken by a door of glass at the center.

The house sits atop a flat rise, surrounded by a wooded valley. To reach the house, there is no direct route. Arriving up the drive to find a solid brick wall, the visitor approaches the house on the diagonal, following first one 45-degree angle path and then another, never confronting the house directly.

Although the Glass House obviously has no rooms in the traditional sense, they are suggested by the placement of the few interior constructions. An entrance hall emerges between the brick cylinder and a low walnut cabinet that contains the kitchen. From here, the natural progression leads to a sitting area defined by a white rug and furnished with a Mies van der Rohe lounge and chairs. The brick cylinder encloses the bathroom facilities, and on its outside wall there is a fireplace. Behind the cylinder there is another walnut storage cabinet, this one protecting the sleeping and writing area located on the north side of the house.

Although Johnson would later turn away from the International Style, the Glass House is almost a pure example of the form. Johnson acknowledged his debt to Mies van der Rohe's Farnsworth House (see page 88), but in the end the house was his own.

Over the years Johnson constructed seven structures on the property, including the red and black "Monster" (also called "Monsta"), a Ronchamp-like sculptural structure near the entrance. It became the visitors center for Johnson's expansive complex, which upon the architect's death in 2005 at age 98, passed to the National Trust for Historic Preservation and will be open to the public. For information, call the National Trust at (202) 588-6000.

Frank Lloyd Wright was a man in his seventies and still going strong when he designed Johnson Wax, one of the most impressive buildings of his long career. The center consists of the administrative headquarters of 1939 (the famous golf-tee lobby as pictured) and the laboratory tower of 1949. The tower shows Wright at his best, working new wonders with space and light, brick and glass.

JOHNSON WAX COMPANY RESEARCH AND DEVELOPMENT CENTER, 1949

**1525 Howe Street
Racine, Wisconsin**

Frank Lloyd Wright

The 14-story tower, 40-feet square with rounded corners, rises above a walled courtyard; it is linked to the central administration building by a covered walkway lined with reflecting pools. From outside, the most fascinating feature is the glass tubing that forms glistening wall sections two stories tall, banded in warm red brick. Inside, the laboratory floors are also unique. The labs are segmented into two-story modules: a main floor, which is square, and a mezzanine, which is round. These floors are cantilevered out from a central core containing the elevator, stairs, and mechanical equipment. During the day, the building appears translucent. At night, it glows with an ethereal radiance and the bold shapes of the interior floors are clear.

In designing this building, Wright drew inspiration from two ongoing preoccupations in his pursuit of "organic" architecture—the shape of a tree with its outreaching limbs, and the form of the

circle. Before long, this combination was expressed as a spiral, the basis of his design for the Guggenheim Museum in New York City. In these masterpieces of his late career, Wright moved away from external decoration toward something much more like sculpture.

By reservation only, Johnson Wax hosts tours every Friday at 9:15 and 11:00 AM, and 1:15 PM. The company also hosts tours of Wingspread, the Wright-designed house for a Johnson Wax founder, three miles away. For reservations and information, call (262) 260-2154.

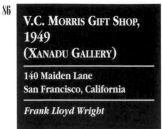

V.C. MORRIS GIFT SHOP, 1949 (XANADU GALLERY)

140 Maiden Lane
San Francisco, California

Frank Lloyd Wright

It would be easy to miss this little gallery on Maiden Lane. The street is tiny and can be hard to find, although it is only a few blocks from Union Square. On this street, the gallery stands out because of its simplicity—an almost-blank wall of rust-colored brick with a simple quarter-round entryway outlined in the same brick, surrounding a quarter-round metal front gate. This must be one of the few stores in American history that has no shop windows and no merchandise on display. The building presents a mystery, but it draws you in nevertheless.

And this, of course, is the point. Frank Lloyd Wright was not only practicing architecture, he was seducing the customer. The building exerts a constant pull from the street through the entry and into the selling space. The design practically guides you through the shop by means of a spiral ramp, a precursor of Wright's integral design for the Guggenheim Museum in New York City some twenty years later. So perhaps it is no irony that the current inhabitant is an art gallery.

An interesting feature of Wright's exterior design is the way he used the ordinary brick coursework to give a sharp edge to the façade. At the left edge of the building, Wright has left alternating brick ends exposed, creating a graphic, punched-out line up the side. As was his practice, Wright signed the building with his red ceramic square logo set into the façade.

The telephone number for Xanadu Gallery is (415) 392-9999.

A well-preserved Schindler house in Los Angeles is Tischler House, a multi-level stucco and wood composition distinguished by a series of triangular extensions—slabs, terraces, and trellises—that rise up the hill into which the house is so cozily situated. Schindler's idea of outdoor rooms, lined with trees and scaled to complement the interior, extends the living area out onto the hillside.

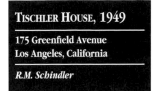
For the construction of the tall, narrow house, Schindler worked with an enlarged concrete block, which he offset in alternating bands to form a simple but distinctive pattern. Blue corrugated fiberglass was used for the roof, but conventional materials later replaced the uppermost portions.

The floor plan is as open as the vertical site permits. The main floor of the house is on the second level, accessible by a lofty flight of stairs up the leafy hillside. Inside the front door,

Schindler positioned a curved wall of concrete block about five feet high that subtly divides the entry from the living room. Its opposite face contains a large fireplace with a beautifully curving metal hood.

The Tischler House owes its design to *Arts and Architecture* magazine, for it was here that Tischler discovered the work of Rudolf Schindler. An artist and silversmith, Tischler's inherent sympathy to Schindler's style is noticeable in the handcrafted hammered silver bowls and tableware he made for the house. These pieces, displayed in the dining area, seem to capture the contemporary spirit of the house, which is now a landmark of the City of Los Angeles.

Tischler House is a private residence.

FARNSWORTH HOUSE, 1950

14520 River Road
Plano, Illinois

Ludwig Mies van der Rohe

In a wooded meadow beside the Fox River, Mies van der Rohe built a one-room house that crystallized his desire to make architecture that strips away nonessentials. The house consisted, he said, of "practically nothing"—a roof, a floor, four glass walls, eight I-beams, and a terrace. But it changed everything. This small weekend retreat, built for Chicago physician Dr. Edith Farnsworth, emerged from thousands of design hours to become the prototype for all glass buildings, from Philip Johnson's glass house (see page 84) in New Canaan to commercial towers everywhere.

Farnsworth House is a rare gem, one of just three Mies houses in America. It looks like a simple white-framed glass box, with one end left open to form a covered porch. Raised four feet above the ground, the house seems to levitate weightlessly. Its combination of large glass walls and white-painted steel performs a magical balancing act: from the outside the house stands in stark contrast to the landscape, while on the inside it feels continuous with the natural suroundings. The physical link between land and house is a floating island of a terrace with two sets of wide steps, also apparently free floating. The front door is the only door.

In this house, Mies inaugurated his use of open, clear-span space, so the interior has no rooms as such. Separate areas for living, eating, and sleeping are suggested by the placement of a few interior structures: a wood-paneled central island containing kitchen and bath facilities, and a free-standing storage wall. The house was not built for air conditioning, and there are only two small, high windows that open.

Mies's architectural advances did not impress Dr. Farnsworth. "Something should be done about such architecture," she wrote in *House Beautiful.* "I thought you could animate a predetermined, classic form like this with your presence. I wanted to do something 'meaningful,' and all I got was this glib, false sophistication." What she got, of course, was a masterpiece.

In 1968, Dr. Farnsworth sold the house to Lord Peter Palumbo, a British "house collector" who maintained it in immaculate condition, restoring it sensitively after a terrible flood. He then decided to sell the property at auction, and preservationists feared a new buyer would move or demolish it. Fortunately, as of 2003, the National Trust for Historic Preservation owns it in perpetuity.

Visits begin at the Visitors' Center and continue along a footpath, both of which were built by Lord Palumbo. The path runs a quarter mile through the woods and along the river, immersing visitors in pure nature for about ten minutes as a prelude to entering one of the purest architectural works of the twentieth century.

Farnsworth House is located about 58 miles from Chicago. From April through November, it is open Tuesday through Sunday, with hourly tours from 10:00 AM to 4:00 PM. Closed Monday and holidays. Off-season visits are limited. Reservations are required. For information, call (630) 552-0052. The Chicago Architectural Foundation offers bus tours twice a month; call (312) 922-3432.

The United Nations Secretariat holds the honor of being New York's first glass skyscraper. It rises high above the East River, two long walls of blue-green glass flanked by two short walls of warm gray marble. A building this big and this different was bound to cause a stir. Everyone had an opinion. While some critics derided it as "a vast marble frame for two enormous windows," and "a cliff of glass," architects tended to look on it in a more positive light. It is "yummy," said one. Another, misquoting Sam Cooke, said, "It sends me." There was no denying the "U.N. look," which would soon spread across the country.

UNITED NATIONS SECRETARIAT, 1950

First Avenue at 46th Street
New York, New York

Wallace K. Harrison with consulting architects Le Corbusier, Oscar Niemeyer, and Sven Markelius

The United Nations Secretariat's 38 stories, 544 feet tall and 287 feet wide, provide office space for 3,500 diplomats and staff as well as a residence for the Secretary General. The Secretariat is a monument to international cooperation and was itself a cooperative enterprise. Prominent New York City architect Wallace K. Harrison, in association with Max Abramovitz, headed a team of designers from around the world, including Le Corbusier from France and Oscar Niemeyer from Brazil.

The final design owes much to Le Corbusier, but the technology that made possible the curtain walls, the central elevator core, and the air-conditioning was clearly American.

"It was a U.N. job—a collaborative job," remarked Wallace K. Harrison, who gained a reputation for forging consensus and getting results when the chips were down. He was also known for

his friends in high places, most notably John D. Rockefeller, Jr., and for his work in designing Rockefeller Center. Although not all his later commissions ended happily, the United Nations Secretariat became quite a symbol of international cooperation. Harrison took professional pride in the fact that modern architecture in the International Style had been used successfully to create a proper building for the international community.

Guided tours are conducted seven days a week from 9:15 AM to 4:45 PM. One-hour English language tours leave every half hour from the Visitor's Center located at First Avenue at 46th Street. For information regarding foreign-language tours, call (212) 963-7539 on the day of the visit. Reservations are required for groups of twelve or more; call (212) 963-4440 during business hours Monday through Friday. For general information, call (212) 963-8687.

Marcel Breuer is best remembered for his masterpiece, the Whitney Museum, and for his classic furniture designs. Less well known, Breuer's houses also rank as modern classics—especially those the Bauhaus architect built for himself. The house on West Road in New Canaan is the third of Breuer's four homes and is said to have been his favorite. It was the one the Hungarian-born architect lived in for the longest duration, from 1951 until 1976. It shows his conviction that the architect's mission begins with discipline and leads to adventure.

Breuer's first American residential adventure was in Lincoln, Massachusetts, in 1937, the year he came to teach at Harvard with Walter Gropius. The two friends built houses next door to each other, a pair of Bauhaus originals with flat roofs, stark white walls, and catalog materials. Blatantly modern, Breuer's design obscured his novel use of traditional material, such as white clapboard. Breuer's severe Bauhaus style softened somewhat in his next house, a large rectangle cantilevered from a concrete podium that was also clad with wood siding, this time laid on the diagonal.

By the time he built the house in New Canaan, Breuer's interest in local materials had turned to stone. On the street façade, slab walls clad with natural stone co-exist with painted brick and glass to provide most of the visual interest. The entry court is paved with stone, as is the rear terrace; interior floors are bluestone and there is a massive stone fireplace in the living room. Because a large wall of glass opens the house at the rear, the stone is a continuous and natural presence throughout the house.

In plan, the house is U-shaped. Parents and children benefit from having separate wings, which Breuer called a "binuclear" plan, but the public areas of the house are designed to be open. One trend of 1950s houses—shallow windows placed at ceiling height—was pioneered here. Interiors were spartan, in keeping with the Breuers' lifestyle.

In 1981, the house was expanded and remodeled for new owners by Breuer and his long-time collaborator, Herbert Beckhard of New York City. In 2004, the house was purchased for its valuable property by a developer as the site of a traditional mega-mansion. In response to the architectural outcry, the house was put up for sale at a high price, and its fate is hanging in the balance. Breuer House is a private residence.

Mies van der Rohe first envisioned the all-glass skyscraper in the 1920s. A true genius, he designed a structure that could not be built at the time, but some thirty years later the technology was at hand. The long-held dream of the crystalline tower was finally realized in these famous apartment towers, 26 stories of black steel and glass.

860-880 LAKESHORE DRIVE, 1951

Chicago, Illinois

Ludwig Mies van der Rohe

Mies described his style of architecture as "skin and bones": evidently nothing more than a steel frame (the bones) with glass inserts (the skin). Streamlined in the extreme, the Lakeshore Drive apartments gain strength in numbers: the two identical towers confront each other at a right angle in a composition of carefully controlled tension. The towers are situated on a travertine base and are elevated two stories above it by columns around the perimeter. At the center of each building, Mies consolidated the elevators and utilities, thereby achieving great freedom in arranging interior living spaces and in designing the outside walls. In a slight elaboration of the skin and bones façade, he added steel "I" mullions, which divide the structural bays. Without this finishing touch to the building, he felt, "It did not look right."

The towers at 860-880 Lakeshore Drive are marvels of precision and refinement, the result of Mies's relentless drive for architectural purity over decades of teaching and practice. The great success of these soaring, flat-roofed glass and steel buildings inspired legions of imitators, changing the face of almost every major city in the world. Unfortunately, very few of the copies hold a candle to the original.

The apartments are private residences, but the Chicago Architecture Foundation includes the towers on their "Architectural Highlights by Bus" tours. For information, call (312) 922-3432.

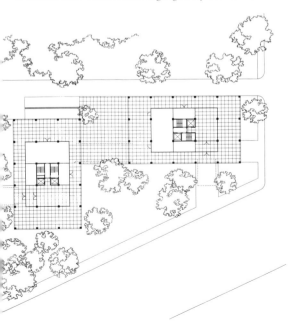

WAYFARER'S CHAPEL, 1951

**5755 Palos Verdes Drive South
Rancho Palos Verdes, California**

Lloyd Wright

This chapel by the sea is a small but elegant structure built of simple materials: glass walls and gables framed in redwood, with a base and altar of stone. The church was intended to increase our appreciation of nature, and the bounty here is almost overwhelming. Taking advantage of its spectacular setting, the chapel seems to merge with the trees and flowers that surround it, and with the Pacific Ocean at its feet.

The chapel owes its existence to Elizabeth Schellenberg, who lived on the Palos Verdes Peninsula in the late 1920s. She first commissioned Ralph Jester to draw up plans for a church to honor Emmanuel Swedenborg, the Swedish theologian and founder of her religion. The church was delayed first by the depression and later by the war.

When the idea resurfaced, Jester felt his mission-style design was not right for the site; he suggested that Lloyd Wright, Frank Lloyd Wright's eldest son, was the architect for the job. It is evident from the chapel that Lloyd Wright shared his father's view of intermingling of site and structure. Also, Lloyd Wright's training in landscape architecture (he worked for a time with Olmstead and Olmstead on the East Coast) was a valuable contribution to the design. After the chapel's completion in 1951, Wright added the stone tower, colonnade, and visitors center to the original design.

The chapel is open daily. Guided tours for groups require advance notice. Sunday services are held at 10:00 AM. For reservations and information, call (310) 377-1650. For group reservations, call (310) 377-1279.

The new look of Lever House revolutionized commercial architecture in New York City with its sleek translucent blue-green glass walls and stainless steel frame. In part, the ground-breaking design resulted from the company's emphasis on cleanliness; for this prominent soap and detergent manufacturer, a clean-looking building was considered essential. Stone and brick become grimy in a city, but glass becomes clean in an instant. To ensure that the building stays that way, a track-mounted gondola system enables two men to wash the entire building in only six days.

LEVER HOUSE, 1952

390 Park Avenue, between 53rd and 54th Streets New York, New York

Skidmore, Owings & Merrill

93

In its massing, the Lever House design was as innovative as the materials. The design separates the 24-story building into two strong slabs, a vertical tower rising out of a horizontal base. This broad, podium-type base is raised one floor above ground level and is supported at the perimeter by rows of columns.

At street level, Lever House offers an open plaza with a courtyard garden in the center, an idea that was highly praised for its sensitivity to pedestrians. This scaled-back design also brought a feeling of airiness to the massive canyons of Park Avenue, and new visual interest from the constantly changing reflections on the glass walls.

By today's standards, Lever House would be considered a small office building, less than 290,000 square feet, but its impact was enormous. Besides setting a trend for New York skyscraper design, the design (by SOM partner Gordon Bunshaft) established Skidmore, Owings & Merrill's signature style and position as a premier source of prestigious commercial architecture.

Lever has left and the new owners completed a massive renovation in 2003, replacing all the glass so the building sparkles anew.

A new liveliness also pervades the ground level. In the plaza, landscape architect Ken Smith has recaptured the spirit of Isamu Noguchi's unrealized original design, and the lobby now hosts rotating art exhibits. A stylish new restaurant designed by Marc Newson, also called Lever House, opened in 2003. The restaurant, like The Four Seasons and The Brasserie across the street in the Seagram Building (see page 105), offers the experience of fine dining in a modern architectural landmark. For restaurant reservations, call (212) 888-2700.

YALE UNIVERSITY ART GALLERY ADDITION, 1953

Yale University
Chapel Street, between York
and High Streets
New Haven, Connecticut

Louis I. Kahn

Louis Kahn's art gallery addition was the first modern building at Yale, and the first prominent masterpiece by the architect whom many view as the towering talent of the late twentieth century. At Yale, where he was teaching at the time, Kahn joined his building to a majestically classic one, maintaining a common sense of scale and grace.

Kahn's gallery is basically a concrete frame warehouse four stories tall. On the garden side, the walls are dark-rimmed glass. A different façade shows its face to the street. Here, a full expanse of beige brick is scored by subtle vertical bands that mark the interior floors. The main entry consists of a sleek, narrow wall of full-height glass. It is set at a right angle to the street, so that this crucial division between the old building and the new one virtually disappears.

As with most of Kahn's buildings, the real excitement lies inside, where space and light are manipulated to powerful effect. The vast concrete floors were deliberately open so that they could be endlessly reconfigured for changing exhibitions by means of movable partitions. This "universal space" is topped by the building's trademark ceiling, an exposed gridwork of concrete tetrahedrons with spotlights mounted within the open struts. In an uncanny way, the rhythmic effect of walking beneath this ceiling enhances the primary purpose of the building: looking at art.

The proverbial late bloomer, Louis Kahn was in his fifth decade when he designed the Yale addition. Many Kahn designs were never built, giving his existing buildings almost "untouchable" status. Still, time takes an architectural toll: over the past fifty years, Kahn's open spaces had been divided, the three-story curtain wall needed replacement, and technical systems demanded upgrading. In 2004, Yale closed the gallery and commissioned James Stewart Polshek, a New York City architect and former Kahn student, to improve the physical structure while restoring Kahn's original vision.

The Yale Art Gallery plans to reopen in 2006. Hours are Tuesday through Saturday from 10:00 AM to 5:00 PM, Sunday 1:00 to 6:00 PM; closed Monday and major holidays. (In the interim, visit Kahn's Yale Center for British Art [see page 15] and Paul Rudolph's Art and Architecture School [see page 119], both across the

street.) The museum hosts a variety of tours; groups require three-weeks notice. For reservations, call (203) 432-8479. For general information, call (203) 432-0600

F rank Lloyd Wright gained fame for his houses and they remained a preoccupation throughout his long and flamboyant career. For wealthy clients, he designed sprawling and highly individualistic structures, such as Fallingwater and Barnsdall House. But the Usonian homes, of which the Bachman-Wilson House is a late example, were meant for average American families.

BACHMAN-WILSON HOUSE, 1954

1423 River Road
Millstone, New Jersey

Frank Lloyd Wright

The name Usonian is Wright's own contrivance, a play on the initials U.S. that expressed his democratic ideals. Usonian homes were small and compact, with flat roofs, open floor plans, and an easy relationship between indoors and out. Not incidentally, these "economical" family homes turned out to cost about twice as much to build as the homes they were intended to replace.

The Bachman-Wilson House is built primarily of undecorated concrete-block. The front is long and flat, with extending eaves. For the entry, Wright employed one of his favorite dramatic devices—a dim, low-ceiling vestibule that ushers visitors into a hall and then into a surprisingly large and light-filled room. This two-story great room, 28 x 35 feet, almost fills the first floor. Its most striking feature is a 10-foot wall of glass and Philippine mahogany that opens to the surrounding forest; four of the panels are doors. Above the glass wall, Wright placed a band of clerestory windows, inset with a repetitive pattern of plywood cutouts, the primary decoration. The radiant-heated concrete floor was originally tinted red.

Wright believed that the hearth was the heart of a home. The Bachman-Wilson House shows how Wright adapted this idea to the Usonian house. It has a core of concrete block, with the kitchen on one side and a fireplace facing the great room on the other. Hallways function as rooms. In the Bachman-Wilson House, the dining room is carved out of such a space. A cantilevered Philippine mahogany balcony wraps the masonry core and forms the hall for the two upstairs bedrooms and the bath. Bedrooms are small, and their ceilings are only 6½-feet high. Balconies of Philippine mahogany are cantilevered off the bedrooms to compensate for their diminutive size.

The house is located about seven miles along River Road, off Highway 544 at Griggstown. The private residence may be accessible on special occasions. For information, write Bachman-Wilson House, 1423 River Road, Millstone, N.J. 08876.

CATALANO HOUSE, 1954

Catalano Drive
Raleigh, North Carolina

Eduardo Catalano

All his life, the Argentine-born architect Eduardo Catalano has pursued new ways of unifying space and structure. His explorations in the 1950s resulted in a remarkable series of theoretical studies for houses; two were actually built, including the 1956 "House of the Decade," one of the few buildings ever praised by Frank Lloyd Wright.

But it is the house that Catalano built for himself that still captures the imagination. It shows Catalano's ability to be both structurally daring and elegantly simple, and to innovate without sacrificing that elusive quality of being genuine, not contrived.

Catalano's astonishing house seems to be all roof, nothing more than a large glider that has drifted into the forest. And in fact, the roof is the key—a 2¼-inch shell of laminated wood lightly tethered to the earth, supported at only two points. The unusual roof shape, a hyperbolic paraboloid, results from Catalano's explorations into the properties of warped surfaces. Using mathematically pure geometry, he designed the house as a continuous and integral structure.

The membrane roof stretches 87 feet above walls of glass. The connection between the roof and the walls seems effortless, partly due to the thinness of the line between them: just two metal angles join these major structural components. By extending the roofline 12 feet beyond the walls of the small (approximately 1,700 square feet) house, Catalano invokes the all-important sense of shelter, the essence of home.

In architecture, Catalano's hyperbolic paraboloid represents the mathematical optimum: the point where the trough of one curve is simultaneously the peak of another. Catalano's composed shape, which seems architecturally unconventional, is satisfying in part because it is mathematically perfect.

Catalano lived in the Raleigh house for about one year, while teaching at North Carolina State University. In 1956, the Harvard-trained architect began teaching at the Massachusetts Institute of Technology, and remained there for decades. The house was demolished in 2001, but a replacement is planned on the campus of North Carolina State University. For information, call (919) 515-8350.

W hen it opened, the Fontainebleau Hotel was probably the most highly criticized building in America, but now it is one of the most highly praised.

FONTAINEBLEAU HOTEL, 1954

4441 Collins Avenue
Miami Beach, Florida

Morris Lapidus

The hotel was the setting for the movie *Goldfinger,* and in fact the Fontainebleau was designed like a movie set, to amaze and to entertain. Built on a curve, the hotel formed a 15-story backdrop for the serpentine swoop of the two-story beachside cabanas (removed in 1979). In between, a formal French parterre garden coexists next to the Olympic-sized swimming pool. "Wonderful nonsense" fills the colorful interior, like the grand lobby staircase to nowhere (now leading to the executive offices) and Lapidus's signature bow-tie pattern inset in the marble lobby floor.

Almost as astonishing as the hotel's ground-breaking design is the fact that it was accomplished for a client who asked for a hotel designed in the French Provincial style. Lapidus soon determined

that his client meant *modern* French Provincial, prompting him to come up with a unique answer to his own crazy question, "What kind of chop suey is this?"

The Fontainebleau was the first building Lapidus ever designed. He says he didn't even consider himself an architect when he got the commission, although for twenty years he had created hundreds of trendsetting store designs in New York City. The short-lived shops allowed Lapidus to experiment in ways that would never fly on a build-

ing project. This design freedom, and the need to attract paying customers, led Lapidus to an architecture of human nature—an architecture based on what people like and respond to. The stores acted as billboards, drawing shoppers in with Lapidus's constants: curving lines, bright lights, and a sense of occasion. The Fontainebleau was the beneficiary of all he had learned.

Despite his unorthodox designs, Lapidus received a classical architectural education at Columbia University in the 1920s. At school, Europe's emerging modern architecture was mentioned only to be dismissed, a looming danger best avoided. But from Mies van der Rohe, Lapidus encountered the possibilities of opening up space, although Lapidus thought not in straight lines but in curves. For the Fontainebleau, his design began as a series of squiggles.

After all these years (he was still practicing in 1999 at 97), Morris Lapidus needed to apologize to no one. The Fontainebleau is a much-studied milestone, as is his Eden Roc Hotel, shown here behind the Fontainebleau. And it is still a beautiful building, world famous, far surpassing its more straightforward rivals. It fulfills Lapidus's wish for all his buildings: do anything, but "By God, don't walk by me."

For information, call (305) 538-2000. For tours, ask for Public Relations.

MANUFACTURERS HANOVER TRUST COMPANY BANK, 1954 (CHASE MANHATTAN BANK)

Fifth Avenue at 43rd Street New York, New York

Skidmore, Owings & Merrill

The opening of the Fifth Avenue branch of Manufacturers Hanover Trust Company caused quite a commotion. For the first time, the hallowed symbol of banking security—the vault—was removed from the hidden reaches of the inner sanctum and positioned right out in the front window.

Manufacturers Hanover Trust was also the first glass-walled bank, and only a half inch of plate (and a 30-ton door) separates the vault from the sidewalk. Skidmore, Owings & Merrill radically reversed traditional bank secrecy with invisible walls, bright light, open teller counters, and a polished, stainless steel vault displayed like jewelry in a store window for all passers-by to see.

The bank's five stories include two customer banking floors, offices, and a penthouse for the president. Sheer glass walls are framed by aluminum mullions, and the 22 x 9⅔-foot panes on the second floor held the record as the largest ever installed at the time. To create the maximum impact of all this glass, SOM intensely illuminated the interior of the building so that the glass appeared invisible.

The interiors, for the most part, are cool and professional. One bright spot is a wall-sized sculptural screen of golden steel by Harry Bertoia located in the great banking room on the second floor.

Now a branch of Chase Manhattan Bank, the building is open during regular business hours. But you can see the vault in the window as you walk down the street.

Outside the mainstream of American architecture, Bruce Goff pursued a career that was mythologically ultra-American—individualistic, innovative, creative, and independent. Bavinger House, a swirling structure set in rugged country, was designed for a sculptor and his family who wanted something different, too.

BAVINGER HOUSE, 1955

730 60th Street
Norman, Oklahoma

Bruce Goff

The Bavingers planned to build the house themselves on a small but beautiful site at the edge of a stream. When cleared, the first level was revealed to be naturally curved, and from this base the shell-like shape of the house emerged. The winding exterior is more than 50 feet tall, 96 feet of continuous wall surface covered with rocks that coils around a steel pole. Cables radiate from this central pole to the spiraling roof, which is covered in copper. Virtually the entire house is suspended from the central mast—the roof, the five principal living areas, an interior stairway, and a suspension bridge that crosses the stream and leads to a garden.

There is no such thing as a room inside; the space evolves upward in a continuous stretch. The five living areas consist of circular pavilions covered in carpet and suspended at various levels from

bottom to top. Goff staggered the pavilions to control visibility. For further privacy, the pavilions are draped with netting and opaque curtains, which can be closed or opened.

The Bavinger design is obviously personal, but it is interesting to note that Frank Lloyd Wright's Guggenheim Museum—also based on the spiral shape—was under construction in New York City. But unlike Wright, Goff's largest commissions came toward the end of his enormously productive life. His last work, the beautiful Japanese pavilion of the Los Angeles County Museum of Art, was completed after his death.

The Bavinger House received the American Institute of Architects Twenty-Five Year Award in 1987. It is a private residence and is shielded by trees, except in winter.

JEWISH COMMUNITY CENTER BATH HOUSE ("TRENTON BATH HOUSE"), 1955

999 Lower Ferry Road
Ewing, New Jersey

Louis I. Kahn

In the off season, the Jewish Community Center Bath House (also referred to as the Trenton Bath House) looks like a tiny compound in an ancient village whose residents long ago moved on. Its four cube-shaped structures with their pyramid roofs sit somewhat forlornly out in an open field. The concrete block cubes cluster around an open-air pavilion in a way that seems tribally protective.

The Bath House is one of Louis Kahn's earliest but most evocative works. It reflects his unique ability to invest ancient forms—the circle, the square, the pyramid, the cross—with new reverence.

Kahn experienced the power of the past while traveling through Italy, Greece, and Egypt in the early 1950s. In visiting ancient sites, he observed that when the architectural details have worn away, only the structure remains. The Bath House design is based on this simple truth. Solid stone-gray walls delineate four large squares, like open columns at each of the corners. Kahn's cross-shaped plan has a circular atrium at the center and a pyramid-shaped roof over each of the hollow columns. The slight space between wall and roof is a masterpiece of dramatic tension. It shows that in Kahn's hands, extreme simplicity can evoke highly complex emotions.

Kahn credited the Trenton Bath House for his earliest insights on organizing space by separating areas that are "served" from areas providing the services, and here it is solved with absolute purity. Services such as restrooms and chlorinating facilities are contained within the "hollow columns" of the walls. These hollow columns, which provide both support and service, also fascinated Kahn as an organizing principle and a source of inspiration. He intended to elaborate these ideas in the community center itself, which unfortunately was never built.

By the early 1990s, the Bath House was in sad shape. Its walls were discolored, its rooftops deteriorating, and its access denied by buckled chain-link fencing. The Jewish Community Center is considering future renovations.

The Bath House is located off Interstate 95, Scotch Road exit, in Ewing, near the New Jersey-Pennsylvania border. Summer swimming programs are available. For information about visiting or contributing to the renovation effort, call (609) 883-9550.

M assachusetts Institute of Technology entered the twenty-first century on an architectural roll, with exciting new buildings like Frank Gehry's Strata Center and Steven Holl's Simmons Hall dormitory. Half a century earlier, however, Eero Saarinen's Kresge Auditorium was the building making the news.

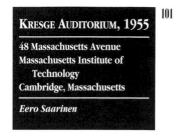

KRESGE AUDITORIUM, 1955

48 Massachusetts Avenue
Massachusetts Institute of
  Technology
Cambridge, Massachusetts

Eero Saarinen

Saarinen became known as the master of unusual forms, and his renegade explorations began with Kresge Auditorium. The design is based on the sphere—actually, a one-eighth slice of it. The dome is made of white thin-shell concrete and is mirrored by an interior floor that cups upward, in a reverse dome, which the architect described as "two shell shapes, like a clam."

The dome roof appears to float above its brick base, but it is ingeniously supported at three points by concrete and steel abutments. Weighing 1,200 tons, the structure encloses a concert hall on the main floor and a small theater on the lower level. The main auditorium is a wonder of column-free space, with free-hanging structures the architect called "floating clouds" on the ceiling. The clouds house lights and ventilation, as well as the acoustical baffling that assures the auditorium's sublime sound.

Saarinen embraced the spherical shape wholeheartedly, continuing it on the front glass wall and the brick podium that surrounds the building. The nonrectangular shape had its critics, but Saarinen held fast. "We believed that what was required was a contrasting silhouette," he said, "a form that started from the ground and went up, carrying the eye around its sweeping shape . . . At first it seemed strange, but gradually it became the loved one."

On the MIT campus, Frank Gehry's Strata Center is located on Vassar and Main Streets; Steven Holl's dormitory is at 229 Vassar Street. For general campus information and Kresge programs, call MIT at (617) 253-1000.

S.R. CROWN HALL, 1956

Illinois Institute of Technology
State Street, between 34th and
35th Streets
Chicago, Illinois

Ludwig Mies van der Rohe

Until Rem Koolhaas's audacious new McCormick Tribune Campus Center opened in 2004, with a futuristic tube encasing the train tracks above the building, the architect synonymous with the Illinois Institute of Technology was Ludwig Mies van der Rohe.

IIT is still primarily the product of Mies's vision. Arriving in Chicago from Germany in 1938, he was commissioned to plan a new campus on the city's south side. Over the years, he developed its signature style of boxy glass buildings with black, exposed steel frames and buff-colored brick. The campus is stocked with Mies-designed classroom buildings, dormitories, laboratories, and even a steam-generating plant, interlaced with other structures so respectful of his style that they could easily be mistaken for originals.

Crown Hall is home to the College of Architecture and is considered Mies's campus masterpiece, perhaps because this was his own department and he essentially built it for himself. The first of his steel and glass structures for the school, it advanced his ultimate goal of transforming a building's internal structure into its outward form. Furthermore, the play of vertical and horizontal lines in Crown Hall seems like the beginning of a new architectural order.

Mies envisioned structures as "floating planes," an idea perfected at the Farnsworth House (see page 88) and writ larger here. A glass-walled pavilion 220 feet long by 120 feet wide, Crown Hall has four massive black trusses straddling the roof. The roof is suspended from these girders, which are in turn supported by eight exterior steel columns. On the east and west ends, the roof is cantilevered 20 feet from the outermost columns. Farnsworth House also comes to mind at the building's entrance, a raised slab pavilion with two sets of wide, shallow steps, all apparently free floating.

Visitors ascend these floating stairs and enter an exhibition space with low, free-standing partitions of finely grained wood. It is a prelude to one of the most majestic spaces in contemporary architecture: a light-filled clear-span expanse 220 feet by 120 feet and 18 feet high. The open span is made possible by the four great roof trusses, which also contribute so mightily to the outside form. It's a space that seems made for the ages, and for the generations of architecture students who continue to dream up new ways to use it.

For information, call (312) 567-3230. Rem Koolhaas's McCormick Tribune Center is located one block away on State Street. The Chicago Architecture Foundation also includes IIT on its tours. For information, call CAF at (312) 922-3432.

In this wooded, 1000-acre "Industrial Versailles," the automotive giant carries on research and development, engineering, and styling of the cars of tomorrow.

The complex of long, low buildings was designed over a ten-year period by Eero Saarinen in partnership with his father, Eliel, who died in 1950. The Tech Center's splashiest feature is its futuristic stainless steel water tower in a 22-acre pool with Alexander Calder's spectacular "water sculpture," a water wall fountain 155 feet wide and 50 feet high.

Eero tried to design "variety within unity" for the multibuilding complex. Unity is established by the five-foot module, horizontal proportions, dark-gray steel frames, green-tinted glass, and green belt surroundings that are common to all. For variety, Saarinen alternated high buildings with low ones, glass walls with brick walls, and buildings seen through trees versus those which open onto the central court. The bright spots include the bril-

liantly colored glazed ceramic brick of the end walls—blue, red, yellow, and orange—which were fired on site. Dramatic blue-black exhaust stacks placed outside of certain buildings add visual punch.

A number of technical firsts also occurred here: the use of brilliantly colored glazed brick; the prefabricated porcelain sandwich panel that integrates interior and exterior walls; the luminous ceiling with lighting covered by modular plastic pans; and especially the neoprene gasket weather seal to mount windows or metal panels, which soon became a construction standard.

The influence of Mies van der Rohe's rigorous steel and glass method is evident at the Technical Center, but Saarinen soon moved on to experiment with a great diversity of architectural forms that were his alone. His independent career was short but energetic and influential; he was posthumously awarded the American Institute of Architects Gold Medal in 1962.

At this writing, the center is not open to the public. For information, call (313) 556-5000.

INLAND STEEL BUILDING, 1958

30 West Monroe Street
Chicago, Illinois

Skidmore, Owings & Merrill

Inland Steel's corporate headquarters building is quite a showcase for the company's main product: steel. Structural steel columns, ordinarily positioned inside the glass curtain wall, are here placed prominently on the outside of the long façade of this corner site. Stainless steel panels are used to clad the adjacent service tower, and steel strips are utilized to form the building's window mullions, transoms, and spandrels.

The building's primary technical advances, however, are on the inside. The offices are separated from the service functions by the creation of two adjacent but distinctly different towers. The glass-walled tower houses the corporate offices on nineteen stories, each 10,000 square feet. Elevators, stairs, lavatory facilities, and air-conditioning ductwork are grouped inside the 25-story blank-walled tower. As a result, the office floors are free of structural constraints, thus greatly increasing the possibilities for interior spatial arrangements.

With the Inland Steel building, Skidmore, Owings & Merrill followed the astounding success of their Lever House design in New York City earlier in the decade. During these years, the firm (which had been formed in the 1930s) gained international acclaim for their refined, Mies-inspired steel and glass style, which became a hallmark of corporate wealth and power.

The Inland Steel lobby is open during business hours. The building is included on the Chicago Architecture Foundation's Walking Tours as well as their "Architectural Highlights by Bus." For information, call CAF at (312) 922-3432.

The Seagram Building is an acknowledged masterpiece, and as with buildings of such stature, there are a number of "firsts" associated with it. Seagram is Mies van der Rohe's first building in New York City, the first bronze-colored skyscraper, and the first skyscraper of glass walls from floor to ceiling. Although it was not the first International Style arrival on Park Avenue (Lever House across the street claims this distinction), it is certainly one of the most elegant skyscrapers ever built.

105

SEAGRAM BUILDING, 1958

375 Park Avenue
New York, New York

Ludwig Mies van der Rohe
and Philip Johnson

The precision of Seagram's design and construction reminds us why International Style architecture was so captivating when it appeared. The design's strength results from its simplicity. The 38-story tower of bronze glass and hand-rubbed bronze mullions and spandrels rises straight up from an elevated granite podium flanked by a pair of reflecting pools with fountains. The soaring quality of the building is achieved by the continuous lines of the bronze mullions, which have been placed outside the glass walls to emphasize the vertical sweep. Because of the delicate way these I-beam mullions create line and shadow, they have been compared to the Ionic columns of classical architecture.

No expense was spared in constructing this building, and the rich materials used outside are continued throughout the interiors, designed by Philip Johnson (including the famous Four Seasons Restaurant). The luxuriousness of the "less is more" architecture at the Seagram Building prompted Henry-Russell Hitchcock to remark after a visit that he had "never seen more of less."

Mies van der Rohe designed the Seagram Building to be a freestanding monument, best to be viewed in pristine isolation. Its success was surely gratifying, but the sheer number of poor imitations came to obscure the contribution of this icon of modernism. In the 1980s, the building itself was compromised by the construction of a new office tower abutting its eastern façade. The Brasserie restaurant by Diller + Scofidio (see page 247) respectfully challenges Mies's modernism with lively video technology.

UNION TANK CAR DOME, 1958

Brooklawn Road
Baton Rouge, Louisiana

R. Buckminster Fuller

Many architects dream of incorporating experimental technology into their buildings, but Buckminster Fuller made a lifetime career of it. His brainchild, the geodesic dome, is his ingenious solution to the problem of enclosing the maximum amount of space with the minimum amount of material and expense.

The largest geodesic dome ever built is the Union Tank Car Dome, a roundhouse where railroad tank cars are maintained, repaired, and painted. With a volume twenty-three times that of St. Peter's Cathedral in Rome, the dome spans a 384-foot clear span interior and is 120 feet high at its apex.

The igloo-like building consists of 320 interlocking hexagonal steel panels, painted goldenrod, which are braced by steel rods on the exterior, which are painted blue. Three tracks bring railroad cars into the building to a rotating table, which transfers them to one of the fourteen repair bays in the roundhouse. Adjoining the main dome is the painting shed, a half-round extension 200 feet long and 40 feet wide. Inside the central dome, there is a second dome with an open geodesic frame that encompasses the storehouse, offices, and a restaurant. In terms of construction economy, the facility is astounding—only two ounces of steel are used for each cubic foot of enclosed space.

Buckminster Fuller succeeded in proving that we could build more with less. Although Fuller's cheerful counterculture proclamations enthralled the media, his geodesic dome failed to gain widespread acceptance as a building type. But for his real contributions to building technology, Fuller received the American Institute of Architects Gold Medal in 1970.

The Union Tank Car facility, about a mile off Scenic Highway, has lain fallow for many years. In 1990, Kansas City Southern Railway Company bought it with the expectation of re-opening it. Since 1992, however, the yard has remained all but abandoned as the company tries to find a buyer for this unconventional but imaginative masterpiece of industrial design. For information, call Kansas City Southern at (816) 983-1224.

It is a rare architectural photograph that captures not only the essence of a building but also the essence of a generation. Here, photographer Julius Shulman's famous nighttime shot stops the clock to show us the beautiful dream of progressive domestic architecture in the late 1950s.

Pierre Koenig's minimal masterpiece represents the most advanced stage of the Case Study Houses, a post-war program sponsored by *Arts and Architecture* magazine to encourage affordable domestic architecture using the latest materials, techniques, and furnishings.

The one-story house is a study in horizontal planes. It turns a solid wall to the street but opens completely with floor-to-ceiling glass walls in the back to favor the breathtaking view of the city at its feet. Koenig's L-shaped plan features two wings flanking the terrace and pool. The public wing houses the living room, dining room, and kitchen; the private wing contains a master bedroom, children's bedroom, and bath. A central core containing the master bath, dressing room, and service areas connects the two. Surprisingly, the pool abuts the edge of the house in two places, where it is bridged to provide access from the carport to the entry.

In this house, Koenig realized his ideal of the glass pavilion. His design is also true to the goals of the Case Study program: a simple but refined modular design of standardized materials and an open floor plan with minimal hallways. But Koenig brought the best of nature to this somewhat austere program— the freshness of sunlight for the inside and the tranquility of water for the terrace.

In 2000, with the original owners still in residence, the sleek little house was named a Historical Cultural Monument. Case Study House #22 is a private residence.

SOLOMON R. GUGGENHEIM MUSEUM, 1959

1071 Fifth Avenue at 88th Street
New York, New York

Frank Lloyd Wright
Gwathmey Siegel (1992
Museum Addition)

For the man who devoted his life to breaking architecture out of the box, the Guggenheim Museum is the final victory. In this last great work, Frank Lloyd Wright created a giant spiral that rises up from its corner site in ever-increasing circles, culminating in a glass dome 100 feet across at the top. This corkscrew building is hollow at the center; on the inside the spiral becomes a continuous ramp of gallery floors surrounding a light-filled central atrium.

The smooth beige concrete walls are angled outward and correspond to the interior gallery walls, where Wright envisioned the paintings tilted slightly back as on the artist's easel—a romantic notion that has given fits to nearly every museum director who has tried to mount an exhibition. The vantage point for visitors is also unusual. Wright meant for museum-goers to take an elevator to the uppermost floor and walk down. Wright's design presents the exhibition and the architecture as a single entity, and when the art is right the combination can be extremely effective.

The Guggenheim has often been criticized, the standard joke being, "They've got the museum, now they'll just have to build a building to show the pictures." The wish was fulfilled in a 1992 expansion and renovation by Gwathmey Siegel & Associates of New York. A 10-story limestone tower rises discreetly behind the museum, its cool gray stone blocks laid in a subtle "tartan grid" pattern. Four new gallery floors, three of them double height, nearly triple the

museum's exhibition space—and provide flat walls. Wright's small rotunda is open to the public for the first time; a new outdoor roof terrace opens onto the trees of Central Park across the street.

Frank Lloyd Wright never lived to see the completion of his final masterpiece, which he designed in the mid-1940s. But he gets the last laugh. The outrage over "landmark tampering" that greeted plans for the annex surely surpassed the original outcry over the flying saucer New Yorkers said had landed in their midst. New York's only building by Frank Lloyd Wright, after all these years, is proudly acclaimed as the museum's own best work of art.

A new stainless steel banner-like sculpture by Frank Gehry ripples across the upper façade, thanks to a six-year Landmarks Commission reprieve.

The Guggenheim is open daily, except Thursday and holidays (Thanksgiving and Christmas), from 9:00 AM to 6:00 PM, Friday until 8:00 PM. For information, call (212) 423-3500.

This small gem of an office building is a classic in the SOM style of the 1950s. The building stands just 11 stories tall on a tight corner site, a shimmery rectangle of glass and aluminum floating above a one-story base of transparent glass. In contrast to the gargantuan office towers in the International Style, the Pepsi-Cola Building is comprehensible in size and scale, and perhaps this is why its subtle refinements make a stronger impression.

PEPSI-COLA WORLD HEADQUARTERS, 1959 (WALT DISNEY CORPORATION)

500 Park Avenue
New York, New York

Skidmore, Owings & Merrill

The design consists of minimal materials in perfect proportion. On the office floors, outside walls are single panes of half-inch glass, 9 feet high and 13 feet wide. Wide, sleek aluminum spandrels divide the building horizontally, while slender aluminum mullions against the glass provide vertical definition. The overall transparency of the building is underscored by the placement of steel support beams immediately inside the window walls, where they are clearly visible from the street. Vertical venetian blinds on all windows provide privacy and sun control, and contribute to the building's unified exterior appearance. Building services are unobtrusively grouped within a slim tower of black granite that virtually disappears.

For Skidmore, Owings & Merrill, Pepsi-Cola World Headquarters marked the end of an architectural era—the ultimate perfection of corporate headquarters buildings created in the International Style. By the end of the 1950s, the firm was already moving in new directions. The Pepsi-Cola building changed too, greatly expanded in 1984 to a design by James Stewart Polshek and Partners: a 40-story granite stone tower at its side and a 25-story aluminum and glass structure cantilevered above it. The expansion, which contains both residences and offices, has been praised for respecting the quality and style of the original structure. (Unfortunately, though, the older building's beautifully proportioned lobby has been split into two retail spaces.)

The Pepsi-Cola building is now New York headquarters for the Walt Disney Corporation. The building is open during regular business hours.

MALIN HOUSE ("CHEMOSPHERE"), 1960

776 Torreyson Drive
Los Angeles, California

John Lautner

New architectural ideas—and new building techniques—often show up first in small houses, where limited budgets call for innovative solutions. In the late 1950s, when Malin House was designed, "the future" was a source of architectural inspiration, especially themes about outer space. In this context, many people look at Malin House (nicknamed "Chemosphere") and see a hovering spacecraft. But John Lautner designed it as an organic response to an unbuildable site, which can't even be reached by conventional means. To compensate for these problems, the house is mounted on a stout pedestal with steel bracing. The "driveway" is a private funicular (the hill-a-vator) that goes up and down the mountainside, and the carport is located at the base of the pedestal.

"I realized," said the Michigan-born architect John Lautner, "that I could leave the whole natural terrain underneath the house and not disturb the nature at all and just have this house up in the air on one column. The aircraft engineer liked it and I went ahead and did it."

Lautner moved to Los Angeles in 1939 to work with Frank Lloyd Wright and practiced there until his death in 1994. He was known for imaginative residential designs. In this case, the 2,200 square-foot house takes the unusual shape of an octagon with a redwood base. On the inside, Lautner divided the house in half, with pie-shaped bedrooms and baths on one side and a single large, open living area on the other. The living area is completely surrounded by sliding glass windows with a magnificent 360-degree view of the San Fernando Valley. The roof is an independent, curved structure that allows for unlimited internal room arrangements.

In 1998, the architectural book publisher Benedikt Taschen bought and renovated the house as his personal residence. For visitor information, call (212) 683-3377.

T he architectural community was literally stunned by the first sight of Guild House, a Quaker home for the elderly in Philadelphia. Sitting starkly behind its chain link fence up against the pavement on a gritty edge-of-downtown street, the dark brick six-story building had a storefront façade, a billboard sign, and an outsized anodized bronze television antenna prominently placed on the roof. If the building seemed "ordinary and ugly," well, that was the point.

III

GUILD HOUSE, 1961

711 Spring Garden Street
Philadelphia, Pennsylvania

Venturi & Rauch

Guild House was the first pre-postmodern building, a renunciation of almost everything the modern movement had represented for more than forty years. As Venturi explained in his two revolutionary books, *Complexity and Contradictions in Architecture* (Museum of Modern Art, 1977) and *Learning from Las Vegas* (with Denise Scott Brown and Steven Izenour, MIT Press, 1977), architecture is a language with something important to say. This language is complicated and full of contradictions, which cannot be ignored.

So, if Guild House is speaking to us, what is it saying? On the most pedestrian level, it attests to kinship with neighboring inner-city structures. The building's size, setbacks and inelegant windows of different sizes recall public housing blocks. The television antenna was meant to be an ironic commentary on the primary leisure activity of the inhabitants.

On a higher plane, Guild House is classically ordered. The main façade is anchored by a polished marble column centered at the entry, and the façade rises all of a piece to the semicircular lunette window on the top floor. Along the way, there are references to Le Corbusier's Villa Stein in France and Bruno Taut's Horseshoe Housing Development in Berlin, both from the 1920s, to Palladio, to Kahn, and to Frank Furness, the nineteenth-century Philadelphia architect admired by Venturi, who also practices in Philadelphia.

In the years since Guild House, Robert Venturi has evolved from a pop iconoclast to an elder statesman. His firm of Venturi, Rauch & Scott Brown received the American Institute of Architects Firm of the Year Award in 1985. And in 1991, Venturi was awarded the prestigious Pritzker Prize for architecture.

Guild House is still open, but the television antenna has been removed. For general information, call (215) 923-1539.

DULLES INTERNATIONAL AIRPORT, 1962

Chantilly, Virginia

Eero Saarinen

As the gateway to America's capital city—and the country's first big jet-age airport—Dulles International called for a distinguished national monument, and Eero Saarinen clearly provided one. Surreal by day, ethereal at night, the airport is defined by two massive rows of tapered concrete columns that reach up and out, in tautly controlled tension that gives a beautiful curve to the roof. In a continuous line, the columns pierce the roof and arc up above it. Saarinen likened his design to "a huge, continuous hammock suspended between concrete trees."

To give special significance to the entry, the front façade rises 65 feet, versus 40 feet in back; columns are 40 feet apart on both sides, inset with walls of dark-framed glass.

In designing Dulles Airport, Saarinen continued to push the technological possibilities of molded concrete forms, which he helped pioneer in the Kresge Auditorium and the TWA Terminal in New York. At Dulles, he used light suspension-bridge cables to gird the roof, with concrete roof panels sandwiched between them, which in turn affected the whole design. "The concrete piers are sloped outward to counteract the pull of the cables," he noted. "But we exaggerated and dramatized this outward slope . . . to give the colonnade a dynamic and soaring look as well as a stately and dignified one . . . I think this airport is the best thing I have done."

Saarinen correctly identified Dulles as the masterpiece of his career, which was brief but extremely influential and ended with his untimely death in 1961, before the terminal's completion.

In the late 1990s, an SOM expansion nearly doubled the length of the original catenary structure. For information, call (703) 572-2700.

The showpiece of Seattle's 1962 World's Fair, Space Needle jubilantly expresses the "Man in Space" theme of a futuristic fair devoted to the wonders of UFOs, the United States space program, Sputnik, and the prospect of men on the moon. Designed, engineered, constructed, and financed by a small group of private investors, Space Needle was also intended to counter Germany's Stuttgart Tower and France's Eiffel Tower. Today it symbolizes Seattle's development as a major metropolitan presence.

SPACE NEEDLE, 1962

**219 Fourth Avenue North
Seattle, Washington**

John Graham Associates

Seattle architect John Graham and his team faced a significant challenge in pure conceptual design. No one had ever seen a Space Needle, its form could take any shape, and there was no precedent for its design or construction. John Graham invited concepts from his collaborators, and the ideas ranged from spears with halos to hot air balloon shapes supported by intricate tether designs.

The final design is an elegant steel tripod tower soaring 605 feet into the air, with a high-pinched waist crowned by the flying saucer-like tophouse. Five distinct, layered discs form the tophouse (bottom to top): 1) a revolving restaurant, 2) a mezzanine disk, 3) the observation deck, 4) the mechanical equipment level, and 5) the elevator penthouse. A 50-foot natural gas torch tower topped the penthouse. The underground foundation supporting this fantastic structure weighs as much as the tower itself.

Seattle residents take delight in "dressing up" the Space Needle. It has been a Christmas Tree, a UFO for the UFO Expo, crowned with a crab for Seafood Month, and a birthday cake for its own tenth birthday.

The Space Needle is open daily from 9:00 AM to midnight, and 8:00 AM to midnight on weekends. Three elevators spirit visitors to the observation deck—in about forty-three seconds—for spectacular views of downtown, Elliott Bay, and Puget Sound. The restaurant is also open to the public. For Space Needle information and reservations, call (206) 443-2111.

TWA Terminal, 1962

John F. Kennedy International
Airport
New York, New York

Eero Saarinen

At the start of the jet age, the TWA Terminal was a monument to the wonder of flight—people came just to watch the planes take off. Its eagle-has-landed appearance gave shape to the exterior, while the interiors continued the feeling of motion in a smoothly integrated design.

This remarkable structure consists of a vast concrete shell constructed of four enormous barrel vaults canted upward, over rounded glass walls that rise at an outward angle to meet them. The vaulted forms, which are separated by skylights and supported on four Y-shaped columns, create a building that is 50 feet high and 315 feet long, and exceptionally light and airy inside.

Entering this building is like walking into the sculpture promised by the exterior form. Curved and molded shapes are everywhere—the ceiling, stairways, ramps, and counters. The evocation of movement also carries over inside, as you pass through a progression of spaces that are alternately closed and open.

Eero Saarinen considered the fact that some people saw the building as a bird in flight to be coincidental. "That was the last thing we ever thought about," he maintained. His goal, instead, was "to design a building in which the architecture itself would express the drama and specialness and excitement of travel . . . a place of movement and transition . . . The shapes were deliberately chosen in order to emphasize an upward-soaring quality of line. We wanted an uplift."

TWA closed in 2001. In 2004, Jet Blue announced plans to build a new terminal next door to TWA and to renovate Saarinen's bird-shaped structure, which would be connected to their new facility. Pending final approval, the new terminal complex will be open in 2008.

T he United States Air Force Academy Chapel exerts a powerful spiritual presence as well as a physical one. Its gleaming aluminum wedge-shaped profile dominates flat, rectangular buildings on campus, and holds its own against the Rocky Mountain range in the background.

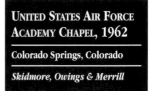

UNITED STATES AIR FORCE ACADEMY CHAPEL, 1962

Colorado Springs, Colorado

Skidmore, Owings & Merrill

As a religious symbol, the Chapel is especially remarkable because three distinct congregations—Protestant, Jewish, and Catholic—worship within separate chapels. And each is consistent with the heritage of its faith. This commonality was achieved by combining two ancient religious conventions, the cathedral spire and stained glass, in a new synthesis. The sources are easy to recognize, but their combined power is mysteriously moving.

Viewed from the front entrance, the Chapel's origami-like image suggests hands raised in prayer. From the side, the image changes to reveal a row of seventeen pointed aluminum spires in regimental lock step, a squadron in formation.

The spires consist of 100 tetrahedrons, each 75 feet long. The spaces between the spires are filled with stained-glass strips in twenty-four colors (but no green), shaded from dark to light, which produce vivid interior hues in the daytime and intensely glowing colors at night. The stained-glass windows depict Paul's conversion on the road to Damascus, described by the Chapel's designer, Walter Netsche, as "a strong story, not sweet."

The U.S. Air Force Academy is located at the northern outskirts of Colorado Springs, about sixty miles south of Denver. The Chapel is open Monday through Saturday from 9:00 AM to 5:00 PM

and Sunday from 3:00 to 5:00 PM, except for special religious services and holidays. Tours are self-guided, although the Visitor's Center, located at 2346 Academy Drive, conducts campus tours during the summer. For information, call (719) 333-2025.

ASSEMBLY HALL, 1963

University of Illinois
First Street, between Kirby and
St. Mary's Roads
Champaign-Urbana, Illinois

Harrison & Abramovitz

The American domed stadium has become a metropolitan set piece. Houston has its Astrodome, New Orleans its Superdome, Seattle its Kingdome, Minneapolis its Metrodome. The ancestor of these ubiquitous mushroom-shaped structures is the Assembly Hall at the University of Illinois.

This early domed hall, with its boldly ribbed roof, was conceived in the late 1950s. It was built using concrete post-stressing machinery that had been developed, in that cold war decade, for the construction of Titan ballistic missile silos.

The domed roof, which weighs 4,400 tons, is a clear span structure without any internal columns or supports to block the spectators' views. The load of the roof is borne by a massive compression ring girdling the dome. This ring around the rim of "the oyster" is itself girdled by 614 miles of steel wire. The wire was tensioned up to 130,000 pounds per square inch, and it is the centripetal squeeze of this ring that holds the roof aloft.

The building is architecturally admirable, but its construction was an heroic process of inventing and improvising new tools and techniques. Not least of the problem was thinking through the sequence of construction. For example, the contractor did not fully excavate the structure, which is deeply dished into the earth, until the dome was already finished overhead. In this way, he was able to use shorter, more robust internal supports while the roof was under construction.

The unusual construction process was carefully documented by a faculty member who shot a 35mm photograph from the same spot each day. These slides were discovered after his retirement and compiled into a fascinating slide show. In just forty-five seconds you can watch the dome blossom out of the flat plain in this semi-animated presentation. Ask about it.

In the intervening decades the domed stadium concept has succeeded too well; in Baltimore, for example, in the early 1990s, the new Orioles Stadium at Camden Yards proclaimed proudly that it was *not* a domed stadium. The University of Illinois Assembly Hall is a reminder that in the beginning, a domed stadium really was a novelty and an intricate, tricky structure to erect. Year in and year out, the roof continues to stay aloft without any visible means of support.

For visitor information, call (217) 333-2923; for information about upcoming events at Assembly Hall, call (217) 333-5000.

With its mission to preserve a valuable cache of rare books and manuscripts, it makes sense that the building housing the Beinecke Library is exceptionally protective—self-contained and almost entirely closed from the outside world. The white marble monument forms the first line of defense. The rare book stacks are further enclosed in bronze glass climate-controlled cages occupying the central core of the library floors; an exhibition gallery surrounds the stacks. The lower level houses reading rooms and offices, as well as an open court enlivened by an Isamu Noguchi sculpture.

BEINECKE RARE BOOK AND MANUSCRIPT LIBRARY, 1963

Yale University
New Haven, Connecticut

Skidmore, Owings & Merrill

The bright white bulk of the library building is lifted above its surrounding pavilion by concrete piers that also frame the gray glass shell of the ground-level entrance. Marble panes, shirred thin to produce a remarkable translucence, are recessed into the overall steel grid. The play of light and shadow transforms the building as the day wears on; at night the interior light produces a continuous glow.

Beinecke Rare Book and Manuscript Library marks a significant transformation in the architectural style of its creators, the architectural firm of Skidmore, Owings & Merrill and Gordon Bunshaft, the library's designer. Turning away from the transparent glass corporate headquarters towers that made them famous in the 1950s, the architects moved on to new kinds of buildings and an increasing diversity of style.

Yale hosts campus tours daily. For information, call (203) 432-2300.

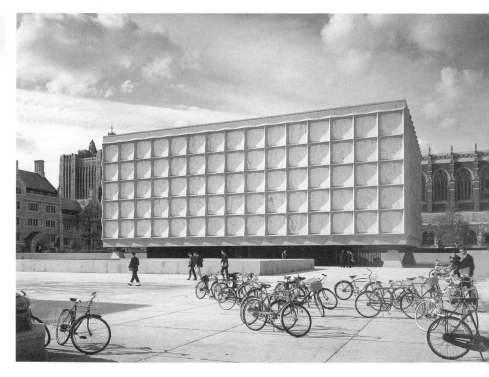

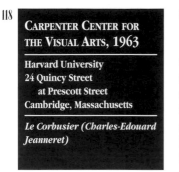

CARPENTER CENTER FOR THE VISUAL ARTS, 1963

Harvard University
24 Quincy Street
    at Prescott Street
Cambridge, Massachusetts

Le Corbusier (Charles-Edouard Jeanneret)

The legendary Swiss-French architect who called himself Le Corbusier ("the crow") designed only one American building, the Carpenter Center for the Visual Arts at Harvard University. The great modern master was seventy-six years old at the time, and the building became an abridged dictionary of his long and eventful career. There are the flat roof and walls of the early days, the *brise-soleil* sunshades of the middle years, and the exposed concrete of the late period. Curving processional ramps like those at Carpenter were a constant theme for a man intensely concerned with how people would experience his buildings as they moved in, around, and through them.

The Carpenter Center for the Visual Arts contains classrooms and studio space for students in architecture, painting, and sculpture—and Le Corbusier was accomplished in all three disciplines. The building has been compared to a cubist painting because of the interlocking forms: a square central structure, a rectangular tower, and ramps shaped like guitar picks slotted in at either side. Carpenter Center features a large open space at the center with a skewed square skylight over-

head. Studios are located at the perimeter, where light and views are controlled by the spacing of windows in various sizes and by the huge *brise-soleil* sunscreens. It is considered the best constructed of Le Corbusier's buildings.

One of three giants of twentieth-century architecture—along with Frank Lloyd Wright and Mies van der Rohe—Le Corbusier revolutionized architecture again and again. In the 1920s and 1930s, he called for a modern architectural purity of his own devising: weightless-looking white stucco buildings on stilts with smooth walls, flat roofs for terraces, ribbon windows, and no applied decoration. By the 1950s, he was using rough concrete in bulging freeform shapes that seemed ancient and primitive. The last buildings, erected like Carpenter Center in the 1960s, used concrete in a more refined but still powerful way.

The Carpenter Center for the Visual Arts is open daily from 9:00 AM to 11:45 PM, except holidays. Exhibits are mounted in the autumn and spring. For information, call (617) 495-3251.

In the 1960s, Yale University's School of Art and Architecture provoked such extremes of praise and outrage that it was difficult to see how the critics could have been describing the same building. Proponents hailed it for introducing a brilliant new style of modernism, with its massive striated concrete columns and interlocking planes, a building that seemed rugged and sophisticated and like nothing else in America. To the students who used it, the building seemed so imposing and hostile that they tried to burn it to the ground. Now, of course, it is an established monument.

YALE SCHOOL OF ART AND ARCHITECTURE, 1963

Yale University
Chapel at York Street
New Haven, Connecticut

Paul Rudolph

"I want a building to move people," explained Paul Rudolph, who was Dean of the School of Art and Architecture at Yale as well as the architect of record. A Gropius-trained Harvard graduate, he designed the school's exterior in a complex asymmetrical series of thick vertical columns, and these masses serve as the organizing principle of the building. The columns are varied in height and juxtaposed against thin, horizontal floor slabs, balcony rails, and walls of tinted glass.

The building is entered from a wide concrete stair that gives onto the second level of an astoundingly complex interior, also raw concrete. There are seven main levels of space for exhibitions, classrooms, and studios, plus a number of partial floors. They are intricately connected and often confounding: in some cases, it is necessary to go upstairs in order to come back down to reach a lower floor. Paul Rudolph used the pinwheel to describe the internal dynamics of horizontally thrusting wings working against the vertical thrust of the center. Quality of light was clearly a prime consideration, both inside and in the intricate changing play of light and shadow on the columns outside.

By the early 1990s the reinforcing steel had begun to rust through the concrete spandrel beams, and the building looked grim. Beyer Blinder Belle, a New York City architectural firm, conducted a three-year renovation that included replacing almost every window, and improving the ventilation.

Yale hosts campus tours daily. For information, call (203) 432-2300.

HUNTINGTON HARTFORD MUSEUM, 1964 (MUSEUM OF ARTS & DESIGN)

2 Columbus Circle
New York, New York

*Edward Durrell Stone
Redesign, Allied Works
Architecture*

After a lifetime of mixed reviews, New York's oddest architectural landmark is scheduled to disappear, but the ten-story white marble elephant will be hiding in partially plain sight. In its new life as the Museum of Arts & Design, the gently curved walls will peek through a veil of terra cotta scrim, by Brad Cloepfil of Allied Works Architecture.

The original building designed by pioneering modernist Edward Durrell Stone was famously characterized by Ada Louise Huxtable as "a die-cut Venetian palazzo on lollipops." It was a private museum for A&P heir Huntington Hartford, a man who knew what he didn't like about art: abstraction. Hartford wanted to exhibit representational art and show it in a home-like setting. (Stone's avant-garde approach at the Museum of Modern Art—Hartford's nemesis—apparently didn't daunt him.)

Curiously, on a site offering some of Manhattan's most cherished views, Stone designed a mostly windowless structure, its closed mass relieved with openings around the base and the top. The museum's galleries were arranged like landings on a great staircase, and the interiors were richly finished. The dream of a homestyle museum ran out of steam when Hartford ran out of cash. The museum lasted only five years.

The luxurious interiors were stripped by the subsequent tenant, New York City's Department of Cultural Affairs, which filled it with offices until 1998, when the building was vacated. In 2004, after a strident tug of war between preservationists and new development advocates, there was a compromise. The city sold the building to the Museum of Arts & Design (formerly the American Craft Museum), which announced it would redesign the building as its new home.

Cloepfil's design brings an ephemeral touch to the old white elephant. The terra cotta scrim, which symbolizes the warp and woof of the museum's textile collections, allows daylight to filter in. New openings and windows (some as high as 70 feet) pierce the solid wall, giving pedestrians a view inside while museum-goers can see out. Large, uninterrupted vertical glass channels, inserted through multiple floors, provide luminous display cases for the museum's collection.

The Museum of Arts & Design is scheduled to open in early 2007. For information, call (212) 956-3535.

In the early 1960s, the twin towers of Chicago's Marina City administered two shocks to the American system. Most obviously, the tall, rounded cylinders with their petal-shaped balconies astonished viewers accustomed to buildings in rectilinear forms. But the mixture of uses was equally revolutionary: the towers are the focal point of a five-building city within a city where residents can live, work, park, shop, bowl, ice skate, go to the theater, or go boating—a modern urban version of living above the store.

MARINA CITY, 1964

State Street at the Chicago River
Chicago, Illinois

Bertrand Goldberg

The 60-story twin towers each have 450 apartments on the top forty floors, stacked on top of twenty floors of parking. The apartments radiate out from a central core 35 feet in diameter; since walls angle out to an open horizon, residents experience the sensation of living in boundless space, just barely defined by the curved railings on the semi-circular cantilevered balconies.

Bertram Goldberg's innovative design results from his explorations of the possibilities of concrete shell construction and a desire to depart from rectilinear shapes. The tubular core houses services and utilities. It also accepts about seventy percent of the weight, while a post and beam cage around the perimeter bears the remainder. The "corn on the cob" towers share the three-acre site with two commercial buildings and a theater of the traditional straight-sided variety.

A native Chicagoan, Goldberg said that a strong wind could "blow the martini right out of your glass" in a traditional tower. For him, the curving forms were not affectations but a source of greater strength and stability in the tall towers—the tallest concrete structures in the world at the time of their construction. Goldberg trained at Harvard and at the Bauhaus in Germany; he was both an architect and an engineer. His inventive use of the concrete shell at Marina City introduced a new phase of modern architecture in America, along with an expanded vision of city living.

The rectangular structure is now a hotel. The Chicago Architecture Foundation includes Marina City on its "Architecture Highlights by Bus" tour; call the foundation at (312) 922-3432.

122

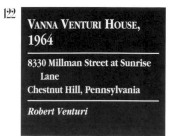

Vanna Venturi House, 1964

8330 Millman Street at Sunrise Lane
Chestnut Hill, Pennsylvania

Robert Venturi

Robert Venturi's house for his mother shows that there's no place like home: it is not an office or a factory, and has no business trying to look like one. Thus, in his first house—and the first postmodern house—he began to overturn decades of modernist doctrine based on the idea of universal space. In returning to a traditional symbolism, Venturi used forms and images that people could recognize. But the "homeyness" is exaggerated and playful. It is, as Paul Goldberger says, "home as a child would draw it."

The house was designed while Venturi was writing *Complexity and Contradiction in Architecture* (Museum of Modern Art, 1977), and it illustrates many of his anti-modern principles: Architecture is a language, full of signs and symbols. Architectural purity is unobtainable in the real world. Contradictions and complexity are inevitable and even welcome.

Although the house is small, it communicates in a big way. The front façade becomes an oversized gable, split in two to reveal the tower and chimney of the upper level. The cheerfully painted stucco walls are ornamented with wood moldings whimsically applied, especially the upsidedown smile above the front entry. Windows are asymmetrically placed in the symmetrical front façade. Under a sloping roof, the outside walls are as flat and smooth as in any modernist building. In the rear, the outer wall has been sliced off to create an outdoor porch on the second floor.

Venturi makes an especially pointed criticism of modernism's disdain for the front door. Here, the entrance is marked by a large square opening front and center. Inside, the homelike elements give way to rooms defined by angular walls that contort their dimensions and seem to deny the coziness implied on the outside.

Venturi ushered in a new architecture at a time when people were clearly ready for a change, and for a revival of the human qualities modern buildings ignored. Since then, he and his wife, Denise Scott Brown, have continued to influence architecture with both their ideas and their buildings. They received the American Institute of Architects Firm of the Year Award in 1985, and in 1991, Venturi won the Pritzker Prize for lifetime achievement.

The house is a private residence.

C lassical architecture never completely disappears, but it assumes different guises that sometimes provoke a shock of recognition, and sometimes just a shock. The Woodrow Wilson School at Princeton offers a little of each. The bright white temple-like colonnaded structure is startling in contrast to Princeton's mostly stone-gray Gothic campus. But the particular way in which Minoru Yamasaki has interpreted the classical temple—with tall, slender, tapered columns set against dark glass walls—now seems more emblematic of the idealistic 1960s rather than the verities of ancient Greece.

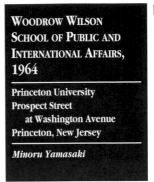

WOODROW WILSON SCHOOL OF PUBLIC AND INTERNATIONAL AFFAIRS, 1964

Princeton University
Prospect Street
    at Washington Avenue
Princeton, New Jersey

Minoru Yamasaki

Although the Woodrow Wilson School looks like a two-story structure, there are three floors above ground and one below. The main floor opens to Prospect Street on one side and to a reflecting pool on the other. The lobby is open all the way through, surfaced in cool white marble and furnished with large seating pieces. This floor also contains the library with a double mezzanine, an auditorium, and a dining room. Faculty offices are located on the top floor, and small conference rooms and service areas are located on the lower level.

By the time Yamasaki designed Woodrow Wilson School, the Washington State native had achieved national prominence for his streamlined classic style. His greatest fame would come in the 1970s with the completion of World Trade Center in New York City. These two mega-structures, 110-stories each, towered over the smaller buildings of lower Manhattan. Now, in Princeton, Yamasaki's delicate columns and classical restraint exist in the shadow of a larger and taller new neighbor. For information, call (609) 258-3000.

DANZIGER STUDIO, 1965

**7001 Melrose Avenue
at Sycamore Avenue
Hollywood, California**

Frank O. Gehry and Associates

Not far from Rudolph Schindler's house of 1922 on Kings Way, one of the first modern homes in America, stands Danziger Studio, an early modern house in the career of Frank Gehry. Schindler's house was astonishing in comparison with the architecture that came before it, but Gehry's early modern house is surprising because of Gehry's own work that came after it. In the intervening years, we have become accustomed to Gehry's exhuberant architecture, where anything from chain-link fencing to titanium billows is likely to turn up.

Danziger Studio could hardly be simpler, and this is its strength. The artist's studio and residence consists of linked cubes—a pair of offset towers that form a small courtyard. A closed compound of gray painted stucco, the building turns a blank face to both Melrose and Sycamore Avenues; its street-smart walls seem to rise right out of the sidewalk. A one-story wall encloses the courtyard of the main entrance on Melrose; the Sycamore side shows the garage doors and high windows in its otherwise blank façade.

Gehry lightens the interior with large loft-style windows on the private side of the house, and with skylights that beam light into the two-story interiors.

Since Danziger Studio was built, Melrose Avenue has become a "where the action is" kind of street and the blank-walled building is an island of calm. A few blocks away, at 8365 Melrose Avenue, Gehry's Gemini G.E.L. Studios of 1976 show Gehry on the way to something much wilder.

Danziger Studio is a private residence.

The design of this modern research facility was inspired by the centuries-old towers Louis Kahn discovered in the northern Italian hill town of San Gimignano in 1951. Kahn's uncanny ability to tap the power of ancient structures for his resonant new forms would soon become legendary. But here, at the brink of his influential career, Kahn was searching for a new order.

He found his new order in the simple, rational distinction between "servant" and "served" spaces, between the parts of a building that provide utilitarian functions, such as stairways or air-conditioning, and those that receive the benefits. This distinction explains the organization and configuration of the Richards Medical Research Building. Three eight-story towers of offices and laboratories—the served spaces—are clustered around a ten-story tower containing elevators, restrooms, and facilities for lab animals—the servant spaces.

RICHARDS MEDICAL RESEARCH BUILDING, 1965

University of Pennsylvania
Hamilton Walk
Philadelphia, Pennsylvania

Louis I. Kahn

In terms of construction technique, Richards Medical Research Building breaks new ground as one of the first high-rise buildings made of interlocking precast, pre-stressed concrete parts. The concrete is exposed in some places; walls are faced in a sandy-colored brick veneer. At Richards Medical Research Building, Kahn's insights into design and structure are pointing architecture in a new direction.

Louis Kahn taught architecture at the University of Pennsylvania from 1955 until his death in 1974. On campus, the Richards building is part of the University's Medical School complex, and is next door to the nation's first medical college building. For general information, call (215) 898-5000.

JONAS SALK INSTITUTE FOR BIOLOGICAL STUDIES, 1965

10010 North Torrey Pines Road
La Jolla, California

Louis I. Kahn

All architecture begins with the making of a room, said Louis Kahn, and he saw the street as a room as well, just located outdoors. Somewhere between these ancient ideas of the room and the street lies the great travertine central plaza of the Salk Institute, which opens to the Pacific Ocean and is one of the most spellbinding sights in American architecture.

The Salk Institute is a unique research center conceived by Nobel Laureate and polio vaccine inventor Dr. Jonas Salk as a place where scientists and artists could work together in pursuit of progress, a place where diverse disciplines could find unity. To Salk, the center should be vibrant and alive, the kind of place where you could hang a Picasso.

It is hard to imagine anyone more sympathetic than Louis Kahn for this human but mystical work. Kahn cared deeply about what a building "wanted to be," and he was profoundly in touch with elemental powers that allowed him to bring forth new forms.

Kahn created a masterpiece, with the central garden plaza at the heart of it. Flanking the plaza are two symmetrical laboratory buildings with concrete walls and teak wood insets. Studies for the scientists are contained in separate wings, connected to the main laboratory space with the intention that these new ideas will be "injected" back to the body of the building for further evaluation.

The Salk Institute won the American Institute of Architects Twenty-Five Year Award in 1992. That same year the Institute broke ground for a new building sited in the eucalyptus grove in front of Kahn's masterpiece. The new addition by Anshen & Allen (former Kahn associates) sets a pair of laboratory buildings on either side of a large open space aligned with Kahn's central axis. While the intent is to respect the original, most critics find it diminishing because it disrupts the sequence of entry from the parking lot through a eucalyptus grove into Kahn's riveting Pacific-view plaza.

The Salk Institute offers guided tours daily. For reservations and information, call (853) 453-4100, extension 1287.

Before Sea Ranch, this stretch of Sonoma County coast about 110 miles north of San Francisco was a remote but spectacular expanse of rocky terrain, fields, and forests above a crashing ocean. The special grandeur of the site evoked strong protective instincts and a sense of responsibility for developing the land without denaturing it.

SEA RANCH, 1965

Sea Walk
Sea Ranch, California

Moore, Lyndon, Turnbull & Whitaker, Architects

Charles Moore and his partners responded by working with nature rather than against it. His revolutionary design for the first condominiums seems indigenous—it plays to the slope and scale of the surrounding mountains with barnlike shapes, angled rooflines, and unpainted redwood siding. The original condominium complex is a carefully integrated whole harboring ten residences and two courtyards within a composite structure. Individual homes are oriented toward the sun, away from the wind, and to frame exceptional views.

Each home begins as a 24-foot redwood cube—one large room with a tall ceiling—in which a second level is created by mounting a four-poster pavilion against the main wall. Glass bays with window seats, solariums, terraces, decks, and walled gardens elaborate the basic structure and open the homes to the ocean views. To brighten the overwhelming woodiness of the interiors, graphic artist Barbara Stauffacher Solomon painted big, colorful designs on the walls, marking the invention of supergraphics.

Sea Ranch condo No. 9 belonged to Charles Moore, and he kept it as his personal getaway-cum-architectural salon until his death in 1993.

Only residents and guests have access to Sea Ranch, a private community now consisting of 2,000 homesites being developed along the sympathetic lines of Charles Moore's original vision. Rentals are available through the Sea Ranch Escape (707-785-2426) and other local agencies. Visitors are welcome at the Sea Ranch Lodge (707-785-2371), a twenty-room inn with swimming pools, tennis courts, and a nine-hole golf course, although the Charles Moore condominiums cannot be seen from this vantage point.

WHITNEY MUSEUM OF AMERICAN ART, 1966

945 Madison Avenue
at 75th Street
New York, New York

Marcel Breuer

The Whitney Museum—like the Guggenheim—houses its art in a building that is among the greatest works of its collection. But unlike Frank Lloyd Wright, Marcel Breuer was charged with producing a monumental, memorable building on a tiny corner site. For the Whitney, the Bauhaus-trained architect created a bold but severe Brutalist design.

Starting with a gray granite box, Breuer carved an upside-down zigzag of broad cantilevered masses that protrude progressively upward and outward toward Madison Avenue. The 75th Street sidewall, by contrast, is flat and blank, except for six trapezoidal windows. (A lone trapezoidal window reigns high on the main façade.)

At the entrance, Breuer provokes an amazing experience of architectural space with a short concrete bridge that spans a sunken sculpture court. The bridge's thick, chest-high walls, together with the massive cantilevers looming overhead, give visitors a feeling of weight and compression, which is countered by the sensation of floating over the open courtyard below. This brief but strong progression culminates in a large, glass-walled lobby, where the ceiling is covered with witty saucer-shaped light fixtures with naked bulbs—the ultimate in mid-'60s cool.

Inside, Breuer softened the hardest edges of his Brutalist exterior. Interior walls are warm-colored concrete with aggregate so richly textured that it begs to be touched. The museum was outfitted like a private club, befitting its aristocratic sponsors, with wood-paneled walls, plush carpets, and fine furnishings that included sofas, chairs, and desks. Most are gone now, but the luxurious bluestone floors and hefty wood stair banisters remain. In recent years, the courtyard level has been animated with a delightful café and gift shop, and with intriguing installations of art and architecture in the sunken outdoor space.

Since 1981, the museum has wrestled with expansion plans. A series of design schemes, first by Michael Graves and later by Rem Koolhaas, came to naught. In 2004, Renzo Piano was commissioned to rework Breuer's 76,830 square feet, and to integrate it with four adjacent landmarked brownstones on Madison Avenue and two townhouses around the corner on 74th Street.

The Whitney Museum is open Wednesday, Thursday, Saturday, and Sunday from 11:00 AM to 6:00 PM, and Friday from 1:00 to 9:00 PM; closed Monday and Tuesday. For information about tours and exhibits, call (212) 570-3676.

Vienna-born architect Richard Neutra came to Los Angeles in 1925 and began changing the course of residential architecture in the city—and the country—from the moment he arrived. Settling with his wife into the famous King's Road house of R.M. Schindler, a fellow Austrian, Neutra began designing houses that offered a new way of living in light, airy spaces that merged inside and out. His iconic 1929 Lovell House (see page 52) was a stunning example of trend-setting European modernism, and in 1932 he completed his own home and studio overlooking Silver Lake in the hills beyond Hollywood.

NEUTRA/VDL II HOUSE, 1966

2300 Silverlake Boulevard
Los Angeles, California

*Richard Neutra and
Dion Neutra*

First built in 1932, the VDL house and studio was named for Dutchman Cornelius H. van de Leeuw, whose $4,000 grant encouraged Neutra's experimental ideas. After the house burned down in 1963, Neutra, with his son Dion, rebuilt this revised design on the original footprint and called it VDL II. (A small outbuilding to the rear of the property survived the fire.)

The house is a wonder of openness on a tight urban site. On a lot that measures just 60 by 70 feet, three levels ramp up a hill, with large expanses of glass on each floor multiplying the views toward the lake and to an interior courtyard. Mirrors and glass further expand the spaces, which include a ground-floor office, second-level living area, and a penthouse. Water is also used ingeniously to add a sense of spaciousness. From some angles, a pool on the living room terrace seems continuous with the lake across the street.

At VDL II, like VDL I, experimental ideas and materials came into play. For example, the house faces west, and the Neutras used the LemLar Sun Louver System—a set of white vertical louvers two stories tall—to shade the large glass walls. In contrast to the many blithely experimental features, its traditional, metal, post-mounted mailbox is surprisingly utilitarian, but in keeping with Neutra's preference for simplicity.

Richard Neutra lived here until his death in 1970; his wife, Dione, continued in residence until she died in 1990. At Mrs. Neutra's bequest, the house is now owned by California Polytechnic University, College of Environmental Design, in Pomona. The university is in the process of restoring the house and as many of its then-innovative materials as can be replicated today.

VDL II is the only Neutra house open to the public. Visits are by appointment only; call Director Ken McCown at (323) 953-0224. The house is also available for seminars, conferences, and retreats. The Silver Lake neighborhood also offers a rare Neutra constellation: three houses built on spec at the corner of Silverlake Boulevard and Earl Street, one block from VDL II.

The Smith House is meant to be at home in its natural setting, but clearly it doesn't "grow out of the ground" in the manner envisioned by Frank Lloyd Wright. Here the aim is not to mimic the natural characteristics of the landscape, but to receive them. The sun shines more brightly on these pure white-painted wood walls, and pours into the house through its large glass windows. As the day progresses, changing colors of light and the shadow patterns of the trees are played out on its walls. A spectacular view of Long Island Sound is also part of the setting, and the house opens out to it on every level.

The overall composition of the house begins with the site, a gentle hill sloping down to the rocky shore, with the house situated at the highest point. The street façade is flat and reveals little of the interior drama. Beyond the entry façade, the house rotates briskly toward the water view. From the rear elevation, it becomes more clear that the four-level section has prompted the intricate, abstract design. In the vertical stacking, public rooms are separated from private ones, and every resident is allocated an individual private space. Levels and spaces are interlocked—horizontally and vertically—to emphasize the dynamics of moving through light as well as through space.

Smith House is the first in Richard Meier's series of all-white houses, built in the late 1960s and early 1970s. These houses advanced the modernist approach of past avant-gardists, including Richard Neutra and Rudolf Schindler in California, Walter Gropius and Marcel Breuer in the Northeast, and, of course, Le Corbusier in France.

Meier has remained a modernist, and for his body of work he received the Royal Gold Medal and the 1984 Pritzker Architecture Prize.

The house is a private residence and is visible only from Long Island Sound.

In midtown Manhattan, the most densely developed real estate in America, the Ford Foundation headquarters pioneered the idea of building offices around a lushly planted skylighted garden atrium. Encased in glass braced by rust-colored steel and dramatic overhead trusses, the building's one-third acre semitropical garden with lily pond is one of the city's most spectacular interiors. It is all the more impressive because it visually extends to an adjoining outdoor park.

FORD FOUNDATION, 1967

320 East 43rd Street
New York, New York

*Kevin Roche, John Dinkeloo &
Associates*

In 1968, *Architectural Record* hailed the building as "a new kind of urban space." Twelve L-shaped floors of offices overlook the 130-foot atrium, and their floor-to-ceiling sliding glass doors open onto the courtyard. This total openness (only the chairman's office is not on view) is meant to stress the importance of teamwork in reaching the foundation's goals. Architecturally, the open arrangement unifies the building's interiors and blurs the distinction between indoors and out.

The dusky pink granite building has two main entrances, and Kevin Roche and John Dinkeloo have created two distinct faces and personalities. The 43rd Street façade is more formal, with a tall *porte cochere* formed by stepping back the first four floors. This relatively blank-walled entrance sets up the surprise of the unseen garden that awaits the visitor. On the 42nd Street

side, the garden is strikingly visible through the glass walls, and the entrance leads directly into the garden atrium.

In 1995, Ford Foundation received the AIA's 25-year Award, with the jury citing in particular its "outstanding collaboration of landscape and architecture." The inner courtyard terraces up one full floor, from 42nd to 43rd Street. This atrium is an indoor public park, and is open from 9:00 AM to 5:00 PM, Monday through Friday. For information call (212) 573-5000.

LAKE POINT TOWER, 1968

**505 North Lakeshore Drive
Chicago, Illinois**

*Schipporeit-Heinrich
Associates*

The first skyscraper with an undulating glass wall, Lake Point Tower opened its doors as the tallest reinforced concrete building in the world. Its curved, curtain walls of bronze-tinted glass are set in a framework of bronze anodized aluminum, making it look like a sleek bronze sculpture. The tower is especially striking because of its free-standing location on the Navy Pier promontory, which projects into Lake Michigan. There is the luxury of open space all around.

Apartments at the perimeter have rounded walls and panoramic views. This openness is possible because of the ingenious prism-shaped core, extending the full 645-foot height of the structure. The prism contains elevator shafts, stairwells, corridor supply ducts, and the main electrical distribution systems. It is also designed to withstand all horizontal movements and shear forces—only vertical compression forces are transmitted, through columns, to the caissons.

Lake Point Tower's architects had been students and, later, staff associates of Mies van der Rohe, who had conceived and modeled a similar concept in 1921 in Berlin. It is often remarked that Mies's basic idea was finally realized in Lake Point Tower, but it seems more realistic to view the building as a very largely original use of technology and materials available in the late 1960s.

Because the Lake Point Tower apartments are privately owned, there are no interior tours of the building. However, you can walk into the ground-floor rotunda, which gives a view to the top. A 70th-floor restaurant (currently called Cité) is open for lunch and dinner, and for breathtaking views of the city. The Chicago Architecture Foundation includes Lake Point Tower on its Architectural Highlights by Bus and River Cruise tours; for information, call CAF at (312) 922-3432.

T he symbolic religious power of Paul Rudolph's inter-
denominational chapel at Tuskegee University is often
compared to Le Corbusier's famous pilgrimage chapel
at Ronchamps. With flat, reddish-brick walls arranged in a
geometrical spiral—all planes and angles—Rudolph captures
the kind of intensity Le Corbusier generated with sensuous
concrete curves.

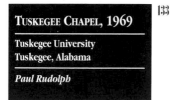

TUSKEGEE CHAPEL, 1969

Tuskegee University
Tuskegee, Alabama

Paul Rudolph

Tuskegee Chapel was originally designed of poured-in-place concrete. Like Ronchamps, the
roof of Tuskegee Chapel slopes boldly upward on one side and down on the other, extending to
a broad overhang of the entry porch with an outdoor pulpit.

Inside, the tall sheer walls enclose a great asymmetrical room that is mystically—almost magi-

cally—illuminated from peripheral skylights in its
celestial ceiling. The solid, central part of the ceiling is accordion-shaped, dotted with artificial lights,
and appears to float above the congregation like a
canopy. Furthermore, this central ceiling curves in
two directions, its warped surfaces seemingly on a
plane with the incoming light. The roof is formed
by open-web steel joists, closely spaced; no two of
these joists are parallel.

A balcony cantilevers into this main body of the
chapel, and the pulpit has its own angled canopy.
The famous Tuskegee choir is framed by the
angled walls of the chancel, behind the pulpit and
facing the congregation. A separate meditation
chapel, enclosed by the main spiral form, is lighted
by skylights and colored glass windows.

Tours are held Monday to Friday at 1:00 PM and
3:00 PM, and Saturday at 10:00 AM; closed University
holidays. Because the chapel is also designed as a
concert hall, musical events are held here as well.
For tours, call the Public Information Office at (334)
727-8347.

JOHN HANCOCK CENTER, 1970

875 North Michigan Avenue Chicago, Illinois

Skidmore, Owings & Merrill

The 100-story John Hancock tower is distinguished by prominently displayed diagonal braces, dark glass, and a tapering monolithic appearance. It is one of the buildings that says "Chicago" to most people.

John Hancock Center works visually like a full-sized cut-away model, showing exactly how the designer solved the structural problem of stabilizing such a very tall building against the wind loads and against its own weight. Hiding the diagonal bracing has been traditional, not because of any secret of engineering—it is commonplace—but because it is usually so busy-looking. On a truly enormous building like this one, however, the long and high-reaching diagonal lines have a novel and unexpected grace. They also provide a strong visual reassurance that the building is good and solid, in the same way great bridges are solid.

The rigidity achieved in the John Hancock Center comes from geometry—and geometry weighs nothing. Consider that the structural steel in a typical medium-rise Chicago building weighs about 50 pounds for each square foot of area. Yet in this extreme high-rise, the ratio is only 29.7 pounds of steel per square foot of area, a statistic almost as impressive as the building's height.

The first 41 floors are office and commercial space, with condominiums, an observatory, a restaurant, and broadcast facilities on the upper floors. For these various uses, the external bracing is a great advantage: the absence of internal columns gives tenants nearly complete flexibility in adapting and partitioning their floor spaces for their own use. Rising 100 stories, John Hancock's altitude is prodigious. One bright day a squadron of open cockpit biplanes, en route to an exhibition in Wisconsin, flew by the waistline of the tower. The sport pilots waved *up* at stylish and interested apartment dwellers on the topmost floors, who peered down from their windows at the passing procession of aircraft.

The observation deck on the John Hancock Center is open daily from 9:00 AM to 11:00 PM except on major holidays; for information, call (312) 751-3681. The building is also featured on Chicago Architecture Foundation tours; for information, call the foundation at (312) 922-3432.

I n 1963, the monks of Mount Angel Abbey wrote a heart-
felt letter to Alvar Aalto, the Finnish architect renowned
for the natural beauty and grace he brought to modern
architecture. "We need you," the monks implored. "We have
a magnificent monastic site. We don't want to spoil it. . . .
Give us a building that will fill our needs in a beautiful and
intelligent way." Almost ten years later, the monks' dream
was fulfilled, making their library one of only two Alvar Aalto
buildings in the United States.

MOUNT ANGEL LIBRARY,
1970

Mount Angel Abbey
East End of College Street
St. Benedict, Oregon

Alvar Aalto

As with most of Aalto's buildings, the Mount Angel Library
appears deceptively simple. Entered at the crest of the hill, it
looks like a rather plain one-story structure of pale yellow
brick. The only ornamentation is an open canopy of redwood,
fir and teak, and thin redwood slats screening the windows.

But immediately inside, the building practically explodes
with light and space, and the full wonder and complexity of
the library's design makes itself clear. At the center is an
open well surrounded by two stories and a mezzanine,
which ramp down the hill. The rear wall is fan-shaped and

overlooks the surrounding view. A curving skylight at the roof floods the library with light by
day. At night, Aalto's signature parabolic fixtures provide the illumination.

The main level of the 44,000-square-foot building is an open floor with a low curving wall
that echoes the contours of the fan-shaped exterior wall. Besides the entry lobby, this level contains the control desk, the periodical room, and the monastery's treasured rare book collection.
Carrels line the outer walls, and the low balcony wall is ringed with a long reading counter
outfitted with Aalto-designed lights and stools. The mezzanine and lower floors are primarily giv-
en over to stacks positioned like spokes on a wheel. All the furnishings were designed by Aalto
down to the door handles. Aalto's way with wood and other natural materials is legendary. His

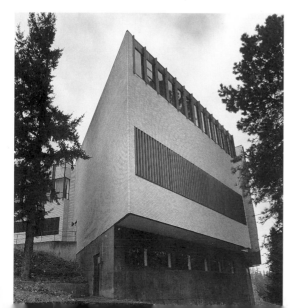

signature slatted wood ceilings
appear in the library's control
area and auditorium.

The Abbey is forty-five miles
south of Portland off Interstate
5's Woodburn exit. Library
hours are Monday through Friday, 8:30 AM to 5:00 PM, Monday
through Thursday evenings, and
on weekends. The library is
closed on major holidays and
runs on a shorter schedule during the summer. For information
and to request guided tours, call
(503) 845-3303.

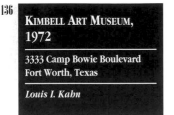

The architecture of Louis Kahn arises from a mysterious source he called "the realm of the senses," and this is the real territory occupied by his buildings when they have been built. The Kimbell Art Museum, with its fine collection, appeals to more than just our sensual appreciation of sight and space. It reaches all the way to the more mystical associations we invest in buildings, drawing on the collective memory of ancient forms and recognizing how satisfying the forces of rhythm and repetition can be.

At the Kimbell Art Museum, Kahn found his solution in the strong southwestern sun, seeing light as the essence of a museum, the common ground between the viewer and the art. He gave the museum its light, and its form, by resurrecting the vault as his organizing principal and the source of the building's interior luminosity.

The building's apparently simple structure and materials are immediately evident. Kahn laid out six pale-colored concrete vaults side by side: an entrance court, the galleries, a series of garden courts, and a reflecting pool. He created an outside porch by leaving open the two vaults that flank the museum's entrance.

The vaults become building blocks: each 100 x 23-foot clear span module has a concrete frame, concrete exterior walls, travertine interior walls, and a lead roof. Even so, this building is much too sophisticated to be considered modular.

A soft, silvery light fills the museum throughout the day. Kahn achieved this luminosity by turning the vaulted roof into what he called a "natural light fixture." He sliced the vault's apex with a full-length skylight and fitted it with a curved, perforated aluminum screen for diffusion. The art can be seen in natural light without suffering damage from the exposure.

The Kimbell Art Museum is the last work completed under Kahn's personal supervision. In the late 1980s, a plan to expand Kahn's design by adding more "modules" was protested so vehemently that the trustees agreed to relent. The museum will remain as Kahn intended. The new Modern Art Museum by Tadao Ando (see page 254) is across the street.

The museum is open Tuesday to Thursday and Saturday from 10:00 AM to 5:00 PM; Friday from noon to 8:00 PM; Sunday from noon to 5:00 PM; and closed Monday, New Year's Day, the Fourth of July, Thanksgiving, and Christmas Day. For information and reservations (two weeks in advance for groups), call (817) 332-8451.

T he Marin County Civic Center is Frank Lloyd Wright's testament to democratic government, although he was accused of being a communist for having designed it. The building was designed in 1958 but not completed until 1972. And like all of Wright's architecture, the setting was the starting point. He saw the beautiful hills north of San Francisco and knew at once that he would span them with three graceful arches.

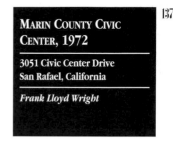

MARIN COUNTY CIVIC CENTER, 1972

3051 Civic Center Drive
San Rafael, California

Frank Lloyd Wright

From this first insight, an amazing complex of buildings evolved in a vast horizontal stretch nearly a quarter of a mile long, tiered with arches, and resembling a Roman aqueduct. This infinite expanse actually consists of two main wings—the Administration Building and the Hall of Justice, with its courts, sheriff's office, and jail. The two wings meet at the dome, a massive and elaborately ornamented structure that houses a library and conference center; a continuous skylight joins the curved roofs of the entire assemblage. Near the dome, mechanical equipment is exotically concealed in a totem-like 217-foot spire.

Using simple materials, Wright has achieved an effect that is fantastic: a composition of tawny pink stucco, a blue plastic-coated roof, bright red and gold window panels, and gold anodized aluminum for the balcony rails, the entrance gate, and the rows of globes that hang from the building's extended eaves. The concrete shell roof is covered with decorative circles, arches, and spheres.

With Marin's long skylighted atrium corridors, Wright unwittingly pioneered an idea that would become a cliché of shopping center design from coast to coast. But here, the skylights work as Wright intended, bringing light and openness to all levels of the interior. Arches open up the exterior walls all around, and balconies provide continuous mobility as outside corridors. Offices have full-height glass walls that expose them to the central atriums, fulfilling Wright's belief that the people's government should be visible and accessible.

The Marin County Civic Center is open from 7:00 AM to 6:00 PM, Monday through Friday. Visitors can wander through the public areas. Tours are available on Wednesday at 10:30 AM, leaving from the second floor gift shop. To arrange a tour, call (415) 499-6646.

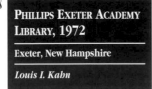

PHILLIPS EXETER ACADEMY LIBRARY, 1972

Exeter, New Hampshire

Louis I. Kahn

One of Louis Kahn's last completed American buildings is the library for Phillips Exeter Academy. On campus, Georgian brick buildings bespeak of tradition; the library manages to coexist peacefully with the older structures while maintaining the clarity and integrity that make a Kahn building special.

Kahn's sympathy with the surroundings affects the exterior, where the walls are brick, flat, rhythmic, and unadorned—a modern complement to the Georgian style. By means of a ground-level arcade, the library confirms its association with the campus by reaching out on all four sides. The entrances can be found at the four corners, sliced off on the diagonal, which Kahn compared to a book with dog-eared pages that tell you where the important parts are located.

On the inside, the almost mystical power of Kahn's architecture is fully exposed in the monumental concrete forms: the curving stairs, the cross-beamed ceiling, and, especially, the mammoth open unframed circles that expose the stacks. The vast interior, almost 90,000 square feet of floor space, is defined by exposed concrete, raw and finished at the same time. It is hard to imagine that anyone but Kahn could have created such a large and open concrete place where the prospect of settling down with a good book still maintains its intimacy.

A dining hall, also designed by Louis Kahn, is adjacent to the library and is faced with the same brick. Its primary features are the large windows in all four dining rooms, and overscaled

fireplaces in two of them. The clean lines and towering chimneys of the dining hall complete the strong geometry of Kahn's overall composition.

Throughout most of the year, the library is open Monday through Friday, 7:30 AM to 9:30 PM; Saturday from 7:30 AM to 4:00 PM, and Sunday from 1:00 to 9:00 PM. The library is closed for major holidays; accessibility is also affected by school vacations and other academic schedules, so it is advisable to call first at (603) 772-4311.

Twenty years ago, professional critics and San Francisco residents alike were convinced that Transamerica's 835-foot pyramid with flippers would permanently devastate the city skyline. But Transamerica has had the opposite effect: its image is now so linked with San Francisco that it often appears on map and guidebook covers for the famous city by the bay.

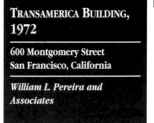

TRANSAMERICA BUILDING, 1972

600 Montgomery Street
San Francisco, California

William L. Pereira and Associates

The Los Angeles firm of William L. Pereira and Associates, known for the space-age restaurant "pods" at the Los Angeles Airport, decided on a pyramid shape, and stuck to it. The base of the building is ringed with huge concrete pillars angled together like tripods in a series of open strutwork pyramids. These strong diagonals point upward, to the bronze-tinted windows set in exposed concrete walls that become increasingly narrow toward the top. And at the top, of course, there is the building's grand gesture, the once-controversial, now-landmark pinnacle.

Transamerica's late-blooming success as a landmark is partly due to the comfort of familiarity, but also to a realization that its design is truly sensible: the pyramid shape admits far more space, air, and light into the area than a bulky box. These considerations add to the vitality of an already bustling scene where three distinctly different neighborhoods come together: the busy financial district, the theme-park bohemian North Beach, and colorful Chinatown. Because San Francisco is a city of hills, arresting views of Transamerica suddenly appear from unexpected vantage points. There are also arresting views from Transamerica's 27th-floor observation area, shot by cameras on the top that are shown on monitors in the lobby. For information, call (415) 983-4000.

**WORLD TRADE CENTER/
FREEDOM TOWER
1972–2008**

Church to West Streets,
 Liberty to Vesey Streets
New York, New York

*Minoru Yamasaki/Daniel
Libeskind,
Skidmore, Owings & Merrill*

When the Twin Towers went up, they made architectural history as the world's tallest buildings. At 110 stories, they became ready landmarks, not as breathtaking beauties, but for their towering graphic presence on the skyline. But their tall walls, which were load bearing, could not bear the unparalleled weight of airliners crashing into them on September 11, 2001. When the buildings came down, it marked a turning point that went far beyond the bounds of architectural history. With the devastating loss of life in this catastrophe, people around the globe felt deeply invested in the reconstruction.

"People wanted something extraordinary," said Daniel Libeskind, "something to lay the ghosts to rest." Libeskind also recognized that buildings tell stories, and his competition-winning design established the master plan with a message: a spiral of towers that culminate in a building 1,776 feet tall (to commemorate the year of America's independence), and to acknowledge the Statue of Liberty just offshore in New York Harbor. His design also left the old slurry walls exposed in remembrance.

The design of the new icon, named Freedom Tower, incorporated Libeskind's emotionally resonant vision. But it was realized—and watered down—in collaboration with Skidmore, Owings & Merrill. The so-called collaboration was an arranged marriage fraught with in-fighting between architects with vastly different styles. The resulting design reclaimed the original title of world's tallest tower: 70 stories of commercial space, with restaurants and a viewing platform on the uppermost three floors. These floors will be topped by an open lattice of cables holding wind turbines that generate about 20 percent of the building's energy, and at the top, a 276-foot spire.

The new design calls for blast resistant glass and its concrete core is encased in a diagonal grid of steel cable netting for stability. The tower is slightly torqued on its east and west sides for extra strength.

Freedom Tower will be situated at the northwest corner of the 16-acre site. The footprints of the fallen towers will be commemorated as twin reflecting pools, in a memorial designed by Michael Arad, which was also chosen in competition. Libeskind's spire—an unabashed gesture of defiance—will be the design's high point. On the ground, Arad's trees will fill the remainder of the site, signifying renewal.

Visitors seeking the most profound approach to the tower should proceed via Santiago Calatrava's PATH terminal, an all-white steel structure resembling the dove of peace. The Freedom Tower's completion is expected in late 2008 or early 2009. For information, call the Lower Manhattan Development Corporation, (212) 962-2300.

T he old fortress-like bank has been supplanted in recent decades by the open, receptive, and unobstructed look of modern banking facilities. But the new openness sets up a paradox for bank architects—they must provide the absolute security of a bastion with the wide open feel of a loggia.

In the Federal Reserve Bank the problem was solved by splitting the bank into two distinct zones. Activities requiring security were simply buried. Fully sixty percent of the facility's square footage is hidden underground beneath the sloped, landscaped plane of a plaza. Poised above this plaza, suspended in midair between two great vertical towers, is the "airy" part of the bank—its public face—as represented by the administrative and clerical office spaces.

The structure above ground looks like a catenary suspension bridge and works on the same principle. The concrete slab floors are supported by a pair of rigid framed catenaries. The catenary members are hung, sixty feet apart, on either side of the building, and the glass curtain walls are designed to emphasize them visually. Above the curve, the glass is inset into the curve; below the curve, the glass stands forward.

Because floors are supported in this fashion, there is no need for columns. The span of the floors is 275 feet, all of it completely clear and uninterrupted. No one had ever before constructed an office building with such an imposingly long clear span.

On a real bridge, the catenaries are deeply anchored ashore. In this building there are no remote anchors. The tendency for the two towers to topple inward is countered by a pair of 28-foot deep beams that span the top of the building. The load of the floors is thus turned into compression on these beams, which also function as channels to contain the building's mechanical equipment.

The Federal Reserve Bank moved to new quarters in 1997. The building, now called Marquette Plaza, has been redeveloped by FRM for office tenants. For information, call FRM at (612) 332-6300.

KRESGE COLLEGE, 1973

University of California
    at Santa Cruz
Santa Cruz, California

Moore, Lyndon, Turnbull, &
Whitaker, Architects

To create a college of dormitories, dining halls, and classrooms, Charles Moore took the idea of an Italian hill town and brought it up to date. The white stucco buildings accented in bright primary colors are organized around a 1,000-foot L-shaped "main street" that twists and turns to ensure a progression of interesting views as well as stopping points to encourage chance encounters among the student villagers.

The most noticeable design element is the stage-set cutout wall, which Moore has inserted like screens in layers along the way. Often the walls appear to be freestanding, whether they are broad, flat, and tall to mark a building entrance, or slender columns substituting for balcony railings. The outside stairs are walled in white stucco to match the buildings, which ties them into the overall design while adding a series of bold angles to the broad, flat squares of the cutout walls.

The layering of freestanding elements is cool and spare. This layered effect turns up in many of Charles Moore's designs, and is most gloriously and classically elaborated at the Piazza d'Italia in New Orleans. Moore's designs frequently summed up the spirit of their times and provided models that would be widely imitated. As Sea Ranch in the 1960s unleashed a decade of timbered townhouses with steeply angled roofs, Kresge College influenced the trend to white stucco construction that was also widely imitated, but not often well, in the 1970s. For information, call (831) 459-2071.

The Sears Tower at the time of its construction held the record as the tallest building in the world. Its 110 stories, 1,468 feet tall, are vertically bundled together in nine rectangularly framed tubes. Each tube is 75 feet square, and can be thought of with some accuracy as nine distinct skyscrapers lashed together.

SEARS TOWER, 1974

Jackson Boulevard, between Franklin Street and Wacker Drive
Chicago, Illinois

Skidmore, Owings & Merrill

The design is called a "Megatube," but not all the component tubes in the bundle rise to the building's full height. Certain tubes terminate at carefully chosen heights to create the visual impression of a naturally occurring crystal, perhaps of calcite or quartz. William Marlin characterized it with a different metaphor: "staggered stacks of catalogs."

Technically, the bundled tube structure handles wind and structural loads without any excess mass. The structural steel weighs just 33 pounds per square foot, which contrasts favorably with the 29-pound-per-square-foot structure of its lean and gracefully cross-braced counterpoint, that other Chicago colossus, the John Hancock Center. Both buildings are virtually airframes compared to conventionally framed Chicago buildings, which require about 50 pounds of steel per square foot to achieve their solidity.

Sears Tower's specification list is a cheerful compendium of gee-whiz statistics. It has 102 high-speed elevators suspended from eight miles of elevator cable; 76,000 tons of structural steel; 17,200 tons of refrigerating equipment; 16,000 bronze-tinted windows; 25 miles of plumbing, 1,500 miles of wiring, and so on. This is a building that has its own zip code.

Sears Tower has recently renovated its 100th-floor Sky Deck and 103rd-floor observatory. There is a new five-minute audio-visual show, as well as exhibits highlighting ten of Chicago's most architecturally significant buildings. The Sky Deck is open daily, from 10:00 AM to 10:00 PM May through September, and from 10:00 AM to 8:00 PM October through April. For more information, call (312) 875-9696.

In a flat, colorless, and tired part of town, the Best Products Showroom arrived flat, colorless, and a total wreck. Built as a brand new, white brick ruin, the "Indeterminate Façade" appeared to be crumbling all around the merchandise mart it housed. An artfully devised cascade of bricks pours down onto the entrance canopy, a pile of rubble advancing toward shoppers' heads.

The Indeterminate Façade was created by extending the brick veneer arbitrarily beyond the logical edge of the roofline, resulting in the appearance of architecture arrested somewhere between construction and demolition. Like the high concept for a Hollywood movie, the Houston showroom introduced a big idea—build the ruin—which struck a surprisingly responsive chord. Once the initial shock and apocalyptic prophesies subsided, the business and artistic success was undeniable. Best erected seven more "unbuilt" showrooms, and the mail order chain became internationally famous for its fantasy stores in the notoriously downmarket arena of discount merchandising.

SITE is a group of New York artists, and they approached the Best store design as conceptual art at the urban scale. Although the buildings were initially shocking, James Wines has said that this was not their purpose. Rather, their "unfinished" state is meant as a counterpoint to both over-packaging in our consumer economy and to the demand for completeness. Wines describes SITE's design process as "de-architecturisation;" today we would call it deconstruction.

In the 1970s, Best was the nation's largest catalog-showroom merchandiser. The company commissioned SITE to design a series of "unbuilt" showrooms: the store with the gouged-out sliding corner entrance in Baltimore, Maryland; the store with "peeling brick" corners in Richmond, Virginia; the abandoned-looking, overgrown façade in Henrico, Virginia; the Ghost Parking Lot in Hamden, Connecticut, and the Inside/Outside Building in Milwaukee, Wisconsin.

After years of success, Best fell on hard times and the collapsing buildings seem eerily prophetic. In the 1990s, an audiovisual store moved in, staving off actual demolition, but at an architectural price: pulsing neon lights now drape the façade's broken edge.

T he Pacific Design Center is called "The Blue Whale," a big blue building that has now been joined by a green whale (and a red cloud-like structure is on the way). Conceived as an enormous home furnishings showroom, the vivid blue 750,000-square-foot colossus broke the scale of its formerly residential neighborhood. The *Los Angeles Times* said it was like trying "to hide a whale in a backyard swimming pool."

PACIFIC DESIGN CENTER, 1975

8687 Melrose Avenue
West Hollywood, California

Cesar Pelli, Gruen Associates

Cesar Pelli designed the building (now called the Blue Center) as an enormous six-story extrusion of glass, color, and form. Its blue glass walls rise up to a barrel-vaulted, partially glazed gallery at the top, which helps to streamline the building's massiveness on the outside and gives a sense of destination to the interior. The intense, fade-proof color comes from the old technique of grinding paint and baking it into the glass.

As a business idea, the buildings were too far ahead of their time. Occupancy languished, and in 1999 Charles S. Cohen bought the center, which was down on its luck. An owner of furniture showrooms in New York City and Houston, he began to humanize the overpowering effects. He commissioned Pelli to "edit" the massive exterior, which included adding see-through windows on the green building. Area updated the interiors and Thomas Balsey designed the new Wave Park landscape. Design-oriented advertising and public relations firms have joined the showroom tenants, and the Museum of Contemporary Art (see page 180) has opened a satellite gallery. As planned decades ago, the colorful complex finally finds itself at the center of a thriving design district that has sprung up around it, primarily in shops on Melrose and Beverly.

The Pacific Design Center is open Monday through Friday from 9:00 AM to 5:00 PM, closed weekends and major holidays. The center also hosts a schedule of design-oriented programs and exhibitions throughout the year, including their big, annual Westweek show held in March. For information and tours, call (310) 657-0800.

ARCOSANTI, 1976 (ONGOING)

Interstate 17, Exit 262
Cordes Junction, Arizona

Paolo Soleri

The visionary Italian-born architect Paolo Soleri recognized long ago that suburban sprawl wouldn't always be pretty, that there was a natural limit to unbridled growth. Soleri believes there must be ways for architecture and nature to work in harmony, and he coined the term "arcology" to describe this process, which has become his lifelong preoccupation.

In 1976, with the help of students and volunteers, Soleri began building Arcosanti as a prototype arcology for 5,000 people. It still has the air of a busy architectural workshop where life and work are practically inseparable. There are now enough completed buildings to house workshop participants and guests, and to provide for community activities. A number of intriguing structures have been completed, including large, open hangar-like vaults that serve as town squares, the crafts building, a café, a bakery, and a museum.

Soleri, who trained at Taliesin West with Frank Lloyd Wright, divides his time between Arcosanti and Cosanti, a tiny assemblage of hand-built earth-formed concrete buildings he began in the 1960s. Dome House—his innovative 1950s glass and aluminum sphere on track-mounted rotating sections that cooled itself with water jets— is located midway between the two communities (but it is not open to the public).

Cosanti, an Arizona State Historic Site, is located at 6433 Doubletree Ranch Road in Scottsdale. It is open seven days a week from 9:00 AM to 5:00 PM, closed for major holidays. The phone number at Cosanti is (480) 948-6145.

Arcosanti is located about sixty-five miles north of Phoenix, off the intersection of I-17 and Highway 69 (Cordes Junction exit 262). Arcosanti is open seven days a week from 9:00 AM to 5:00 PM, closed Thanksgiving and Christmas. Guided tours are held every hour on the hour from 10:00 AM until 4:00 PM. Special architectural tours also go behind the scenes in the design office. The café and gallery are pleasant places to wait if meeting the quorum causes a delay. Arcosanti also has a few inexpensive guest rooms for overnight stays. Workshops include a six-week program and a new one-day workshop as well. For reservations and information, call (928) 632-6217.

Not too long ago, John Hancock Tower was probably the most ridiculed building in America, a national symbol of architectural trouble. Now it is widely acclaimed as one of the last great skyscrapers of the modern age, a dazzling mirrored parallelogram that is intellectually honest and geometrically pure.

JOHN HANCOCK TOWER, 1976

200 Clarendon Street
Boston, Massachusetts

I.M. Pei & Partners

Clearly, this building has had a tumultuous history. But it started in an ordinary way, as a corporate rivalry played out architecturally. In the mid-1960s, one enormous corporation—the John Hancock Mutual Insurance Company—determined to out-build its competitor, Prudential. John Hancock's plan to erect a 60-story, 2-million-square-foot tower on a single block next to Copley Square ignited fierce protest. How could this monolith respect the neighborhood's human-scale architectural treasures: Trinity Church by H.H. Richardson; the Boston Public Library by McKim, Mead & White; and the Copley Plaza Hotel?

A reflective glass skin intended to minimize the tremendous mass and reflect the surrounding landmarks on its surface proved to be the start of something much worse. While under construction in 1973, the tower was ravaged by a storm that blew out one-third of the 10,000 windows, each weighing 500 pounds. With plywood filling the gaps, the building became a scandal and a joke: the tallest wooden building in the world.

The building's prominent corporate architects and its designer, Henry Cobb, were able to solve the problems and to emerge with reputations intact. In the final analysis, John Hancock Tower can now be seen as a high-water mark of minimalism: a sleek mirrored column with notched sides offering elegant proportions and considerable dignity. Holding a mirror to the landmarks that surround it, John Hancock Tower has finally become one of them.

For information, call (617) 572-6000.

NATIONAL AIR AND SPACE MUSEUM, 1976

Independence Avenue, on the Mall between Fourth and Seventh Street S.W. Washington, D.C.

Helmuth Obata & Kassabaum

On any given day, as many as 50,000 people will visit the National Air and Space Museum; they will enter, circulate, mill around, stare at great length in wonder, study, shop for souvenirs, attend theaters, and finally exit.

America's most popular museum is a mammoth structure: 685 x 225 feet, with the long dimension facing Independence Avenue. From the Mall, the building looks like a linked series of four distinct buildings, each a 90-foot-tall monolith in pink Tennessee marble, all interconnected by three glass galleries. From the street side, the intervening galleries are accented by huge, visually suspended granite-covered blocks that hang like airborne monuments between the buildings.

The museum building is a wise and thoughtful design. It identifies and solves the real problem of putting airplanes on display, which is to allow visibility from every direction, including above and below. Moreover, planes have complicated shapes that actively resist boxing. No two aircraft are alike in size and configuration—wings, wheels, tails, struts, and engines poke out in every direction.

The sophisticated design solution is the same one kids use for their model planes—they hang them on strong threads from the ceiling. The sky enters the picture thanks to great, glassed-in, display bays. A full panoply of stairs, catwalks, and open mezzanine hallways lets visitors move freely about the place in all three dimensions, to get an excellent look at the exhibits.

The open galleries are framed using pipe trusses, and the airplanes hang on steel cables from these structural devices. The architectural allusion made by these tubular tetrahedrons, longerons, and stringers is precisely that of an aircraft fuselage. It visually

demonstrates the real-world problems that confront aeronautical and aerospace engineers: the static and dynamic stresses the airplane must bear, and the need to add structural strength without adding weight. As a building design element, these truss tubes may not be much of a metaphor for the human spirit taking flight, but they are a perfectly elegant metaphor for the engineering ideas that got us off the ground.

The Air and Space Museum is open daily from 10:00 AM to 5:30 PM. Closed Christmas Day. For information, call (202) 357-2700.

The twin bronze-black towers of Pennzoil Place almost touch. More than the buildings themselves, the ten-foot sliver of sky between them is riveting. Now you see it, and then you don't. The drama is best experienced by car as you curve around downtown on the elevated freeway—a processional view Philip Johnson called "automobilistic."

PENNZOIL PLACE, 1976

**700 Milam Street
Houston, Texas**

Philip Johnson & John Burgee

In terms of commercial architecture, the striking appearance of Pennzoil Place helped launch a trend for designer buildings. In place of the predictable glass box, Johnson and Burgee introduced two identical towers shaped like trapezoids—a square with a triangle appended to it. Instead of the traditional flat roofs, the tops of these buildings are sliced off on the diagonal. There is considerable "wasted" space in the pointy corners of every floor. These buildings defied all traditional real estate expectations, yet 1.2 million square feet leased like hotcakes.

Pennzoil's spectacular atrium-entry also caught on. Here, the street level space between the two towers is enclosed within a triangular sloping glass roof to form a glass courtyard eight stories at its apex, with shops and restaurants in the court.

For eight years Pennzoil Place virtually defined the Houston skyline. But in 1984 the vast Republic Bank Tower went up across the street and stole some of the thunder, despite the fact that the new bank's architects— Philip Johnson and John Burgee —were presumably most sympathetic to the uniqueness of Pennzoil Place.

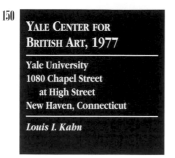

YALE CENTER FOR BRITISH ART, 1977

Yale University
1080 Chapel Street
at High Street
New Haven, Connecticut

Louis I. Kahn

The Yale Center for British Art was Louis Kahn's final commission. And in one of modern architecture's most striking coincidences, it is located across the street from the Yale Art Gallery, the first major work of Kahn's career.

At the Yale Center for British Art, Kahn's life-long determination to simplify is evident inside and out. The grid-like exterior consists of a four-story concrete frame filled with panels of dark glass and pewter-toned stainless steel; on the interior, the concrete grid is inset with oak panels. A recessed corner cutout at Chapel and High Streets marks the entry, and it propels visitors into a glorious interior court that rises full height, naturally illuminated by a clear glass roof. Skylights on the roof diffuse natural light throughout the top floor galleries and the second interior courtyard of the library.

Kahn respected all parts of a building, and perhaps for this reason the vertical stainless steel shafts of the mechanical systems occupy an exposed position right in the middle of it. Another central feature is the cylindrical stairway, with walls of concrete and floors of travertine. Interior colors and materials—travertine marble, white oak, undyed wool carpeting, and natural linen wall coverings—provide a subtle background in which the works of art become paramount.

Kahn expected the pewter-paneled museum to "look like a moth on a cloudy day and on a sunny day like a butterfly." Sadly, he died before its completion. Kahn's former associates, Anthony Pellechia and Marshall Meyers, assumed the tricky task of figuring out the final details of what Kahn would have wanted. They surely succeeded; and almost mystically, the reflection of Kahn's first great building can be seen in the dark glass panes of his concluding one.

Paul Mellon donated the building and the core collection. Today, the Center houses the most comprehensive body of English paintings, prints, drawings, rare books, and sculpture outside Great Britain.

The center is open Tuesday through Saturday from 10:00 AM to 5:00 PM and Sunday from noon to 5:00 PM; closed Monday and major holidays. Scheduled gallery tours take place Saturday at 11:00 AM; one Saturday every month (usually the third Saturday), an architectural tour is also conducted at 11:00 AM. For information, call (203) 432-2858.

I n Paul Rudolph's complex and powerful design for the Bass House are echoes of two of modern architecture's most important residences. There are the tantalizing overlapping cantilevers reminiscent of Fallingwater (see page 67), and the elevated, translucent quality of the Farnsworth House (see page 88). But more importantly, the

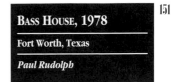
house is a continuation of Rudolph's own concerns: the interactions of vertical and horizontal thrusts, and how strongly opposing forces can be brought into balance to achieve serenity.

Rudolph's landmark Art and Architecture building at Yale University (see page 119) used a pinwheel concept to contain these forces, which are solidly grounded in vertical towers of massive striated concrete. At the Bass House, commissioned in the early 1970s, the pinwheel recurs as an organizing principle: there is a central courtyard and the cantilevers extend outward on all sides. The balance this time is a delicate one. A series of light-looking horizontal layers amount to something incredibly strong.

Bass House is built up in three dimensions, layer upon layer, with white enameled, wide-flange structural steel, aluminum sheathing, glass, and white porcelain. The overall structure basically consists of three main levels, which Rudolph subdivided into twelve floor levels, fourteen ceiling heights, and a small penthouse. At the core of the house is a fireplace that rises exposed through all levels, with the two-story living room, the upper study, the library, and the stairs arrayed around it.

The intricately layered structure accomplished Rudolph's primary goal of space-making, by which he meant the whole space, inside and out. The house becomes a series of interlocking volumes that creates both bright spaces and dark ones, high and low spaces, and exhilarating progressions in, around, and through them.

Integral to the design are the outdoor spaces: terraces on many levels, the central courtyard, a swimming pool, and an auto court. The spatial dynamics, inside and out, would not be complete without the superb collection of contemporary artwork and the evocative gardens designed by Robert Zion, Russell Page, and Anne Bass.

The house is a private residence.

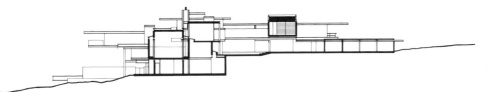

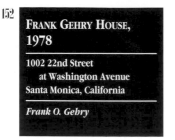

**FRANK GEHRY HOUSE,
1978**

1002 22nd Street
   at Washington Avenue
Santa Monica, California

Frank O. Gehry

The shock of the new was nowhere more startling than in Frank Gehry's house in Santa Monica. Starting with a traditional Dutch cottage in a conventional Los Angeles neighborhood, Gehry literally tore the house apart. When the pieces came together again, the traditional façade vanished behind a new one: a jagged asymmetrical wall of corrugated metal, and panels of raw plywood topped by a cyclone fence. Some of the original studs remained exposed, and the kitchen was paved with asphalt. This was startlingly novel architecture, but it worked, and Gehry's reputation as a major design innovator was secured.

Gehry's architectural bravura launched a fascination for reconfiguring standard industrial materials in abstract combinations, although Gehry resisted the trend's designation of "deconstruction." Reacting against the blank modern buildings of the International Style, Gehry chose to move forward with a new and personal vision, rather than to recreate the styles of the more distant past. The Toronto-born architect received the Pritzker Prize in 1989 in honor of his success in bringing art back to architecture. He also showed that serious architecture can be fun.

In 2005 Gehry announced plans to build a new house—actually a cluster of houses—for his family in Venice, casting doubt on the fate on this once earth-shaking architectural icon. The house is a private residence.

In contrast to the neoclassical columns and statues of official Washington monuments—including the original National Gallery of Art by John Russell Pope across the street—I.M. Pei's East Building is a study in elegant simplicity. Its dusky-pink marble walls are taut, flat, and smooth, ornamented solely by the razor-sharp precision of the design and construction. But it is also a lively and convivial place that wants to attract large audiences to its constantly changing exhibits.

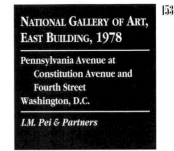

NATIONAL GALLERY OF ART, EAST BUILDING, 1978

Pennsylvania Avenue at
   Constitution Avenue and
   Fourth Street
Washington, D.C.

I.M. Pei & Partners

At the heart of the East Building's apparent simplicity is the triangle, a complicated shape that requires intricate design skill to carry off at large scale. And the East Building is more than just a single building; it is a complex of almost 300,000 square feet that includes an underground connection to the old museum. Pei has used the triangle scheme to organize the major functions. The largest triangle houses the seven-level museum; beside it a study center for scholars occupies a smaller triangle. They are linked by yet another triangle, a skylighted court with an immense, red Calder mobile suspended from the center of this 60-foot-high space. Because the main entrance is purposefully low and compressed, this spectacular light-filled court seems to explode into view. Not just a visual surprise, this central courtyard serves as a primary conduit to the museum galleries by means of elevated walkways and a grand staircase.

For all the differences between the old neoclassical museum and the new contemporary one, there are also similarities. Both buildings exist because of the unparalleled generosity of the Mellon family. In sympathy with the old museum, I.M. Pei decided to clad the new building with marble from the same Tennessee quarry.

I.M. Pei studied under Walter Gropius at Harvard University, and the modern architectural principles he learned there have stayed with him throughout his career. But unlike many modern architects, Pei is sensitive to surroundings. The East Building is precisely aligned with Pope's National Gallery building, and their entrances face each other across Fourth Street.

The museum is open Monday to Saturday from 10:00 AM to 5:00 PM, Sunday from 11:00 AM to 6:00 PM, closed Christmas and New Year's Day. For information, call (202) 737-4215.

PIAZZA D'ITALIA, 1979

**300 Block of Poydras Street
New Orleans, Louisiana**

*Charles Moore with August
Perez and Associates and Ron
Filson*

The Piazza d'Italia celebrates New Orleans's Italian community, and it is hard to imagine a better setup for a postmodern masterpiece. Not only was Italian Renaissance architecture an inspiration for the 1970s architectural movement, the city itself has always embraced "postmodern" ideals: a lively historical tradition, an affection for color, a love of humor, and a delight in theatrical mischief.

The Piazza d'Italia is an open-air stage set, with a triumphal arch as a centerpiece and a series of curved, freestanding walls in the classical Italian orders arrayed before it. Punched-out walls with columns (some of stainless steel) straddle the fountain, which cuts a wide swath as it cascades down various steps and levels. From a high vantage point, the plaza is revealed to be a big bull's-eye of concentric brick paving, and the fountain is a map of Italy, the waters recreating the Po, the Tiber, and the Arno. At night, the plaza is illuminated with neon.

"We try to make it happy," Charles Moore said of his impish architecture, which he managed to infuse with humor while keeping high standards. His respected work as an "art" architect and force for change elevated him to the top of his profession; in 1991, he received the American Institute of Architects Gold Medal, the equivalent of a lifetime achievement award. Teaching at the University of Texas School of Architecture in Austin when he died unexpectedly at age 68 in 1993, the architect's face is cast into fountains spouting water jets, added by Moore's associate architects on the project to honor his contribution.

For many years, the New Orleans tradition of genteel decay afflicted the Piazza. And although the postmodern style became an architectural outcast, this work was different. Preservationists from New Orleans and elsewhere fought hard to save it. Finally, in a 2004 development deal for the adjacent site, Loews Hotels salvaged the Piazza, restored its brilliant, sunny colors and wacky structure, and began using the space for outdoor receptions.

Because it is an outdoor pavilion, the Piazza is always open.

There are now approximately 900 residents of New Harmony, Indiana (the same number present at the utopian community's creation in 1814), but this small population has generated a fascinating and innovative history. New Harmony claims the first kindergarten, the first vocational school, the first free public school system, and the first free library in the country. This history is preserved and displayed with exhibits and films here in the New Harmony visitors center, itself a prime tourist attraction.

THE ATHENEUM, 1980

**North and Arthur Streets
New Harmony, Indiana**

Richard Meier & Associates

The Atheneum's gleaming, hyper-white modernism—its sharp angles, undulating curves, bold ramps, and striking stairs—present quite a contrast to the surroundings: quiet, green cornfields on the banks of the Wabash River. The prominence of ramps and stairs on the outside alerts viewers to the importance of procession, from outside to inside, and within the interior as well. You can move through the porcelain-clad building via the central spiral stair or the taut ramp system. Either way, exhibits of New Harmony's past are intercut with views of its present—the landscape framed by carefully positioned windows. Because the internal ramp rotates five degrees off the main grid, spaces seem to compress and expand as you move through the intricately layered structure. The final destination of this elaborate journey is the rooftop observation terrace overlooking the town; the exposed exterior stairs make an appropriately dramatic exit from this lofty perch.

The building's largest space, the auditorium, is impressive and austere. White walls, a charcoal carpet, an aluminum slatted ceiling, and wooden pews call to mind the themes of modernism, Alvar Aalto, and Shaker design.

Richard Meier's sophisticated modern architecture has been uniquely influential, both in this country and internationally. Meier's career has consistently explored the limits of modern architecture, and the Atheneum marks a transition from the early houses (which were white) to more commercial commissions, like the High Museum in Atlanta (also white).

The Atheneum is open daily from 9:30 AM to 5:00 PM from March 15 to December 30, except major holidays. Tours are available daily, with special tours year round by appointment. Individuals and small groups are welcome during these hours; arrangements for large groups should be made in advance. For information, call (800) 231-2168.

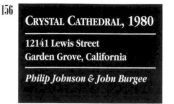

CRYSTAL CATHEDRAL, 1980

12141 Lewis Street
Garden Grove, California

Philip Johnson & John Burgee

few blocks from Disneyland, the glittering silver geometry of the Crystal Cathedral appears on the flat Orange County landscape. From certain angles, this all-glass mirrored structure might be mistaken for an early-1980s suburban office building. But there is a giant cross atop the tower next door that begins to reveal the religious context.

Inside, the architecture takes over completely. Churchgoers are dazzled by special effects, particularly the giant bright white honeycomb of a ceiling that admits subdued light, which seems to be emitted from some great beyond. This effect is achieved by a structural network of painted steel tubes that brace opposing planes of the glass ceiling to its full height. Stunning effects thus result from the unusual plan, an elongated four-point star 415 feet long and 207 feet wide, and from the angled roof that rises to 128 feet at its apex.

Designed for television minister Reverend Robert M. Schuller of drive-in church fame, the Crystal Cathedral ministers to a large congregation. The church proper seats almost 3,000 congregants in pews on the main floor and in triangular balconies; during services, glass doors 90-feet high swing open to accommodate the drive-in participants.

Church tours are conducted Monday through Saturday every half hour from 9:00 AM to 3:30 PM; Sunday services take place at 9:30 and 11:00 AM, and at 6:30 PM. For information, call (213) 971-4000. For tours, call (213) 971-4013.

T his tiny chapel in the Ozark woods makes up in grandeur what it lacks in size. With a stunning virtue of simplicity, Fay Jones has used just a few materials—which could be carried up the hillside site by two workmen—to create an abstract nondenominational church as impressive and timeless as a Gothic cathedral. In 1991, the results of an American Institute of Architects survey of its national membership overwhelmingly named this

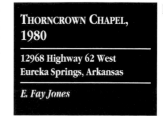

THORNCROWN CHAPEL, 1980

12968 Highway 62 West
Eureka Springs, Arkansas

E. Fay Jones

travelers' chapel as the best American building since 1980. It is one of those very few structures that appeals to both the public and to the architectural profession.

The little chapel is just 24 feet wide, 60 feet long, and 48 feet high. And while it is tucked into a wooded site, its composition is almost totally revealed, and completely focused. Its most arresting feature is the cross-braced ceiling, with timbers sequentially layered to create an open framework pattern of rhythmic repetition that carries the eye the whole length of the chapel. Everything serves to enhance, or not detract from, this dramatic effect: the chapel walls are glass and wood, the floors and side-wall supports are fieldstone. Nature provides the ornamentation. And the lighting seems supernatural.

In fact, Jones described the chapel as being "aligned with nature." This naturalistic approach, and the geometric, handcrafted woodwork of the chapel, calls to mind the work of Frank Lloyd Wright, with whom Jones apprenticed at Taliesin in Spring Green, Wisconsin, in 1953. Later that year, Jones established his practice in Fayetteville and began a thirty-five-year teaching career at his alma mater, the University of Arkansas. Jones's residential designs employed many of the

same natural themes found in Thorncrown, and with the publication of the chapel his early work found a wider audience to admire them. For his lifetime achievements, Jones was awarded the American Institute of Architects Gold Medal in 1990.

The chapel is located one mile west of Eureka Springs on Highway 62 West, and its hours are seasonal: April to November, 9:00 AM to 5:00 PM; March and December, 11:00 AM to 4:00 PM; closed January and February. Nondenominational Sunday services also vary according to the season. In 1989, the Jones-designed Worship Center was completed at Thorncrown. For information on tours and times, call (479) 253-7401.

M.D. ANDERSON HALL, 1981

Rice University School of Architecture
Houston, Texas

James Stirling, Michael Wilford and Associates

James Stirling won the Pritzker Prize in 1981. Anderson Hall, the London architect's first American project, opened later that year, and the spotlight naturally turned to it. How had Stirling applied his forthright, imaginative, mostly high-tech approach to the renovation and expansion of a 1940s building on a campus with an emphasis on context?

The simple answer is that Stirling and Wilford took a contextual approach to the outside and a modern approach to the interiors, using the building's public spaces as a connection. Adopting the "Rice style," a somewhat Mediterranean mix of banded terra-cotta brick with limestone trim, red tile roofs, and arched arcades, the architects make it difficult to tell where the old building stops and the new one begins. But there are clues to the work of Stirling and Wilford: the gabled west façade with a tall recessed arch, an off-set round window high inside the arch, a column in the middle of the entrance, and two conical skylights rising from the roof.

A pleasant courtyard is formed by the extension of the new Anderson Hall wing, and an arched arcade makes a fine transition from the campus to the building. The two main entrances are topped by the conical skylights. Inside, the galleries, jury room, studios, and offices seem cool, white-walled, and primarily functional.

Stirling died in 1992 at the age of 66, still enjoying the enormous renown that came to him for his Neue Staatsgalerie in

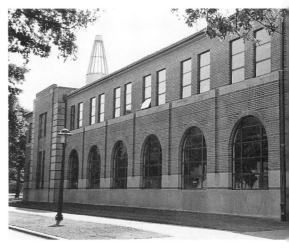

Stuttgart, Germany, of 1984, considered to be one of the most important new museum designs in the world. There will be, then, only a handful of buildings in America designed by James Stirling: Anderson Hall at Rice University; the Arthur M. Sackler Museum at Harvard University (see page 177), completed in 1985; and the Performing Arts Center at Cornell University, which opened in 1989. For visitor information, call (713) 348-0000.

Columbus takes great pride in its architecture, and for good reason. This small town of about 30,000 people is home to more than fifty architecturally noteworthy buildings, a collection that includes churches by Eliel and Eero Saarinen, a school by Richard Meier, and a library by I.M. Pei. The architectural heritage is no accident; it results from the enlightened support of the Cummins Engine Foundation, which contributes to the fees of prominent architects to ensure buildings of stature.

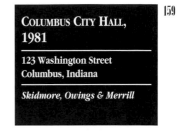

COLUMBUS CITY HALL, 1981

123 Washington Street
Columbus, Indiana

Skidmore, Owings & Merrill

The San Francisco office of Skidmore, Owings & Merrill won the commission to design Columbus's primary civic building. Edward Charles Bassett, who designed it, created a triangular-shaped building with a symbolically welcoming entrance. A broad flight of steps invites visitors up into a semi-enclosed forecourt. This procession into the court—and the building—is made spatially interesting by framing the view with a pair of cantilevered brick-faced steel beams that

seem to hang in space, not quite touching. Visually framed by these beams is a curved glass wall, rising the full height of the building, and containing the entrance.

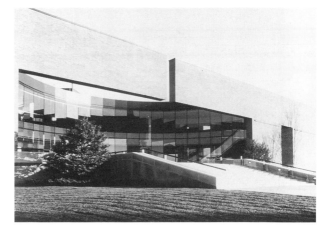

The three-story building is simply clad, with Indiana limestone for the base, and brick for the upper stories. Behind the tall curved glass façade, a two-story gallery rises to a second floor balcony, and there are staircases at either end of the main floor. The upper level houses city government offices, conference rooms, and the Council Chamber. A meeting hall is located at court level of the 60,000-square-foot building, and the Police Department is located on the east side.

The life and times of the city of Columbus are depicted in various ways inside the building. There are Amish quilts, photographs, and renderings of local buildings—for which Columbus is famous—and commissioned paintings by Robert Indiana and William T. Wiley.

The Columbus Visitors Center, 506 Fifth Street, provides comprehensive information. Open daily (except Sundays from December to February), the center hosts guided architectural bus tours Monday through Friday at 10:00 AM, Saturday at 10:00 AM and 2:00 PM, and Sunday at 11:00 AM (except December to February). Reservations are recommended. For information, call (800) 468-6564.

Seaside, Florida, 1981 (Ongoing)

County Road 30-A
Near Panama City, Florida

*Andres Duany and Elizabeth
Plater-Zyberk, Master Planners*

Seaside introduces a radical new vision of an American town, and the point is how faithfully it resembles the small cities of fifty to one hundred years past. The straight, narrow brick-paved streets are lined with neat houses built in recognizable shapes, with familiar materials, and painted in pastel colors. Front porches, clapboard walls, and tin roofs are design staples. White picket fences and rows of palm trees border the streets, which lead to the town center and to the beach. You can walk where you're going.

These simple virtues, abandoned for decades, have given way to sprawling, car-crazy suburbs with wide curving streets and complicated culs-de-sac; they all look alike. Lost in the process: a sense of place and a feeling of community, intangibles sorely missed. To undo perceived wrong-headed development practices, Andres Duany and his wife, Elizabeth Plater-Zyberk, peeled back

the layers until they hit bedrock: the authenticity of the small-town prototype that provided America's collective memory of home.

Working with a sympathetic developer, Robert Davis, Duany, and Plater-Zyberk designed Seaside's master plan for the 80-acre site with 2,300 feet of frontage along the Gulf of Mexico. The plan calls for about 450 houses, a town center with hotels, offices, shops, and a workshop/ware-

house area. Such civic buildings as the post office are dispersed throughout the various neighborhoods where they act as focal points. The central role of the beach in this resort community is highlighted by the beach pavilion, a gazebo, and a small park. The main features of Seaside's plan have been incorporated into a town zoning code, which ensures continuity but also allows for individuality.

Along with the picturesque houses, there are now prominent new architectural works: Steven Holl's retail/hotel/office complex on the central square; Walter Chatham's rooming house on the ocean; and the house of famed British classicist architect and theorist, Leon Krier, on Tupelo Circle are a few of them.

Seaside is located between Panama City and Destin, on County Road 30-A between Grayton State Park and Seagrove Beach. Cottages can be rented. For information, call (888) 732-7433.

H ouston's Memorial Drive is the city's most pleasant parkway, winding along Buffalo Bayou west of downtown and continuing through the cool-looking forests of Memorial Park. Fortunately, instead of spoiling an otherwise pristine view, the YWCA adds a popular destination.

YWCA MASTERSON BRANCH AND METROPOLITAN OFFICES, 1981

3615 Willa (off Memorial Drive)
Houston, Texas

Taft Architects

Like its site, the YWCA is long and narrow. Its two main façades are distinctly different, but equally interesting. Most visitors arrive from Memorial Drive and see the back view first: a series of big, multi-colored projecting boxes and a wide open space—accurately reflecting how the sports rooms, swimming pool, offices, and courtyard are arranged on the inside. The entry façade, on the other hand, is flat and smooth, a continuous wall 350 feet long. It tells less about the 20,000-square-foot structure behind it and more about the surface decoration, a convivial graphic design of arches and gables rendered in rich terra-cotta tilework against beige stucco, a blue-gray stucco, and bright blue for lettering and accent bands. This colorful decoration also serves an important purpose by highlighting the entrances into the three separate but connected parts of the building: the office wing, the walled garden, and the recreational pavilion.

Inside there is the bracing, spartan feel of a no-nonsense gym, combined with the indulgence and friendliness of a good health club. The plan is airy and open, with big windows and tinted concrete floors. A large atrium is the heart of the recreational pavilion; its most compelling feature is a snaky open ramp that doubles back on itself, providing views of the interiors, the pool, and the park. Vivid ceramic tile accents, in the same terra-cotta and blue used on the outside, add spark to the interiors. Especially interesting is the way large overhead doors (garage doors with windows) are imaginatively deployed to create movable walls.

Visitors are welcome at the YWCA, which is open every day: Monday to Friday, 5:45 AM to 8:45 PM; Friday until 7:00 PM; Saturday 8:30 AM to 2:30 PM; and Sunday 1:00 to 6:00 PM. One-day passes are available for a small fee to women and men who would like to use the exercise facilities. For information, call (713) 868-6075.

NATIONAL AQUARIUM, 1981

Pier 3, 501 E. Pratt Street
Baltimore, Maryland

Cambridge Seven

Baltimore was born by the sea and reborn there in the 1980s with the amazing transformation of the Inner Harbor into a major tourist attraction and source of civic pride. In the waterfront renewal process, the creation of a National Aquarium proved especially inspired. A cross between a zoo and a natural history museum, the aquarium has attracted huge crowds from day one. Its astonishing popularity provided a new model for many waterside cities in need of shoreline revitalization.

Unique as the aquarium is, it's hard to approach it without thinking of Charles Moore's Sea Ranch: the aquarium's glass-peaked roofs have similar pitch; its rough-scored concrete resembles Sea Ranch's weathered wood siding; and a bright supergraphic plays to the harbor view. Inside, however, the aquarium immediately becomes its own colorful but shadowy undersea world. There's a feeling of total immersion, heightened by the early sight of a deep clear-walled pool where stingrays perform a mysterious ballet.

This waterworld isn't limited to water creatures. Its subject is water as the basis for all life, and exhibits feature a wide range of aquatic life—mammals, birds, amphibians, and plants—as well as fish. The museum recreates habitats from all over the world and houses more than 5,000 animals in over two million gallons of water.

The aquarium presents its major exhibits in a five-level atrium gallery topped by a triangular glass pyramid that roofs a simulated rain forest. Interconnected to the atrium is a four-level oval-shaped ring tank. A separate structure houses the Marine Mammal Pavilion and the 1300-seat Sound Theater auditorium. Moving people from the elevated entrance platform through the complicated structure is the key. "Circulation is what it's all about," Cambridge Seven's Peter Chermayeff explained. Escalators crisscross upward thorough the atrium exhibits, culminating at the rain forest. Visitors wind back down on scissored ramps through the center of the huge ring tank. A glass-enclosed bridge conveys visitors to the Marine Mammal Pavilion.

The architectural challenge of controlling so much water was complicated by the aquarium's pier location. Below grade placement of mechanical equipment was unfeasible, so the facilities occupy the plaza level and part of the mezzanine.

In July and August, hours are Sunday to Thursday from 9:00 AM to 6:00 PM; Friday and Saturday 9:00 AM to 8:00 PM. From September to June, hours are Sunday to Thursday from 10:00 AM to 5:00 PM; Friday 10:00 AM to 8:00 PM (except March to October, when it opens at 9:00 AM). For information, call (410) 576-3800.

V isiting the Vietnam Veterans Memorial is a profoundly emotional experience unlike that of any other work of architecture in this country.

The initial approach to the monument recreates the progression of infantry marching into battle. In the company of friendly strangers, visitors advance across open ground, going up and over a slightly rising hill before descending slowly into a valley of darkness and death. The soldier's fate is cast in the monument's design, a black granite wall and walkway cut deeply into the earth. It's like walking into an open grave. The tombstone seems endless, panel after panel of polished black granite engraved with the names of over 58,000 Americans who lost their lives in Vietnam. As "the Wall" slopes downward it also rises higher, showing how casu-

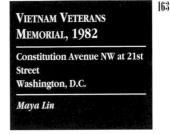

VIETNAM VETERANS MEMORIAL, 1982

Constitution Avenue NW at 21st Street Washington, D.C.

Maya Lin

alties mount as conflicts escalate. Reviewing these columns of war-dead names, known or unknown, visitors experience a heart-wrenching jolt of recognition and accountability: the face you see in these reflective walls is your own.

"I knew that when you saw it you would cry," confirms Maya Lin. An architect, sculptor, and monument maker, she designed the Vietnam Veterans Memorial at age 21, an architectural student at Yale. Architecturally, Lin describes the memorial as a study in surface and dimension, a cutting and polishing of the earth to achieve pure

surface with no dimension. In material terms it surely is that: a wall, a walk, rows of text impressed into flat planes, a bare minimum. Yet this architecture affects like an artwork. An ethereal silence resides here, blocking out the sounds of the city and the other visitors, but there is really no peace to be found.

The Vietnam Veterans Memorial, with its outdoor location adjacent to the Lincoln Memorial, is always "open." Street parking is available, but finding a spot requires patience. Take the Metro for best results. From 8:00 AM until midnight, National Parks Service Rangers are on duty. The officers will provide assistance in finding a name, as well as paper and instructions for tracing names on the Wall. For visitor information, call (202) 426-6841.

ATLANTIS ON BRICKELL, 1982

**2025 Brickell Avenue
Miami, Florida**

Arquitectonica

The Atlantis on Brickell Avenue makes you think that Arquitectonica looked over the whole history of architecture and decided it was time to have some fun. In this bright, colorful, and intriguing design, the main attraction is Atlantis's astonishing sight gag: a 37-foot-square hole punched out of its mirrored walls. The audacious see-through cutout frames an exotic, bright-red spiral staircase, vivid yellow walls, and a gigantic palm tree hovering many stories in the air.

On either side of the "skycourt," the building's façades are different in design but unified by bright colors and a bold graphic look. Along Brickell Avenue, the center hole is visually balanced by a big red triangle on the roof to the right, and by four bright-yellow triangular balconies extending from the mirrored wall to the lower left. At ground level, the main entry is defined by four large red columns under a canopy; a matching set of columns reappears just inside the lobby doors.

The opposite side of the building attracts attention with a giant-scale brilliant blue-painted stucco grid superimposed over a smaller, light gray grid of balconies and railings. On this side observers also discover the fate of the "missing" hole: it appears to have landed by the tennis courts, a 37-foot yellow cube housing an exercise room and squash courts.

There are twenty floors of apartments in Atlantis, ninety apartments and six duplexes. Four of the floors open onto the surreal skycourt, with a whirlpool, a hot tub, and a spectacular view.

The lighthearted but sophisticated quality of Atlantis set a new style for Miami Beach. At the time Atlantis opened, Arquitectonica's principals—Laurinda Spear, Bernardo Fort-Brescia, and Hervin Romney—were in their thirties, and their relatively youthful success made almost as many headlines as the building. On their follow-up commissions along Brickell Avenue, Arquitectonica continued the colorful Atlantis themes.

For visitor information, call (305) 285-1269.

In contrast to the cool, unadorned steel and glass towers of modern architecture, the Portland Building ushered in a new era: a return to classical themes and forms, traditional shapes, riotous color, and yes, even ornament. Appearing on the covers of *Time* and *Newsweek* as the first major public building of the postmodern movement, it also showed that a building—and its architect—could be a celebrity. Practically overnight, Michael Graves—modern architect, artist, and Princeton professor—became *Michael Graves,* a superstar whose new signature style broke through traditional architectural reserve and captured the popular imagination.

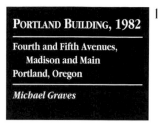

PORTLAND BUILDING, 1982

Fourth and Fifth Avenues, Madison and Main Portland, Oregon

Michael Graves

Graves's design was meant to convey the building's civic importance. The 15-story tower rises from a base covered in celadon-green ceramic tiles, and the entry is emphasized with enormous columns. Above this base, a cream-colored midsection is visually heightened by terra-cotta colored columns topped by giant-scale keystones. Small, widely spaced windows with terra-cotta frames in red impose a strict graphic regimen on the imaginative façades, which are decorated with blue-ribboned garlands. At the penthouse level, the building steps back to allow a balcony on all sides, with a view of Mount Hood in the distance. The three-story statue of "Portlandia," an image taken from the city seal, announces the main entry with a civic zestfulness not seen for many a year.

The Portland Building brought a new aura of architectural sophistication to the city. Graves's design also struck a popular chord nationwide and he advanced his vision of a contemporary architecture in league with ideals and images of the past, and leavened with humor. Graves continued breaking architecture's traditional bounds, first with the teapots he designed for Alessi (still in production in 2005), a comprehensive line of housewares for Target, and a shop across the street from his offices in Princeton. Long after postmodernism lost its allure, Graves's visionary products, and his beautiful drawings and watercolor renderings of buildings, remained highly prized.

The Portland Building is open weekdays during business hours, except major holidays. Much of Graves's interior design has been renovated away, but the lobby remains true to the original conception. City walking tours visit the building. For tour information, call (503) 774-4522. To reach the building, call (503) 823-3990.

**GENERAL FOODS
HEADQUARTERS, 1983
(800 WESTCHESTER
BUILDING)**

800 Westchester Avenue
Rye Brook, New York

*Kevin Roche, John Dinkeloo &
Associates*

oel Garreau's book *Edge Cities* (Doubleday, 1991) chart-
ed America's vast post-war migration: city dwellers
moved to the suburbs, and before long businesses
began to follow people out to where they lived. The idea of
building a corporate home in a natural environment seems to
have inspired the design of the headquarters of General
Foods in Rye Brook, New York. As if to underscore the point
of a corporate residence, the building is clad in white aluminum siding. But at 560,000 square feet, it is, without a
doubt, a very big "house."

Classically composed, the building features a central
rotunda flanked by two symmetrical wings, and the symmetry is compounded by the building's
image reflected in the man-made pond in the foreground. The main driveway bisects the pond,
running up to and through the center of the building before disappearing into the parking
garage.

The central rotunda is likened to the corporate living room, and its seven stories make an

exceptionally grand entrance.
The rotunda lobby soars 95 feet
and it shimmers from top to bottom with mirrors and mirrored
finishes; even the atrium's inner
dome is reflective. Despite all
this glitz, the basic interior structure retains the classical, formal
intent introduced outside. The
most luxurious executive space is
called the "tiara"—a seventh-floor
gallery that rings the rotunda and
overlooks the atrium.

The idea of the corporate
home resurfaces in the general
offices, which strive to keep a residential quality with soft colors and built-in furniture. Clerestory
windows ensure that the people who work here are not deprived of natural light.

Kevin Roche and John Dinkeloo became partners in the 1960s, when they worked in the
offices of Eero Saarinen. Their successful building designs include headquarters for the Ford
Foundation, John Deere, and Union Carbide.

In 2004, the General Foods building was purchased by RPW Associates of White Plains, and
reopened as offices for multiple tenants.

For visitor information, call (914) 285-1700.

The High Museum of Art is that rare building that impresses and welcomes at the same time. This is partly because Richard Meier's design offers the best-orchestrated procession of any museum since the Guggenheim.

HIGH MUSEUM OF ART, 1983

1280 Peachtree Street N.E.
Atlanta, Georgia

Richard Meier & Partners

From beginning to end, people in motion are considered part of the picture. The main approach leads you directly up a ceremonial entrance ramp that makes a twist near the door. From here you are funneled through a low, dark entry that dramatizes your arrival into the lobby: a luminous four-story skylighted atrium that seems designed to encourage mixing and mingling. From this bright and busy central fan-shaped atrium, a series of ramps that wrap the glass atrium walls will take you through the three gallery floors. Finally, exiting visitors share the long central ramp with the new arrivals.

A fascinating aspect of traveling the atrium ramp is Meier's placement of large white panels—like blank canvases—along the way. Sunlight and shadow from the atrium skylight cast constantly changing patterns on these panels, and your movement past the panels causes the patterns to change in response.

White, in dozens of shades, is the chosen color inside the museum. In the free-flowing galleries, Southern artists receive special attention. The museum's permanent collection occupies a stunning installation by Scogin, Elam and Bray.

Adding three new buldings by Renzo Piano (opening in Fall 2005), the museum expanded into an "art village." Piano's new buildings are clad in marmorino, a plaster of slaked lime and marble dust.

High Museum of Art is open Tuesday through Saturday, 10:00 AM to 5:00 PM; Sunday, noon to 5:00 PM; closed Monday. For general information, call (404) 733-4444. To arrange special tours, call (404) 733-4556.

333 WACKER DRIVE, 1983

Wacker Drive, Lake and
  Franklin Streets
Chicago, Illinois

Kohn Pederson Fox

The starting point for 333 Wacker Drive is its one-of-a-kind triangular site, formed by a bend in the Chicago River, which intersects the city's rectilinear grid. Wacker Drive runs along the river, and the river and the street cut diagonally across the site. What is left is a neat little triangular half-block with the hypotenuse facing the riverfront.

The 35-story speculative office building that the firm of Kohn Pederson Fox designed to take advantage of this site is fan-shaped; its most arresting feature is a curved green glass curtain wall facing the river. The green glass mirrors the color of the river, and flat walls on either side frame it against the sky.

333 Wacker Drive sits across the river from the Merchandise Mart, an emphatically vertical neighbor. For their design, KPF chose to emphasize the horizontal lines. The building's curved face is horizontally banded with stainless steel bullnoses spaced six feet apart. In contrast, the sides and back of the building are flat, except for a vertical notch that rises the entire length of the building on the city side and a sawtooth configuration across the top.

The building uses geometrical optics in amazing ways. Because the site is triangular, the side walls of the building retreat sharply from the curved front face. From certain points of view, this creates the illusion that the building is breathtakingly thin—a sliver of glass projecting from the cityscape.

At the base, bands of colored granite and marble are used to create the impression of massively stacked strata. Inside, the two-story lobby is highly polished—with stainless steel ceilings that reflect marble terrazzo floors, and theatrical concentric stairs. The adjacent building at 225 West Wacker is also by Kohn Pederson Fox.

The building is open during business hours. 333 Wacker Drive is also featured on two Chicago Architecture Foundation tours (West Loop and Architecture River Cruise). For tour information, call CAF at (312) 922-3432.

T ransco Tower resembles a classic limestone building of the 1920s that has been sheathed in reflective glass the color of stone. But here, the tall, stepped back piers are mirrored. They face each other at the corners, so that the building takes on a faceted appearance. Visual effects can be dazzling: on a cloudy day, it is fascinating to circle this building on the nearby freeway to catch the animated reflections; in a storm, the building appears moody and electric.

TRANSCO TOWER, 1983 (WILLIAMS TOWER)

2800 Post Oak Boulevard at Westheimer
Houston, Texas

Philip Johnson & John Burgee

A pyramid tops the 1.6 million square foot building, and the base features a huge, ceremonial arched entry faced in pink granite, although most visitors arrive by car and enter from the garage across the street through a glass-enclosed overhead walkway.

To the south of the tower is a formal park with the popular Transco Fountain, a 60-foot-high water wall also designed by Philip Johnson and John Burgee. Water cascades down both the interior and exterior sides of the arc, creating both a mesmerizing sense of vertical motion and a cooling breeze. A freestanding portal frames the water view.

The building is open during regular business hours, and there is an observation deck at the top, but it has been closed. For more information, call (800) 945-5426.

GORDON WU HALL, 1983

Princeton University Campus
College Walk at Butler Walk
Princeton, New Jersey

Venturi, Rauch & Scott Brown

Gordon Wu Hall is slipped into a site that, like Frank Lloyd Wright's Fallingwater, did not even seem to be there until Venturi, Rauch & Scott Brown erected a building on it. The building is necessarily long and narrow, and bracketed by existing structures, prompting Robert Venturi to call it "a hyphen." This characterization is especially apt given Venturi's well-known conception of architecture as literature, a special language of signs and symbols.

The purpose of Gordon Wu Hall was to establish a new residential college entity that would include several surrounding structures. Although one of the existing dormitories is aggressively modern, the main inspiration for Gordon Wu Hall comes from the collegiate Gothic style that set the tone of Princeton's 250-year-old campus, which in turn takes its cues from Oxford and Cambridge. Venturi has pointed out that while we can no longer build classical buildings, we can represent them in our own time and our own ways.

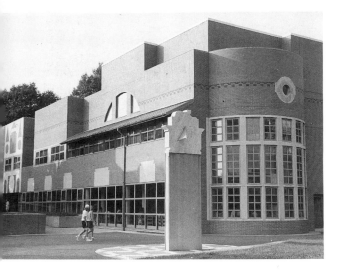

The "modern Gothic" three-story orange brick building with limestone trim satisfyingly complements the size, colors, and rhythms of the older neighbors. It is also stimulating in its individuality—most notably for the "billboard," entry façade inset with gray granite and white marble the students describe as a cat's face with whiskers.

In contrast to the lively exterior, the interior seems suddenly subdued. But it also appears inordinately spacious because of the open views from one end to the other through the rounded bay windows. Most of the first floor is given over to a long dining room, part diner and part "great hall." A wide staircase, called the "grand bleacher," provides an indoor amphitheater as well as access to a lounge, administrative offices, and a library on the second floor.

The Philadelphia firm of Venturi, Rauch & Scott Brown is internationally known for its architecture and writings, and its aphorisms ("Main Street is almost alright") are legendary. The firm's principal designer, Robert Venturi, graduated from Princeton University and was awarded the Pritzker Prize in 1991. Following the success of Gordon Wu Hall, the firm completed two additional buildings at Princeton University: the Lewis Thomas Molecular Biology Laboratory Building (exteriors only) and the Fuller Building adjacent to the Woodrow Wilson School.

For visitor information, call (609) 258-3000.

Philip Johnson said that you cannot *not* know history. As if to prove the point, the design for the 36-story AT&T corporate headquarters provokes instant recall of the Chippendale highboy that seems to reside in our nation's collective memory. The architectural in-joke quickly became an icon.

The revival of historical style on such a grand scale marked an important architectural turning point—the rejection of the cold and anonymous flat glass box in favor of warmth, visual interest, and a strong identity for a prominent American corporation. It is fitting that Philip Johnson, the first American architect to champion the International Style in the 1930s, should be one of the first to bury it forty years later.

The outsized highboy is clad in pink granite, and it meets the street with a tall columned plaza and majestic 65-foot arched main entry. To the rear of the building is a retail arcade.

When the AT&T building opened, it was considered ironic that such a high-technology company resided in an "old-fashion" building. The interiors, it was always stressed, were explicitly up-to-the-minute. In 1992, another high-technology company, Sony Corporation, purchased the building from AT&T. It now houses the offices of Sony Music and a Sony store.

The building is open during regular business hours. For information, call (212) 833-8000.

AT&T BUILDING, 1984 (SONY)

550 Madison Avenue
New York, New York

Philip Johnson and John Burgee

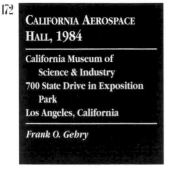

CALIFORNIA AEROSPACE HALL, 1984

California Museum of
    Science & Industry
700 State Drive in Exposition
    Park
Los Angeles, California

Frank O. Gehry

alifornia's heroic test pilots take pride in "pushing the outside of the envelope"—breaking the barriers—and Frank Gehry's design for California Aerospace Hall achieves the architectural equivalent. It pushes museum design to new heights by displaying the "collection" on the outside for all to see.

Harmoniously disharmonious, the museum is a building in two distinct parts. The larger structure is a seven-sided hangar clad in riveted sheet metal that cantilevers out at an arresting angle. More rectangular but no less sedate, the white-stucco museum wing attracts attention with a Lockheed F104 Starfighter braced to one wall, poised to crest the building in flight.

Unlike many museums, this one opens itself to the street, secure in its ability to lure people inside where the planes and aerospace memorabilia are seductively exhibited. Planes hang suspended from the ceiling, and open walkways let you walk around and see them from all sides. Another internal advantage is the quality of the light, in part a result of Gehry's eye-catching windows that modulate the Los Angeles sun.

Frank Gehry's practice is located in Santa Monica, and you can get quite a Gehry education by visiting his buildings in the area: his own famous residence in Santa Monica, the early Danziger Studio on Melrose, Loyola Law School, and the Chiat/Day building in Venice to name just a few. Gehry's prominence has gone international; in 1987 he was awarded the Pritzker Prize and his museum in Bilbao, Spain is an international sensation.

California Aerospace Hall is located in Exposition Park East, near the University of Southern California. It is open daily from 10:00 AM to 5:00 PM, except Thanksgiving, Christmas Day, and New Year's Day. For information about tours and exhibits, call (213) 744-7400.

F rank Gehry designed all but one building on the Loyola Law School campus; he even designed the parking garage. So, as the locals say, this campus is "very Gehry." There are five of the Santa Monica architect's buildings assembled here—three lecture halls, a chapel, and a mid-rise building for classrooms, administrative offices, and a bookstore—and they are make a colorful composition with their walls variously painted yellow, orange, and blue-gray.

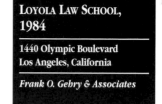

LOYOLA LAW SCHOOL, 1984

1440 Olympic Boulevard
Los Angeles, California

Frank O. Gehry & Associates

The mid-rise is the major structure, and dominates. The smaller buildings—some of them near miniature size—are arrayed in front of the main building and force the perspective. There is a sense of visual upsweep toward an acropolis—and this in close quarters, without the benefit of an actual hill.

Gehry's inventive and artistic touch is everywhere. There is a greenhouse-like temple that appears to be hatching from the top of the classroom building, and the cantilevered, lightning-bolt stairs lead the eye up to the temple through what one might take to be the cracked shell of the building. There is a logical method at work here—a method for startling the beholder. Some of the visual shock-effects come from strong lines that go where it seems they should not, or simply go nowhere. More striking effects are derived from Gehry's trademark use of "cheapskate" materials in unusual or deliberately inappropriate contexts. Still more arise from the technique of

leaving parts of the understructure exposed, or constructing the building in a permanently unfinished look. The seriousness, however, is made clear: the wood may be plywood, but it is *polished* plywood.

Loyola Law School is located just off the Harbor Freeway in midtown Los Angeles, and you can see it while driving by. Tours for prospective students are also open to general visitors, space permitting. To reserve, call Admissions at (213) 736-1074. For general information, call (213) 736-1000.

HERRING HALL, 1985

Rice University
Houston, Texas

Cesar Pelli & Associates

Importation of architects has given Rice University its Beaux Arts sense of style and order, as well as its new, "modern classical" buildings by high-profile practitioners: Cesar Pelli from the East Coast, England's James Stirling, and Ricardo Bofill of Spain. The reknowned New York architects Cram, Goodhue & Ferguson developed the master plan in 1910, with Mediterranean style buildings of terracotta-colored St. Joe's brick and limestone and red tile roofs arranged around a series of open quadrangles and lawns shaded by old oaks.

Cesar Pelli's design for Herring Hall, Rice University's graduate school of business, echoes the Rice style but introduces a new liveliness of design and decorative brickwork. He has divided the building into two long offset rectangles, each with a distinct roofline—one is pitched, the other is vaulted—and the parts are connected by a glass-enclosed central corridor and arcade. The entire exterior is imaginatively clad with brick. The soft terra-cotta of St. Joe's brick is background for

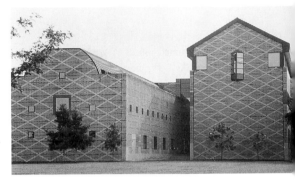

horizontal stripes, including glazed burgundy brick denoting the floor slabs on the long walls. On the short side walls there is an eye-catching overall diamond pattern that has prompted students to call this "Herringbone Hall."

The three-story pitched-roof building, which houses classrooms and lecture halls, sits close to the street. Here the main entrance is marked by a tall triangle of green glass. The flat-topped atrium part of the building contains the library. This side faces an expansive lawn shaded with old oak trees; its ground-level arcade is enlivened with a vaulted ceiling and columns that are half-covered in brick and limestone, half in steel.

On the inside, Herring Hall's light and open quality is a consequence of its many large windows and the balconies and terraces that are worked into the design. The scene stealer inside is the library, a two-story vaulted space with Pelli-designed patterns on the ceiling and tile on the walls.

Pelli is a native of Argentina who holds a Master of Arts degree from the University of Illinois. In his position as Dean of the Yale School of Architecture from 1977 to 1984, he saw campus planning from the inside, which surely contributed to the success of Herring Hall.

For visitor information, call (713) 348-0000.

A fter decades of monochromania, color came back into architecture with Michael Graves's Portland Building of 1984 (see page 165), even though the building was basically boxlike. The Humana Building is different. The design is a three-dimensional extravaganza of shapes, materials, and textures. But color has not been forgotten. Graves's pretty palette appears in the materials he has selected, which include Finnish pink and Brazilian green stone; these provide a nice change from white, black, gray, and beige. Color also identifies important elements of the building, and links the structure to the natural world—browns suggest earth, blue the sky.

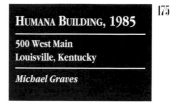

The Humana Building's 26 stories are treated to three different elevations, a complex division between the base, midsection, and the top, and many historically inspired motifs. Each multi-layered element plays a part in this rich mix. The six-story base appears firmly planted on the entire site, with rows of tall square columns at the perimeter creating a street-level arcade. A parapet angles out over the roof of this lower structure, with a glass triangle skylight peaking out above it.

The 525,000-square-foot tower steps back from its full-block base, occupying only about half of the surface area. The midsection, containing tenant-occupied offices, is the plainest part and the most regimental, with its rigorous rows of flat, square windows. The juggernaut top recalls ancient Egyptian and Mayan forms. On the 25th floor at the front of the building, there is an outdoor porch with a bowed balcony braced by trusswork painted deep terra-cotta.

The Humana Building's lobby is accessible weekdays from 8:30 AM to 9:00 PM, and private tours can be arranged. For appointments, call (502) 580-1000.

PA CONSULTING GROUP, 1985

279 Princeton Road
Hightstown, New Jersey

Richard Rogers

For sheer shock value, it is hard to top the first sight of PA Consulting Group's high-tech flagship amidst the fields of suburbia. Nine giant A-frames—tubular steel masts 60-feet high—are aligned along the building's central spine. The structural framework becomes an exposed A-frame exoskeleton tethered with cables seemingly anchored by giant washers. Within this structure, a suspended cradle holds air conditioners, heaters, and plumbing equipment, also exposed. Color coding of the mechanical elements—silver for the air handling, green for sprinklers, orange for electricals—gives the whole composition a festive air. At sunset, the building takes on an otherworldly orange glow.

The British architect Richard Rogers practically invented "high tech," along with Renzo Piano, at Paris's Pompidou Center in the 1970s. There, the wizardry of exposing and color coding structural elements drew attention to the museum and the city's position as a culture capital. At PA, the design was meant to express the advanced technological thinking of a British-based firm of management consultants and product development specialists with international reach.

In Rogers's first work in the United States, the high-tech aesthetics impose a "kit of parts" approach to the one-story 42,600-square-foot rectangle. On the inside, one does not lose sight of the superstructure that makes the exterior so intriguing: a bubble skylight runs along the building's center line, exposing the underside. A practical advantage of Rogers's design is the creation of vast areas of flexible column-free interior space.

It is surprising to learn that the intricate superstructure was not custom fabricated. All the components come right off the shelf. Even so, the industrial aesthetic of a high-tech building does not come cheaply. High costs have certainly dampened the general enthusiasm for high tech. The PA building is the standard bearer in this country.

Driving by will allow a complete view of the building, which is no longer occupied by the far-sighted company that commissioned it.

The internationally renowned British architect James Stirling died in 1992 at the age of 66, leaving a brilliant legacy of building in England and in Germany, but only three works in the United States—all of them on college campuses. And at all three, the biggest surprise is how little they look like Stirling's work at first glance.

The Sackler Museum, an expansion of Harvard University's Fogg Museum across the street, puts most of its architectural interest on the main façade, and inside rather than out.

If you approach the building from the northwest, you'll be greeted by a closed and somewhat forbidding system: two sides and a rounded corner striped with two-toned bands of brick, and dotted by windows placed at irregular intervals. This part of the

ARTHUR M. SACKLER MUSEUM, 1985

**Harvard University
Broadway at Quincy Street
Cambridge, Massachusetts**

James Stirling and Michael Wilford

building represents the five floors of L-shaped administrative space that wraps the three gallery levels that are the heart of the building.

The main façade is infinitely more interesting—it is almost literally a face: a wide square of glass at the brow, a long triangular window below it, and three glass doors at the base. A flanking pair of columns rising about halfway up sport ventilator grilles that look like ears. This façade is meant to work alone, or as background for a covered third-level walkway that is yet to come, which would link the Sackler Museum with the Fogg Museum (but this walkway will probably not be constructed).

All this design activity of the entry façade is prologue to the building's grand gesture just inside the front door: a steep, tall, and narrow processional staircase with a skylight at the top and bright bands of color on the walls. The stair will lead you into the double-height galleries, which occupy 11,000 square feet in the building. On the lower level is a 250-seat auditorium.

The Sackler Museum displays the university's fine permanent collections of Oriental and Islamic art, and hosts temporary exhibits as well. The museum is open Monday through Saturday from 10:00 AM to 5:00 PM, and Sunday 1:00 to 5:00 PM. Closed major holidays. Tours are conducted Monday through Friday at 2:00 PM. For information, call (617) 495-9400. For tours, call (617) 496-8576.

STATE OF ILLINOIS CENTER, 1985

Clark, La Salle, Randolph and Lake Streets
Chicago, Illinois

Helmut Jahn

This building was intended as a new focal point for Chicago's West Loop, and it is surely that. But the attention has cut both ways. Illinois taxpayers, who paid for the construction, sometimes say this relatively short and idiosyncratic 17-story public building cost more, at $172 million, than the very much taller Sear's Tower (arguable bookkeeping, correcting for inflation). Paul Goldberger called it "architecture on amphetamines." On the other hand, it draws praise for its imaginative futuristic form, for its eye-popping full-court atrium, and for co-mingling the government's bureaucracy with retail and office coworkers.

The structure's complex design is difficult to see whole, and it looks different from every angle. But the basic idea is simple: take a block of ice and turn on a sunlamp aimed at one corner. The corner melts away, thus rounding the cube. (Retreating glaciers created Illinois terrain, putting the metaphor on the side of history.)

In real life, the main façade is a curve, stepped back in three tiers, and capped by a cylinder sheared off at a rakish angle. This complicated shape is clad with both colored and clear glass. Color is coded as a function of altitude: deep blue at the base to white at the top, with tinges of salmon. With its curved and angled walls, its variegated colors, and its many mullions, the 1.2-million-square-foot building looks like a faceted colossus.

It should come as no surprise that the interior is not "plain Jane." You walk into a great cylindrical atrium, 160 feet in diameter, rising all 17 stories—and beyond, through the roof into a bevel-topped silo (more Illinois symbolism). This atrium is a riot. Bright red strutwork covers the "skylight" and travels down the walls, which are painted in blue and salmon. Circular office floors ring the great rotunda, and the elevator banks are freestanding towers that soar to the top. Giddy looking stairways cantilever out into the atrium, making for an unforgettable spatial experience.

German-born Helmut Jahn, one of architecture's more flamboyant practitioners, designed the building with his firm, Murphy/Jahn, which is based in Chicago. He pulled out all the stops on this one, making his United Terminal at O'Hare Airport look calm by comparison.

The State of Illinois Center is quite a sight in the daytime; at night its illumination is spectacular. The building is open during regular business hours. It is also featured on the Chicago Architecture Foundation's daily Loop walking tours, "Modern and Beyond." For information, call CAF at (312) 922-3432.

L ike many Houston corporations in the 1970s and 1980s, the University of Houston selected Philip Johnson and John Burgee to crown its growth with a signature building. The signature in this case is that of Claude-Nicholas LeDoux, a French architect who lived from 1763 to 1826, and who is considered the first great architect of the Romantic Classical style.

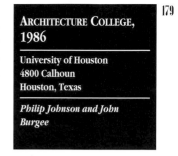

ARCHITECTURE COLLEGE, 1986

University of Houston
4800 Calhoun
Houston, Texas

Philip Johnson and John Burgee

The Architecture College is virtually an exact "quotation" of LeDoux's design for the House of Education in his ideal imaginary town of Chaux. Here the 200-year-old design is produced with modern construction methods. The formal, symmetrical composition consists of a massive cruciform base of flat, beige brick, out of which emerges a central square attic, topped by a white columned temple. Windows also rise in orderly succession: a rectangular row at ground level, superseded by a course of square windows, dominated by the band of tall arched windows, with a single occulus at the top. Each façade follows the same pattern, including the Palladian entry arch and recessed porch. On each side, too, rooflines project over the walls, creating defining lines and casting interesting shadows on the spare, flat walls.

The interior seems both more open and more ornate than the outside. The four-story, five-level central atrium court has a Victorian flavor, with its ornamented staircases, balconies, columns, and skylight. Classrooms, studios, and administrative offices, and a library and gallery are located off the central court, for the most part out of sight.

The College of Architecture is intended to mark a new gateway to the campus, and the building is visible from the I-45 South freeway. The school is open from 8:00 AM to 5:00 PM Monday through Friday. Special exhibitions are often on view in the gallery. Campus tours are held at 10:00 AM and 3:00 PM Monday through Friday. For information, call (713) 743-1000.

The Museum of Contemporary Art was the early arrival in Los Angeles's now-flourishing downtown architectural scene, which includes Frank Gehry's Walt Disney Concert Hall (see page 257), Rafael Moneo's Cathedral of Our Lady of the Angels, and the Caltrans Building by Morphosis. In breaking new ground on a downtown site, MOCA also reached out in selecting Japan's "guerilla architect" and new-wave leader, Arata Isozaki, to design a jewel-like haven to hold its own amidst the looming commercial towers.

Isozaki envisioned the museum as a village among skyscrapers: with strong architecture he would achieve the same presence the neighboring buildings held by size alone. In contrast to the glassy towers, Isozaki's "village" is warm and tactile looking—a cluster of structures clad in seductive red Indian sandstone, with a rough-hewn texture that appears cleaved by hand. Dark-green aluminum panels with bright pink diagonal joining and a barrel-vaulted roof clad in copper contribute to the overall impression of luxurious textures and colors.

Isozaki designed the museum with a combination of Western geometry and Eastern tranquility, and, especially, with an Asian appreciation for how the progression of entry can focus the visitor's frame of mind. MOCA occupies a tight site, and much of the seven-level building is below grade. This layering allowed Isozaki to design a central courtyard, where, like the prelude to entering a Japanese teahouse, you can pause to experience the building before you enter it.

Above ground, flanking this central court, Isozaki divides the facilities. On the north side are the taller buildings, dominated by the barrel-vaulted library wing with its prominent onyx windows and ticket booth cube at the door. The great pyramid skylights mark the south side. These pyramids, together with rows of saw-toothed skylights, help illuminate the upper levels of the galleries concealed below.

Inside, the museum is cool and contemplative. All-white interiors have maple floors and are minimally detailed so as not to detract from the art on view. The main gallery, a 60-foot vaulted room illuminated by the largest skylight, is among the most evocative spaces Isozaki has ever built.

MOCA is open Monday and Friday from 11:00 AM to 5:00 PM; Thursday from 11:00 AM to 8:00 PM; Saturday and Sunday from 11:00 AM to 6:00 PM; closed Tuesday, Wednesday, and major holidays. A satellite gallery is located in the Pacific Design Center at 8687 Melrose Avenue, West Hollywood. For information, call (213) 626-6222.

This deconstructed "roadhouse for the year 2,000" began with the actual deconstruction of a 1950s-modern bank building and the subsequent insertion of an industrially elegant restaurant within the old structural framework. In the multi-layered exterior, the new walls of white ceramic tile, glass block, and plastered cement seem old, while the bank's steel cage looks new. But there is no mistaking the here-and-now nature of the overall design. Among the clues: a sundial's steel fin protruding from the roof, and the stainless steel block letters of Kate Mantilini's marquee, suffused at night in a colorful neon glow.

KATE MANTILINI RESTAURANT, 1986

9109 Wilshire Boulevard
   at Doheny Drive
Beverly Hills, California

*Morphosis/Thom Mayne and
Michael Rotundi*

At the Kate Mantilini Restaurant, Morphosis has created one of the most exciting and engaging spaces in the city. The focal point of the 100-foot-long restaurant is a complicated steel sculpture—an orrery—that appears to be a continuation of the rooftop sundial that is visible through the skylight. In ancient times, astronomers used the clockwork mechanism of the orrery to portray planetary motion. The mechanisms could be earth-centered or sun-centered. The restaurant's contemporary one is self-centered. It culminates in a stylus that has "inscribed" the building's plan onto a steel plate on the floor.

The restaurant's namesake, Kate Mantilini, was a boxing promoter in the 1940s, which explains murals of fighters in the ring. The largest painting, by John Wehrle, spans the curving north wall above the counter; a smaller mural provides a backdrop for the orrery sculpture.

The architecture of Morphosis stands out from the deconstructionist competition in the sophistication of their ideas and the quality of their materials and construction. Also, as Peter Cook observes, Morphosis has the compelling ability to anchor their architecture as well as explode it.

In a town of high-concept restaurants, Kate Mantilini has become a landmark. And, since Thom Mayne and Michael Rotundi dissolved their partnership in 1991, it is one of the last collaborations of this influential pair.

Kate Mantilini is open Monday to Friday from 7:30 AM to 1:00 AM; Saturday, 11:00 AM to 2:00 AM; Sunday, 10:00 AM to midnight. The phone number is (310) 278-3699.

CHARLES MOORE HOUSE, 1986

2102 Quarry Road
Austin, Texas

Charles Moore and Arthur Andersson

Charles Moore always seemed to have a twinkle in his eye. His love of life infused the love of his life, which was architecture, and he could barely keep still pursuing its many possibilities. Designing, building, teaching, lecturing, writing, collaborating—he was constantly working while dashing off to the next exciting thing. Houses were his special love (his book, *The Place of Houses,* is a classic). In the places he settled, the 1991 AIA Gold Medalist built seven homes. Moore moved to Austin in 1984 as O'Neil Ford Professor of Architecture at the University of Texas. This duplex house/studio became his last home, for he died unexpectedly at age 68 in 1993. It survives as a virtual Wonder Wall of Moore's prolific and colorful existence.

A man who loved Disneyland, Charles Moore never owned a Barcelona chair. As a young practitioner, he disputed modernist constrictions. Color, history, ornament, and whimsy were not sins to him, but expressions of life truly lived. There was room for everything in Moore's architecture, and he helped turn a generation of architects his way.

The Austin house and studio complex resembles one of Moore's favorite metaphors, the geode: dull on the outside but colorful on the inside. Its gray exterior wraps a stunning pink interior filled with amazing collections—toys, scenes of the Last Supper, 85,000 slides, and whatever else caught his fancy. The living room alone looks like the set for an exotic stage play. Its curving pink wall presents a ring of totem-like pilasters shaped like suits of armor and decorated with designs painted by students, Kachina figures, and Mexican masks at the top. To Moore's assistant, Kevin Keim, the house is "the fullest expression of [Moore's] quest to completely integrate his spatial motives and his overflowing collections."

The original 1930s bungalow first struck Moore as "semisinister." But he and his architectural partner Arthur Andersson transformed it into a 4,130-square-foot Texas "spread," with a home for Moore, a smaller house for Andersson, and two design studios. A tall tower announces the entrance and leads to a serene lap pool in a central courtyard, with a pergola spanning the pool on the cross axis. The courtyard is wrapped on three sides by the house/studio complex, and large glass windows orient the living and working spaces to this enclosed garden view. In keeping with the Texas theme, the house is sheathed in native materials—stone, board and batten siding, and galvanized metal roofing. Inside, the large architectural gesture is the "lazy oval," an ellipse in plan that encircles the public spaces, leaving the private spaces beyond its borders.

This house and studio was Charles Moore's architectural playhouse and laboratory. Now it is his legacy. The structure, with its contents and collections, is preserved intact, in cluttered magnificence, as the Charles W. Moore Center for the Study of Place. Visits are by appointment only. For information call (512) 692-6862.

For the architectural traveler, O'Hare's United Airlines Terminal is almost a sure thing. Thanks to a hub-and-spoke system that funnels passengers through major airports on the way to their final destinations, this is one key building you'll probably see whether you want to or not.

UNITED AIRLINES TERMINAL, 1987

O'Hare International Airport
Chicago, Illinois

Murphy/Jahn

From the air it's clear this building covers a lot of ground. Two parallel structures, each 1600 feet long, are 800 feet apart and connected by an underground tunnel—for a total of 1,400,000 square feet under roof. These are daunting distances for anyone racing for a plane. But for airport officials, the problem is more like riot control: how to disperse a cranky crowd over vast distances in an orderly way.

Architect Helmut Jahn's design solution is to treat the airport as an interesting part of the trip—a festival marketplace of light, color, music, movement, shops, and views—a destination in itself. The ticketing lobby has the openness of a central plaza, with skylights along its folded truss roof and patterned terrazzo floors. The main lobby leads to Concourse B, a lofty, vaulted hall framed in steel arched bents resting on 8-inch steel pipe columns. These vaults are clad with a system of insulated aluminum sandwich panels and insulated glass assemblies, both fritted and clear. At either end the concourse terminates in curved glass-roofed conservatory style cul de sacs.

Concourse C, the satellite terminal, resembles Concourse B in plan and overall cool. But the 800-foot tunnel between them is red hot. It is here that Helmut Jahn, always the adventurous architect, pulls out all the stops in his "wonderland tech" design. Passengers ride a people-mover conveyor belt flanked by undulating backlighted walls that progress through the color spectrum. Overhead, a mirrored ceiling doubles the fun of a kinetic neon sculpture by Michael Hayden that

runs the entire length of the tunnel, flashing like multicolored lightning. Colors change as you move along, as does the music, which is computer programmed to the light show. The endless pulsing light sculpture amplifies the sense of motion and creates the sensation that you are really going somewhere.

O'Hare Terminal is United's flagship facility in their home city. Designed as the "Terminal of Tomorrow," Jahn's celebration of the concourse set a new standard for airports everywhere. The airport is always open.

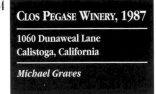

CLOS PEGASE WINERY, 1987

1060 Dunaweal Lane
Calistoga, California

Michael Graves

The classic shapes and muted colors of an old Tuscan farmstead have inspired Michael Graves's design for this wine-making estate located in the heart of the Napa Valley about ninety minutes north of San Francisco. A clustered village of stucco buildings with tile roofs, Clos Pegase is a 50-acre estate that includes wine-making facilities, tasting rooms that are open to the public, and owner Jan Shrem's house on the hill, which is private.

Clos Pegase is the culmination of Shrem's dream of uniting his love of wine, art, and architecture in an "epoch-making" way; this comes through in the entire design, starting with the procession of entry. The complex is approached via a long road, around the long stretch of the winery building, ending up in front of the visitors' wing. This wing will seem well composed but closed, like an old monastery or fortress. Its entry is marked by a single monumental earthen-red Tuscan column positioned dead center in the high-ceilinged entrance portico. Within a few steps, visitors see that the building turns out to be warm and welcoming. It opens to the sculpture garden straight ahead, and to the left is the Napa Valley's most beautiful tasting room, where works from the owner's private art collection are on display.

The estate's production wing, to the east of the visitors' wing, is often mistaken for the main entrance because of its architecturally monumental loading dock: a portico with four pairs of voluptuous 24-foot columns. But Clos Pegase is a working winery, and it is in the production wing that the wine-making takes place. Grapes are brought from the fields, crushed, and then fermented in enormous underground caves.

Now that Clos Pegase has been constructed, its program seems tailor-made for Michael Graves, considering the renowned Princeton-based architect's skill at evoking the classical forms of the Italian countryside and his distinct skill as an artist. But the owner chose the architect by the process of competition, under the auspices of the San Francisco Museum of Modern Art.

Clos Pegase is open seven days a week from 10:30 AM to 5:00 PM for wine tastings and tours. September and October are harvest times, when vineyard activity reaches its peak. Tours take place at 11:00 AM and 2:00 PM daily. For information, call (707) 942-4981.

Many American cities are known for their grandest public buildings—museums, libraries, and city halls—but "functional" buildings deserve their due. Columbus, Indiana, is famed for its outstanding collection of public and private buildings by world-renowned architects, and fire stations seem to be a special source of civic pride. In this town, the now-standard fire station plan of wrapping living quarters around the equipment core was devised in 1941. Susanna Torre's Fire Station No. 5 is the latest in a distinguished line that includes Robert Venturi's 1967 Fire Station No. 4.

Fire Station No. 5 responds to its small-town setting, its functional requirements, and the city's reputation for architectural sophistication. The station occupies a site that is rural on the way to being suburban, and Torre has acknowledged local vernacular styles in her design. Residential in character, the two-story building has yellow brick walls, a seamed, metal barnlike roof, and a hose tower resembling a silo.

Torre, an architect whose practice is located in New York City, organized the fire station into two basic parts: the functional "garage" and the residential "house." Public spaces occupy the ground floor, and living quarters for male and female

FIRE STATION NO. 5, 1987

100 Goeller Court
Columbus, Indiana

Susanna Torre with Wank Adams Slavin Associates

fire fighters are on the upper floor. The two zones are linked by a circular core with stairs and a fire pole—that staple of movie and television fire fighting actually exists. The building is further divided into two wings, forming a rear courtyard, although here the walls of the building and the circular stair tower are clad in metal. More metal appears on the second-story exteriors, where the structural steel columns are clearly exposed.

Columbus calls itself the "Architectural Showplace of America." Today, in terms of the number of buildings designed by noted architects, it ranks fourth in the United States after New York City, Chicago, and Los Angeles. The Columbus Visitors Center, 506 Fifth Street, provides comprehensive information. Open daily (except Sundays from December to February), the center hosts guided architectural bus tours Monday through Friday at 10:00 AM, Saturday at 10:00 AM and 2:00 PM, and Sunday at 11:00 AM (except December to February). Reservations are recommended. For information, call (800) 468-6564.

The Australian-born architects Hank Koning and Julie Eizenberg began making their reputation in Los Angeles in the early 1980s designing small houses with affordable building budgets. From this experience they developed an uncommon skill for generating new ideas in very small spaces and for using inexpensive materials with considerable style. The Hollywood Duplex represents a somewhat larger project and a more handsome budget; the site is in a very desirable area of the Hollywood Hills, with a splendid view to the east.

The space is confined by geography rather than available funds. The site is a slender triangle, and it is mostly vertical. The resulting "twin towers" design is in many ways characteristically Californian: tall rather than deep, and elbow-to-elbow with the neighbors. A particular triumph is that the two houses, angled onto the triangular site with a terraced garden and stairs between them, do not intrude on each other's space or privacy.

Each tower measures 20 feet square and four stories tall, with one room per floor: a garage on one, a studio workroom on two, a living room on three, and a bedroom on top. The kitchen and baths are in a semi-separate structure tucked behind the top floors, linked to the tower by an interior stairwell. With intelligent packing, Koning and Eizenberg have created a sense of spaciousness,

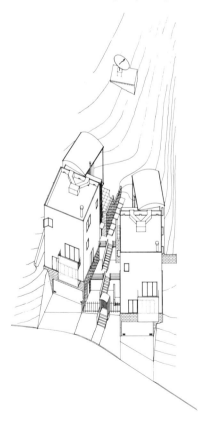

and succeeded in making the beautiful natural setting an important part of the overall design.

The twin towers stand out with their cheerful colors: the concrete walls of one tower are painted mint green with yellow windows, the other is pink with white trim. The walls facing the inner courtyard are clad in sheet metal. On the inside, the houses are basically white and are detailed in a way that seems more European than American. Ceilings are exposed concrete, and the floors were meant to be polished masonite, although in one duplex unsuspecting painting contractors treated them as drop cloths and wood floors were installed instead.

The color, the openness, and the spare interiors tend to give the duplex apartments the feel of beach houses in the hills. And because of the hills and the fine, slender Italian poplars adjacent to the houses, the perch could be a ledge above Lake Como or Lake Garda in Italy.

The apartments are located in Hollywood, north of the intersection of Highland and Franklin, near the Hollywood Bowl. The houses are private residences, but the twin towers are easily seen from the street.

T he Menil Museum offers an atmosphere of calm, refinement, and respect at a time when many museums seek to attract large crowds that make contemplation or even viewing exhibited art almost impossible.

This museum seems personal in every respect, a characteristic announced at the front door where the signatures of principal donors are carved in stone. The collection is highly personal, too, consisting of 10,000 works of antiquities, tribal arts, Surrealism, and late twentieth-century American art assembled by Dominique and John de Menil. The museum is located in a residential neighborhood, and the building is clearly meant to fit in. Like the surrounding houses (belonging to the de Menil family), the museum is gray with white trim and compatibly scaled; interior galleries are room-sized and comprehensible. The Menil Museum even indulges the human impulse to look behind the scenes: framers and conservators work in an open area on the main gallery floor.

Compared to Italian architect Renzo Piano's colorful high-tech extravaganza at the Pompidou Center Museum in Paris (with Richard Rogers), the Menil Museum is cool, spare, and very formal—a long rectangle, 402 x 142 feet, clad in gray-stained cedar siding. The museum's most arresting feature, designed by Piano with Peter Rice of Ove Arup, is the innovative system of cement light-diffusers set in a ductile iron truss. These gracefully curved "leaves" act like stationary venetian blinds above the rooftop skylights. They extend beyond the roof to shade the exterior walkways.

For most of its length, the building consists of a single story that contains the exhibition galleries, some of which are punctuated with windows and others with views of garden courts. High ceilings, white walls, and floors of black-stained pine create an interior that is almost ethereal. Administration offices occupy a mezzanine, and the second floor is given over to the "treasure house," where the collection is accessible to historians and scholars.

In 1995 the Menil opened a companion museum, the Cy Twombly Gallery, across the street. The single-artist museum is also the work of Renzo Piano, but the 9,300-square-foot structure is quite different: a gridded concrete exterior softened by a floating cantilevered roof. The two museums share Piano's exquisite ability to animate the intense Houston light. A specially designed system of grilles, louvers, and tinted skylights modulates light inside the galleries, all eight of them designed as cubes.

The Menil Museum hours are 11:00 AM to 7:00 PM Wednesday to Sunday, closed Monday, Tuesday, and major holidays. The museum shop is housed in a gray bungalow across the street from the main entrance. For museum information, call (713) 525-9400.

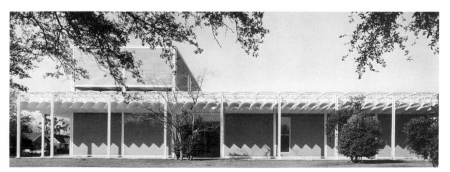

BERKOWITZ-ODGIS HOUSE, 1988

Lighthouse Road
Martha's Vineyard Island,
Massachusetts

Steven Holl

Steven Holl's beach house on Martha's Vineyard island captures the spirit of its austere waterfront as freshly and convincingly as Sea Ranch on the northern California coast did in the 1960s. The Berkowitz-Odgis House occupies three acres of natural shrub land on a bluff overlooking Vineyard Sound, and Holl was inspired by these rugged surroundings.

In designing the beach house, Holl was also drawn to the seafaring legends of Herman Melville's *Moby Dick*, and to the ancient customs of local Indians who built their houses by draping skins over the skeletons of beached whales. With this skeletal image in mind, Holl pushed a traditional wooden balloon frame to the outside, exposed it, and hung the three-bedroom, 1,600-square-foot house within it. The wooden "bones" of the house also allow for verandas along the south and west, and an entrance porch to the north. Wooden members are meant to harbor the natural vines of the island and soften the straight lines of the architecture.

Holl's design runs counter to the conventional wisdom that a waterfront house must first of all face the water. Here, the house is long and narrow, but it is set perpendicular to the shore. This opens up multiple side views rather than a single head-on one. Rooms follow a simple progression as they rise up the site's gentle slope: the living room, dining room (which occupies a glass-enclosed triangular bay), kitchen, two bedrooms, and the exercise room. The house culminates with a tower, with a master bedroom, sun deck, and an expansive view.

The island's building code required that the house be constructed of wood, in a natural, weathered-gray color. Part of Holl's artistry has been in transforming this requirement into one of the house's most delightful characteristics. Wood railings and balustrades, connected by brass rods, are laid out vertically, horizontally, and sometimes on the diagonal. They serve as a continuation of the structure, as well as an intriguing elaboration of it.

Berkowitz-Odgis house is a private residence with no house number, but it is located on the water side of Lighthouse Road, off Lobsterville Road. It is visible from the street.

An architectural fascination of Emilio Ambasz's is the combination of nature with technology, and he often solves the problem by burying his buildings. At this botanical conservatory, much of the structure is constructed below grade and faces a sunken courtyard and its water gardens. Technology appears in the series of glass pyramids and cone-shaped towers that rise out of the underground galleries. One-half acre is enclosed under glass, making this the largest conservatory in the Southwest.

LUCILE HALSELL CONSERVATORY, 1988

San Antonio Botanical Center
555 Funston Place
San Antonio, Texas

Emilio Ambasz

In the galleries, plants grow in man-made computer-controlled approximations of their native climates (spanning the range from a Desert Pavilion to an Alpine Room). Because the building is largely subterranean, these glass projections are essentially sky-lights. The geometries of metal and glass visible from the sur-face are of course artistic state-ments, juxtaposing nature and technology. They are quite strik-ing visually.

But these glass projections also trick the Texas sun, which is ferocious. An expanse of flat glass roof here would be the first essential component of a solar oven, and the last thing one might wish to erect over a building intended to conserve green and delicate living organisms. Ambasz's shelter for the plants has no flat surfaces on top—instead, it presents the smallest conceivable areas to the sun: thin lines and sharp points. The inclined planes of the skylights, surfaced with glass, forcibly bounce the sun away from the building.

The conservatory is Ambasz's first major built work. A native of Argentina, Ambasz works in Bologna, Italy, and in New York City, where he was curator of design at the Museum of Modern Art from 1970 to 1976. In 1989, the museum mounted a show of Ambasz's work along with that of Steven Holl—implying that they were two architects to watch.

The Lucile Halsell Conservatory is open daily from 9:00 AM to 5:00 PM. Closed Christmas and New Year's Day. Guided tours are available by request. For tour information, call (210) 207-3276. For general information, call (210) 207-3250.

MORTON H. MEYERSON SYMPHONY CENTER, 1989

2301 Flora
Dallas, Texas

Pei, Cobb, Freed & Partners

The Meyerson Symphony Center is a building within a building: a separately endowed concert hall situated within the symphony center structure. The striking outer building, designed by I.M. Pei, is a unique construction that appears to be a glass sphere spliced by a masonry plane. Pei has stretched a Cartesian grid over a ball in a way that makes it hard not to think of Mercator projections. But the wall is sliced and stacked to create visual discontinuities to the hemisphere. The glass-walled curve contains the Symphony Center lobby, which wraps the hall. The lobby's broad, curved staircases lead to the concert hall and generate intriguing spatial experiences as one progresses through the vast glass-walled space.

Within Pei's dynamic construction is the 1,800-seat McDermott Concert Hall, which was treated as a distinct design by Artec Consultants because of the specialized nature of the acoustics. To conserve sound quality, Artec Consultants designed the hall shoebox style: 94 feet long, 84 feet wide, and 85 feet high. To maintain seating capacity, Artec used the available vertical space with three tiers of balconies.

Three adjustable elements can be used to tune the hall: a four-piece acoustic canopy, a large reverberation chamber, and two sets of acoustic curtains. The canopy, a monumental feature that projects out over the stage and resembles the Starship Enterprise, weighs 42 tons. It can be adjusted between its lowest stop, 40 feet above the stage, and its highest stop, at 75 feet. The low setting is for chamber music, and the high setting accommodates the heroically proportioned C.B. Fisk pipe organ rising behind the stage.

The meticulous wooden wall panels are actually a veneer over concrete. The paneling conceals no subsurface voids that might deaden sound reflection. Every panel was tapped for hollow spots with a rubber mallet by the consultant, just to make sure.

The Meyerson Symphony Center is home to the Dallas Symphony Orchestra; for performance schedules, call (214) 871-4000; for tickets, call 692-0203. The building is open for events and tours only. Tours are conducted by the Meyerson Symphony Center at 1:00 PM on Monday, Wednesday, Friday, and Saturday, but performances sometimes necessitate a change in tour schedules. Groups of fifteen may arrange private tours with a notice of one month. For tour information and reservations, call (214) 670-3600.

A desert landscape seems especially hospitable to arresting architecture—buildings become virtually the sole scenery on the flat, open, mutely colored terrain. Although the Southwestern setting of the Nelson Fine Arts Center is actually a built-up university campus, Antoine Predock has created a scenic wonder strong enough to hold its own in the open desert.

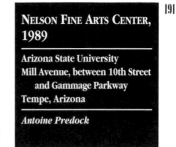

NELSON FINE ARTS CENTER, 1989

Arizona State University
Mill Avenue, between 10th Street and Gammage Parkway
Tempe, Arizona

Antoine Predock

On campus, the fine arts center is like a pueblo within the city. Its pale lavender stucco walls seem to have accrued layer upon layer, rising to a Sphinx-like "mountain" in the middle, and partially ringed by an outer arcade of vivid red brick. Labyrinthian paths and below-grade passages seem to result from ancient but purposeful crossings. The cumulative effect of this layering and seemingly indirect circulation is not haphazard at all. It is Predock's way of drawing you into an adventure where there is much to discover.

Predock's design for the 119,000-square-foot complex is in fact enormously complex—it will take you up and over, around and through. On three levels above and below grade, the center includes five major components: the university art museum, the drama wing, the dance studio and the 496-seat Gavin Playhouse, plus sculpture gardens. The central plaza is a gripping space defined by the tower bridge. (At night, projectors hidden in the bridge beam images onto a tall, facing wall that resembles a drive-in movie screen.) Performances in the dance theater are meant to spill over into the plaza outdoors.

The main public entrance on Mill Avenue leads to the art museum, and it shows Predock's mastery of managing the transition from overpowering sunlight to the cool austerity of the sunken interiors. Aiding the transition, Predock has designed a series of trellises at this entrance to introduce welcome shade and cast geometrically patterned shadows. Once inside the museum, however, you won't be able to proceed directly from the museum to the theaters; these have separate entries.

According to Predock, the Nelson Fine Arts Center is an example of "naked architecture." Its massive blank walls stand up to the strong sun, which obliterates the fine-grained detail that provides definition in other climates. Predock's subtleties work with this climate—for example, the infinite mutations of the building's lavender color in different lights and after it rains. Its interiors harbor a sense of mystery, even for people who know them well.

The Nelson Fine Arts Complex is open Wednesday to Saturday 10:00 AM to 5:00 PM, Tuesday until 9:00 PM, closed Sunday and Monday. Special architectural tours can be arranged for groups of six or more. For information and tour arrangements, call (480) 965-2787.

WEXNER CENTER FOR THE VISUAL ARTS, 1989

Ohio State University
Columbus, Ohio

Peter Eisenman

If you take a map of Columbus, Ohio, and draw a bright red line from 15th Avenue to the campus football stadium, you will see how Peter Eisenman began to conceive the Wexner Center for the Visual Arts. The red line marks the convergence (or collision) of the city's grid with the campus grid, a likely starting point for an art center whose stated goal is to bring avant-garde art to town. Wexner Center's initial display of avant-garde art is obviously the building itself, America's most prominent work of Deconstructionist architecture. Like its illustrious and theoretical architect, Wexner Center speaks its own language, makes its own rules, and seeks to elicit a completely new set of responses.

Wexner Center is slotted between two existing buildings. Although most of the structure is tucked underground, its axis is clearly marked at street level by long, open, white steel framework, which Eisenman calls "scaffolding." It forms an angled outdoor street almost a block long, and a wedge of the main building intrudes into its long, gridded promenade.

Eisenman marks the center's entrance with a set of dark brick towers—the "armory"—in place of an old armory on the site that was demolished after a 1958 fire. This architectural resurrection is not entirely literal; Eisenman's towers are split and peeled away, positioned and angled in novel ways. Inside the main entrance, in the two-story lobby, the campus grid and the city grid collide in framework. Consider yourself alerted to the unconventional effects that will follow: stairs with columns, grids jammed into ceilings, grids hanging in space, windows on the floor. The lobby's grand staircase channels you down to the primary circulation spine, a long ramp off which galleries are arrayed on terraces. The lower level spaces are beautifully illuminated by windows and skylights.

Wexner Center is large—almost 110,000 square feet plus the 155,530 square-foot existing buildings—and its requirements are complex: galleries, experimental theaters, classrooms, offices, an arts library, café, bookstore, and amphitheater. Before Eisenman won the design competition, his built work consisted mainly of houses. The New York architect also had a reputation as the

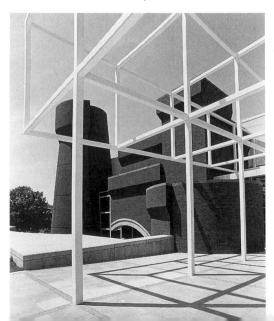

"bad boy of architecture." His ideas work at Wexner Center, and success here has brought Eisenman several large commissions, including a new convention center in Columbus.

In fall 2005, the building reopens following renovations: Tuesday to Saturday, 10:00 AM to 6:00 PM; Thursday until 9:00 PM; Sunday noon to 6:00 PM; closed Monday. Architecture tours are available by request. For information, call (614) 292-0330.

Battery Park City is New York City's newest neighborhood. It occupies a 92-acre strip of manufactured Manhattan real estate, which was created along the banks of the Hudson River by the systematic depositing of landfill from the World Trade Center twin 110-story towers a few blocks west of the site. The master plan by Alexander Cooper and Stanton Eckstut mixes commercial, residential, and retail development with grand public plazas and an esplanade along the river that gives New York the kind of congenial urban space you would expect to find almost anywhere but here.

WORLD FINANCIAL CENTER AND WINTER GARDEN, 1989

Battery Park City
West Street between Chambers Street and Battery Park
New York, New York

Cesar Pelli

The work of several important individual (and highly individualistic) architects is represented, but the most prominent buildings to date are the four World Financial Center Buildings and the Winter Garden, all of which were designed by Cesar Pelli and developed by Olympia & York Companies (U.S.A.). The statistics: 6,000,000 square feet of offices, 300,000 square feet of retail space, and 200,000 square feet of lobby and circulation space. The four octagonal office towers vary in height from 34 to 51 stories, creating a cluster of buildings housing prominent financial corporations like Merrill Lynch and Dow Jones. The Winter Garden, the centerpiece, is a magnificent glassed-in park containing shops and restaurants, and providing space for concerts and other events. For the Winter Garden's 120-foot-high vaulted roof, the glazing was put into place over a ring and stringer steel structure of heroic proportions, strongly reminiscent of a zeppelin frame. In front of the Winter Garden, there is a fine plaza created by Pelli, Siah Armanjani, Scott Burton, and M. Paul Friedbert.

The apartments in Battery Park City are masonry with stone bases, and seem inspired by the beloved 1920s apartment houses along Central Park West. The choice of material brings a continuity to the new development, a little bit of old New York for this new New York.

The office buildings of World Financial Center are open during business hours. The Winter Garden is open seven days a week: Monday through Friday from 10:00 AM to 7:00 PM and Saturday and Sunday from noon to 5:00 PM. Restaurant hours vary. For information, call (212) 945-0505.

ASTRONAUTS MEMORIAL, 1989
"SPACE MIRROR"

Kennedy Space Center
Kennedy Space Center, Florida

Holt, Hinshaw, Pfau, Jones

As proof of modern technology's power and glory, nothing compares with the launch of a spaceship. Rockets as tall as multi-story buildings blast off with megaton force to pierce the sky and orbit the Earth. When all goes well, "technology" gets much of the credit. Unfortunately, the 1986 Challenger disaster brought home technology's human cost of pursuing superhuman ideals. The Astronauts Memorial, in response to that tragedy, was initiated to honor U.S. astronauts who die in the line of duty.

Space Mirror commemorates the astronauts' heroism with no apology for their faith in technological prowess. The monument's base resembles a rocket launcher, but in place of a spaceship it holds an unflinching mirror up to the sky. Four stories high by fifty feet wide, the mirror consists of black granite panels polished to a highly reflective surface. The astronauts' names are cut through the granite, inscribed in the sky's reflection. Letter spaces are filled with crystal-clear acrylic, minutely jagged on the front side to diffuse the light. Like an eternal flame, the names always glow. Mirrors positioned behind the engravings draw the sun's rays during the day; lights on these rear mirrors illuminate the astronauts' names in the night.

The slab-like mirror sits on a white-painted steel framework, controlled by computer to track the sun. This framework tilts and rotates the huge polished slab to ensure that the granite reflects only empty sky, without glare, and that the sun will strike the backlighting mirrors at the correct angle to light up the names.

Space Mirror's designers, Holt Hinshaw Pfau Jones, tend to a high-tech approach. At the memorial, structure and mechanics are integral to the architecture—and in full view: the 18-foot-diameter slewing ring; the two screwjacks that tilt the wall; the large counterweight for stability; the mirror-and-light assemblies mounted on white-painted steel trusses behind the rotating wall. A ramp runs behind the wall, cantilevers over a lake, and brings visitors around to the back for a closer look at this complex technology.

Space Mirror stands at the entrance to Spaceport USA, an exhibition complex within Kennedy Space Center. The memorial is open Monday through Saturday from 9:00 AM to 5:00 PM. For visitor information, call (312) 452-2887.

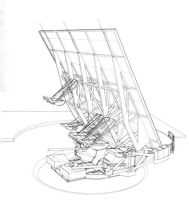

Antoine Predock's architectural journey has taken him far from his native New Mexican desert, but wherever he builds his work becomes site-specific. To Predock, however, "site-specific" means two things—the actual site and the site of his own imagination. This beachhouse overlooking the Pacific Ocean in the land of dreamy dreams occupies both realms.

In real life, the site is amazingly accessible, with a busy boardwalk on one side and a narrow street on the other. It's extremely rare to find a house like this in a place like this. Most architects leave houses behind as they rise to prominence, or they build only for the out-of-sight rich, but not Predock. He continues to work on houses and to pour architectural creativity into them. Venice House proves that even a small Predock house is something to see.

The house, in fact, is made for seeing and being seen. Looking out, the views through the cast-in-place concrete are carefully calibrated from the two-level interior and a rooftop terrace with bleachers. The ingenious pivoting red-steel-framed window-wall of the living room makes the ocean look closer than it is. This is accomplished by a trick of perspective: a 60-foot-long black granite "runway" on the living room floor widens toward the window, foreshortening the view. Next to the 9-by-14-foot pivoting window, Predock positioned a narrow slice of sea-green glass sideways in a foot-thick concrete armature. Sunlight casts a colored beam through the glass strip, and when one looks through there's a kaleidoscope view of the ocean panorama. On the street side, opaque windows predominate, but two small cantilevered balconies within the concrete frame provide lookouts. The garage doors are mirrored to reflect the passing scene, and, Predock muses, to give the car a place to primp.

Forming a visual bridge to the ocean, a black granite "fountain" abuts the concrete frame. A thin film of recirculating water washes over this granite block, creating an ever-changing reflection of sea, sand, and sky. The granite piece solves a technical requirement for railings that would have disturbed the view. As it has turned out, the little black pool is a source of endless fascination for beachgoers, who can walk right up and touch it.

Venice House is a private residence.

VENICE HOUSE, 1990

**2315 Ocean Front Walk
(between 23rd and 24th
Avenues)
Venice, California**

Antoine Predock

THE DOLPHIN HOTEL AND THE SWAN HOTEL, 1990

Walt Disney World/EPCOT Center
Near Orlando, Florida

Michael Graves

Walt Disney World's companion hotels, the Dolphin and the Swan, are like larger-than-life cartoons in which a colorful carnival is in full swing. The playful atmosphere is obvious even from a distance: two gigantic dolphins are doing headstands on top of their namesake hotel, and twin swans 47-feet tall preen against the sky atop the smaller hotel. And each hotel is further "themed" by supergraphic murals—green banana leaves are painted onto the sandy background of the Dolphin Hotel, and cresting blue waves cover the surface of the Swan.

This is architecture as show business, or what Walt Disney called "entertainment architecture," and so the graphic extravaganza never stops. Tented entries, columns of banana trees and palm leaves, beach-scene wall murals, doors striped like cabanas, and carpets designed to resemble boardwalks and lily pads are just a few of the fantasy confections contributing to the tropical resort.

Michael Graves designed the two hotels as part of his master plan for Walt Disney World's new hotel and convention center located between the EPCOT World Showcase and the Disney-MGM Studio theme park. The hotels face each other across a crescent-shaped lake, with a causeway connecting the two lobbies. The larger and more ambitious of the two is the Dolphin Hotel, which is a 1.4-million-square-foot convention center. Its 27-story triangular tower is the focal point of the building, and of the whole complex. Four nine-story wings of guest rooms project from this center out over the lake. The vaulted entry is flanked by clamshell fountains splashing water down either side. The Swan, a 12-story hotel with 615,000 square feet, is divided into the main building with a gently curving roofline; two guest room wings project out toward the water. Big, colorful cabana-striped awnings tent the entry and shade the causeway that ties the hotels together.

Virtually nothing has escaped the Graves graphic touch. The restaurants feature plates ringed in oranges and tabletops painted as slices of oranges, lemons, and limes. In the guest rooms, Graves-designed furniture includes lamps with pineapple bases and furniture stenciled with waves, fruit, and flowers.

To reserve a room at either hotel, call (407) 934-7639.

N o one sees the desert quite like Antoine Predock, or uses its intense light and bleached natural colors so convincingly. His competition-winning design for the Las Vegas Library/Discovery Museum is a complex of strong shapes rendered in subtle colors that stand up to the sun and cast striking shadows. In a town where most buildings compete for attention by turning up the voltage to eye-popping wattages, Predock's work stands out as an oasis of architectural sophistication.

LAS VEGAS LIBRARY/ DISCOVERY MUSEUM, 1990

833 Las Vegas Boulevard North
Las Vegas, Nevada

Antoine Predock

For the approach, Predock lays out a carefully integrated series of graphic elements—cubes, cones, towers, and strategically placed palm trees—that draws you toward the entrance. The pale, bone-colored concrete shapes play off against sandstone walls rendered in pale terra-cotta and earthy red, a subtle combination that mimics the baked-clay feel of the desert and adds just enough color to be enticing. Water, the most precious commodity in the desert, washes one of the outside walls, and continues its flow to the lobby and on to an enclosed outdoor courtyard.

As its name implies, the Library/Discovery Museum is two buildings in one. Predock locates the library in the east wing and the children's museum in the west wing, which is set off at a slight angle. On all three floors of the 110,000-square-foot complex, the wings meet in a stepped-back triangular core that juts out on the north side and houses the facility's common administrative services. On the second and third floors, the wings are spanned by a barrel-vaulted reading room for children.

The cones and towers are places of merry-making and adventure for children. The cone-shaped exterior room at the entrance turns out to be the birthday party room, shaped like a birthday party hat. Gravity experiments take place in the 112-foot tower, which doubles as a lookout post. In the galleries, windows are low to the floor, allowing children to indulge a favorite pastime, spying on the adults and children visible in other rooms.

In dealing with the desert climate from a technical standpoint, Predock has used a number of cooling effects. Some of the windows are shaded with metal grills to help screen out the sun, and some courtyards are outfitted with fabric roofs that block out half the light. Left exposed are the outdoor bleachers, remnants of the baseball field that formerly occupied the site.

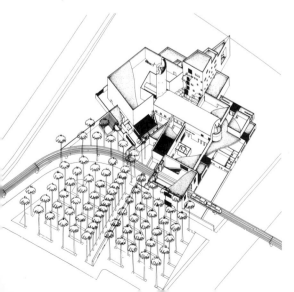

The library is open 9:00 AM to 9:00 PM Monday through Thursday; 10:00 AM to 6:00 PM, Friday to Sunday. Architectural tours can be arranged by calling the library's main number, (702) 507-3500.

MANDELL FUTURES CENTER, 1990

The Franklin Institute
Benjamin Franklin Parkway
at 20th Street
Philadelphia, Pennsylvania

Robert Geddes and Michael Kihn
Geddes, Brecher, Qualls and Cunningham

Since 1933, the Franklin Institute has been famous for its "learning by doing" approach of teaching science to children as well as adults. The spunky new addition adjoins the temple-like original structure (whose depression-era plan was never completed) and adds a bright spot to the formal City Beautiful boulevard that runs alongside it.

The Mandell Futures Center could be the playground of a giant, sophisticated child whose oversized blocks include a limestone cylinder, a pyramid, and a glass cube that have tumbled to rest at a jaunty angle amid brightly painted steel beams. But as it stands, the cylinder is a huge Imax theater showing 70mm movies on a wraparound screen, the pyramid is the theater's roof, and the glass cube jutting out from the second floor is the "Science Overlook" vantage point for the outdoor Science Garden.

The designers, Robert Geddes and Michael Kihn of GBQC in Philadelphia, respected the existing structure while updating it with plentiful light and bright primary colors—a place where learning science seems like fun. The addition adds 90,000 square feet on two levels, plus underground parking. In the galleries, the Franklin Institute's proclivity for dynamic interactive displays continues, even higher tech than before. The central focus of the addition is the new museum entrance, a "Great Hall" atrium with a bright red ramp that spirals around to provide the main circulation. A lecture hall, restaurant, and bookshop were also added.

The Franklin Institute, its planetarium, and the Mandell Futures Center are open seven days a week. For information and hours, call (215) 448-1200.

S tarting with a historic shell—the famous "901" studio occupied for forty years by Charles and Ray Eames—Frank Israel inserted a contemporary office for a corporate design firm that epitomizes southern California's contemporary architectural vivaciousness. Israel's vision was surprising, colorful, mysterious, dramatic, and sophisticated; he seemed to see architecture as serious fun.

BRIGHT & ASSOCIATES, 1991

**901 Hampton Drive
at Washington Blvd.
Venice, California**

*Franklin D. Israel Design
Associates*

A vivid, yellow, flying-wedge canopy calls out the entry into the complex, a composite of three old, industrial structures. Inside the door, the regular, rectangular two-story exterior gives way to something completely different: a tall tower with angled walls, a skylighted roof, and high clerestory windows. This dramatic lighting illuminates mustard-yellow stucco walls with stone-gray ledge-like door frames for an overall effect that is somewhere between the medieval and the modern.

From the entrance, visitors are literally funneled through a dark tunnel to the adjacent building, arriving in an open court, also mustard-colored and modern/medieval in spirit. This court is bounded by the triangular-shaped office of the firm's president on the left and the conical wall of the conference room straight ahead. To the right, an interior arcade contains the firm's design offices. Beyond the arcade, a second set of offices is defined by curving purple walls; the sequence concludes with a mustard-yellow wall at the rear.

Inside and out, the new structure clearly resides within the old one. For example, the original 901 building's façade has been spruced up with a new sheet-metal marquee that looks contemporary but suits the industrial integrity of the older building. On the inside, the sequence of spaces within the L-shaped plan takes place under the exposed trussed roof of the old Eames warehouse.

Frank Israel, who died in 1996 at age 50, was at the forefront of a generation of southern California architects influenced by the imaginative, artistic approach of fellow-California architect Frank Gehry. Israel was born in New York, held a Master of Arts degree from Columbia University, studied at the American Academy in Rome, and worked briefly as an art director in film before opening his Los Angeles practice in 1983. You can compare Israel's work at Bright & Associates with Gehry's office building for Chiat/Day advertising, which is in the neighborhood. The offices now have new tenants and are not open to the public.

CHIAT/DAY BUILDING, 1991

340 Main Street
Venice, California

*Frank O. Gehry & Associates
with Claes Oldenburg and
Coosje van Bruggen*

Is it art or is it architecture? Frank Gehry, a self-contained collaboration of the two, has often designed buildings that confound traditional boundaries. Here the collaboration is easier to decipher. Gehry's architecture is teamed with outdoor sculpture by artists Claes Oldenburg and Coosje van Bruggen, creators of the already famous pair of giant binoculars designating the entrance to this advertising agency's West Coast headquarters. You cannot, of course, miss them.

The black binoculars, 43 feet tall, are an exaggerated focal point for a building replete with visual surprises. On the outside, the façade has two main elements that vie with the binoculars for attention. At one corner is the Tree Building, where sturdy-looking copper-clad beams—the branches—jut out from masonry columns to form a metallic forest above the windows. At the other end, the façade is cool and white; it opens up to reveal layers of walkways. Overall, strong lines forcibly veer away from the eye's foursquare expectations of where a building ought to start, stop, and go.

The three-level, 75,000-square-foot building is designed to encourage creative work. The interiors are organized as a series of spacious open areas, with varied ceiling heights, all receiving natural light from the large windows and generous skylights. Gehry has specified his characteristic commonplace (he says "cheapskate") materials such as plywood and galvanized metal for the interiors and furniture he designed for the building. But here they are contrasted with richer materials such as copper sheeting, maple panels, and stone. The main entrance desk is fashioned from gnarled tree stumps, a continuation of the Tree Building theme.

The binoculars originally contained a pair of small, circular "thinking rooms" on the second level. From overhead, sunlight beams down into each thinking room through a binocular eyepiece, which is also a skylight. The building is sited well and has a fine view of the Pacific Ocean.

Chiat/Day has moved, and the building is not open to the general public.

Culver City's metamorphosis from an industrial has-been into Los Angeles's version of Soho owes much to the architecture of Eric Owen Moss. His 1978 Morganstern Warehouse (now demolished) was the first revival of this architecturally neglected industrial building type. A progressively adventurous series of warehouse conversions for creative businesses has followed. They are clustered around the Culver City Studios, the one-time movie capital of America, where Orson Wells directed *Citizen Kane*.

GARY GROUP OFFICES, 1991

9046 Lindblade Street
Culver City, California

Eric Owen Moss

For Gary Group, a public relations firm, Moss converted a former steel foundry into high-visibility offices. The most prominent exterior wall is on the west side, and it presents a picture made of industrial parts. The old concrete block wall is draped with chains and studded with ladders of steel rebar in a theatrically nautical configuration.

In front, the main entrance is recessed behind a new tilted wall of rust-colored block. This false front extends above the roof line and shows its support: three C-shaped metal ribs attached to three steel columns behind the façade. A shallow balcony juts out, and a metal staircase leads to the top of the "C." This whole construction collides with a white steel grid with a clock centered in the middle. From the parking lot, it looks like a clock tower gone berserk.

There is nothing conventional about the inside either. First-floor offices are grouped around an interior marble pool washed by water from residential shower heads. But the most provocative space is the conference room. Its overlay of geometric shapes, like walls within walls, turns a square room into an octagonal one with tilted metal beams. Above the octagon, a round steel collar supports tilting beams that rise 25 feet through a glass and aluminum pyramid, topped by a cone-shaped skylight. The industrial-strength interiors are soothed by small gardens planted with bamboo.

Another Moss-designed office building, The Samitaur at Corbett Street and Jefferson Boulevard, is elevated twenty-one feet off the ground. It showcases Moss' plan to build a city over abandoned railroad tracks. This hopefully heralds renewed civic pride and economic development in south-central Los Angeles. The offices are not open to the public.

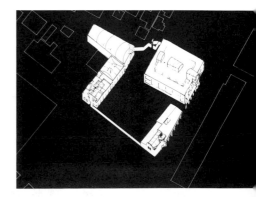

SEATTLE ART MUSEUM, 1991

100 University Avenue
at First Avenue
Seattle, Washington

*Venturi, Scott Brown
& Associates*

The Seattle Art Museum opened in a blaze of glory. Its excellent Asian art collection was newly showcased in a structure designed by postmodernism's reigning godparents, Robert Venturi and his wife, Denise Scott Brown. Opening the same year Venturi won the prestigious Pritzker Prize, the new civic masterpiece also established a strong sense of place meant to jumpstart arts-related downtown development. But when postmodernism became passé, the museum's building suddenly seemed like a historical artifact. Fortunately, time is on the museum's side again. Brad Cloepfil of Allied Works Architecture is designing a sleek new modern tower annex that will feature a futuristic four-story *brise-soleil* of stainless steel louvers that move with the sun.

Venturi and Scott Brown envisioned their building as a return to the traditional museum ideal of a neoclassical palazzo. This approach was possible in part because the museum is small—five stories containing 150,000 square feet. Still, with its cultural significance, the building needed to look suitably monumental.

The museum is set into a gentle hill on a downtown corner, its main façade a massive limestone wall scored with vertical fluting. Along the slanted street-side wall, marching up the hill, is a long arcade of tall windows topped by colorful arches in red sandstone, pink granite, and terra cotta. The building's name is inscribed in giant letters across the top, making a billboard for itself.

The grandest gesture appears just inside the door—a magnificent marble and travertine staircase rising up the entire street-side wall of the building with monumental Ming Dynasty figures (including camels and tigers) posted at intervals along the way. The great stair's ceiling is decorated with a series of colorful Moorish arches, and they create a complementary rhythm overhead. The large windows open the great stair to the street view and provide a natural illumination. In the exhibit galleries, Venturi continues the natural illumination with full walls of glass on the east and west.

The Seattle Art Museum successfully paved the way for a downtown revival of culture and architecture. The 2004 opening of Rem Koolhaas's Seattle Central Library (see page 259) made the city the architectural epicenter of the moment, not unlike the outpouring of praise that greeted the Venturi/Scott Brown building when it opened in 1991.

The museum is open Tuesday through Sunday from 10:00 AM to 5:00 PM, and until 9:00 PM on Thursday; closed Monday and major holidays. When Cloepfil's new building opens in 2007, the main entry moves north to Union Street at First Avenue. For information, call (206) 654-3100.

A nimation is the art of visual surprise. In a cartoon, anything can happen. Elephants can fly. A fake tunnel, painted on a mountainside, might bring forth a train. Ducks are blue and cats turn green. Arata Isozaki's design for Walt Disney Company offices near Orlando presents an intriguing set of illusions worthy of the world's preeminent fabricator of celluloid fantasies.

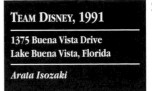

TEAM DISNEY, 1991

1375 Buena Vista Drive
Lake Buena Vista, Florida

Arata Isozaki

Disney's most famous character, Mickey Mouse, is "immortalized" in the front gates, which are Mouseketeer ears in outline. From here, the scene shifts to a work of Isozaki's creation. The bold black-and-white plaid pattern of the two long office wings is an illusion Isozaki devised by com-

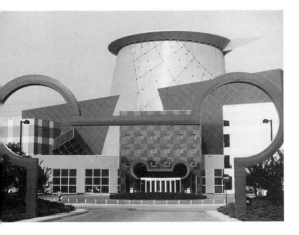

bining dark glass and light-and-dark-colored spandrel panels. This strong black-and-white graphic emphasizes the contrast with the building's exotic centerpiece. Above the main entrance, Isozaki rivets your attention with a cluster of geometric shapes in cartoon colors. A pink and green cone-shaped tower is topped with a bright yellow disc and stylus. A 120-foot-tall tilted curve appears to be "intersected" by a deep, blue wall. It is one illusion after the next. The tower rises above a four-story reddish-brown masonry cube with a flat pink wall running though its forward corner and a bright red tilted cube on its roof.

The enormous tower turns out to be hollow, and open at the top; it is one of the world's largest sundials. The yellow stylus visible on the outside can be seen from inside the tower for what it is: a hand in the clock of the open ceiling's circle. The shadow of the stylus's spun-aluminum "ballpoint" marks solar time on red tile disks on the walls. The floor of the sundial is covered in large, smooth rocks, and the space is bridged along one side, connecting offices and a conference area. Over the door, at the base of the sundial, Mickey Mouse's ears reappear in the form of an elegantly curved steel canopy.

This building is Isozaki's first Disney building. And while Disney's high-profile "entertainment architecture" commissions have made much news, the Tokyo-based Isozaki has been making his mark all over the world. No small creator of fantasies himself, Isozaki has repeatedly astonished the architectural profession—in the east and the west—with work dating back to the 1960s. One of his own celluloid fantasies appears in his design for the Museum of Contemporary Art in Los Angeles, where a curving wall is based on the shape of Marilyn Monroe.

Team Disney is open from 8:00 AM to 6:00 PM Monday through Friday and closed on weekends and holidays. Although there are no tours of the building, the sundial atrium is open to visitors. For information, call (407) 824-4500.

ISLAMIC CULTURAL CENTER, 1992

1711 Third Avenue at 96th Street
New York, New York

Skidmore, Owings & Merrill

New York's first mosque was built by twenty Islamic United Nations countries to serve the city's entire Muslim community. Although the cooperating nations each had individual traditions, their common heritage runs deep. It is a heritage concerned with values that are humanistic, spiritual, and architectural, and the design of the mosque is meant to give contemporary expression to ancient ideals.

Given Islam's prohibition against figurative representation, the mosque is strictly geometrical. A recurrence of squares underlies the design; the mosque is basically square in shape and plan, with a dome on top. Because religious law requires an eastern orientation, the building is rotated twenty-eight degrees to Manhattan's street grid, creating a large open forecourt where worshipers gather prior to prayers.

Square granite panels, evoking endurance, make up the mosque's base. Narrow glazed channels surround these panels, admitting daylight and creating a sense of permeability. In the midsection, large glazed panels are embellished with fired ceramic surface decorations in an overlapping lattice pattern, a modern technological treatment of an ancient material. Skylights at the four corners also admit natural light. The gilded copper dome, separated from the building by a clear glass band, appears to float on a ring of light.

At the portal, geometry is again employed to evoke ancient associations. Flat, rectangular layers of cut glass are overlapped to resemble the arch, but this one is symbolic, abstracted, and modern.

Inside, the mosque is almost purely space and light. Unlike Christian churches or Jewish synagogues, there are no pews, and worshipers sit on carpets. Filling the space is an ethereal light, from the carefully placed glazing and from a circle of lights suspended by brass cords to form a halo above the congregation.

Tours can be scheduled Sunday through Thursday from 10:00 AM to 4:00 PM. The mosque is closed on Saturday. Religious services for the congregation only are held on Friday afternoons, when the mosque is closed to visitors. For appointments and information, call (212) 722-5234.

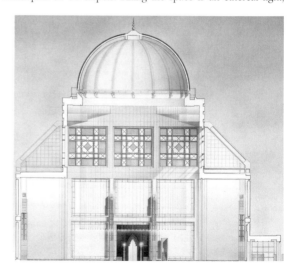

T he Shepherd School of Music at Rice University is devoted to achieving world-class sound quality for the listener, but there is also much here that will interest its viewers. For many Americans, it will be the first opportunity to see first-hand the work of Barcelona-based architect Ricardo Bofill, who is internationally renowned for his Mediterranean classical style.

SHEPHERD SCHOOL OF MUSIC, 1992

Rice University
Houston, Texas

Ricardo Bofill/Taller de Arquitectura

The new music school continues Bofill's tradition of curved colonnades. Facing the main campus across a vast expanse of empty green lawn, the curved, colonnaded façade seems stretched to infinity—it is 465 feet long and two stories high. Massive white concrete columns are set against pale terra-cotta brick to mimic Rice's prevailing building materials. These columns alternate with tall, narrow windows giving outside views to the teaching studios and practice rooms inside. Bofill's grand classical sweep is meant to be mirrored in a reflecting pool, which has yet to be constructed.

Two interior courtyards separate the curved façade from the more public opposite side where the main public entrance is located. Flatter and less rhythmic, this western façade reveals more clearly the building's asymmetrical massing and the outlines of its four performance halls: a 1,000 seat concert hall, a 236-seat recital hall, an opera rehearsal studio, and an organ studio, each acoustically tailored to its intended purpose.

In expanding a campus originally designed by Ralph Adams Cram in 1910, Rice University administrators have commissioned buildings by a number of internationally recognized architects, including Cesar Pelli (Herring Hall) and James Stirling and Michael Wilford (Anderson Hall). Like these architects who built at Rice University shortly before him, Bofill has tried to fit his building into the existing brick and limestone campus tradition without losing his individuality.

Shepherd School of Music is open from 7:00 AM to 7:00 PM when school is in session. Access is limited from mid-May to mid-August, as there is no summer session. Concerts by students and faculty are held during the school year. For visitor information, school schedules, and tour requests, call (713) 348-8000.

HAROLD WASHINGTON LIBRARY CENTER, 1992

400 South State Street
Chicago, Illinois

Hammond, Beeby & Babka, Inc.

hicago's Harold Washington Library is a literary powerhouse holding 1.6 million volumes, making it one of the largest open-stack libraries in the world. The 10-story building occupies a full city block and was completed in a surprisingly short time—just five years, beginning in 1987. But to look at it, you might imagine that work on this solid, robust, classical, ornamented building had begun in the early 1900s, a time when public libraries in the Beaux Arts style were going up all over the country.

Like the classic libraries of the early twentieth century, Harold Washington Library is grand in scale and materials: granite, cast stone, deep-red brick, metal, and glass. It meets the street on all

sides with a heavy base of rusticated stone, with arches framing the doors and ground-floor windows. On each side, a trio of elegant arched windows rises five stories above the base, set off by ornamental cording and garlands cast in stone. The library has a temple-like attic (extravagantly decorated by vertical helical rods) with barrel vaults laid in cruciform on the roof, glazed at the nexus.

From the outside, the library appears to be the very bastion of human knowledge, but on the inside every effort has been made to keep it accessible, easy

to use, and inviting. The stacks on the library's six main levels are open, and the floors are connected by both escalators and elevators. The traditional wood paneling of classic libraries is picked up here in the escalator encasements, which are paneled in maple. Lighting, furniture, and state-of-the-art computer technology all help make the building more helpful to the public. The auditorium on the lower level is especially striking. The most exciting space in the building, however, is on the top floor: the enormous glass-enclosed Winter Garden.

The library was designed by Thomas Beeby, of Hammond, Beeby & Babka, the winner of a competition played out on public television for the whole country to see. As the competition evolved, judges considered the modern proposals. But it was the most resolutely classical design that got the vote.

The Harold Washington Library Center is open Monday to Thursday from 9:00 AM to 7:00 PM; Friday and Saturday from 9:00 AM to 5:00 PM; Sunday 1:00 PM to 5:00 PM; and closed major holidays. For information, call (312) 747-4300. The Chicago Architecture Foundation includes the building on its Loop Walking Tour. For information, call CAF at (312) 922-3432.

There are stadiums, and then there are ballparks. Classic parks like Wrigley and Ebbets Fields, built early in this century, were outmoded by the triumph of the domed stadium in the early 1960s. Thirty years later, the ballpark is back. Oriole Park at Camden Yards proudly revives baseball's most beloved traditions—the open sky, real green grass, a city setting—but with all the modern conveniences and advanced sports design. Its spectacular success with baseball purists and urban defenders now makes the domed stadium seem like a dinosaur.

ORIOLE PARK AT CAMDEN YARDS, 1992

333 Camden Street
Baltimore, Maryland

Hellmuth, Obata and Kassabaum

Like most successful structures, Camden Yards has an intelligent masterplan. The Orioles management and the Maryland Stadium Authority chose to locate the park downtown. Its eighty-five-acre site occupies a former railyard just west of the Inner Harbor, allowing the designers to integrate the park with the city. The plan takes in two old structures—a former train station, which became the ticket booth, and an eight-story 1898 railroad warehouse, which has been converted into team offices, shops, and restaurants. Keeping the warehouse proved particularly fortuitous. The space between it and the stadium became a pedestrian mall with old-time flavor, a perfect prelude to the neo-traditional stadium. Aligned with the downtown street grid, and oriented toward the skyline, Camden Yards is integral with the city, with spectacular nighttime views of the cityscape.

Orioles' owner Eli S. Jacobs envisioned the stadium as "a modern, old-fashioned design" just for baseball. In response, Hellmuth Obata and Kassabaum's Sports Facilities Group in Kansas City designed a three-tiered, 48,000-seat stadium that brings back the warmth and intimacy of baseball's good old days. The curved exterior, with its eight projecting stair towers, is clad with red brick and precast concrete. Arched openings in the facade provide screens for the pedestrian ramps. Steel trusses, not concrete, support the upper deck in another reference to traditional ballpark designs.

The fans' comfort was paramount, so there are no bad seats. The curved seating bowl is column-free, and seats are close to the field. The field itself is asymmetrical, reviving the odd angles and quirky niches that domed stadiums lacked.

Camden Yards is not an exercise in nostalgia for its own sake. The ballpark honors baseball's new traditions, too. Its Sony JumboTron video board, for example, is the latest high-tech scoreboard.

Orioles staff host daily tours: Monday to Saturday at 11:00 AM, noon, 1:00, and 2:00 PM, and Sunday at 12:30, 1:00, 2:00, and 3:00 PM. Advance tickets are required. Call (410) 685-9800 for tour and ballgame tickets and information.

AUDUBON HOUSE, 1993

NATIONAL AUDUBON SOCIETY HEADQUARTERS

700 Broadway at 4th Street New York, New York

Croxton Collaborative

The nature of design is to deal with the visible, with what we see. The *in*-visible or intangible elements are typically overlooked, as if they were, well, invisible. But we know a building's air can help or harm us. Its light can cheer or depress us. On a larger scale, what about the building process itself? Can we construct buildings using resources more wisely, buildings that consume energy more lightly over time?

These concerns confronted the Audubon Society when they bought an abandoned eight-story sandstone and cast-iron 1891 loft building for their headquarters. As a nonprofit organization devoted to the natural world, Audubon wanted this new headquarters to reflect their environmental concern. Croxton Collaborative's Randolph Croxton and interior design partner Kirsten Childs took up the challenge of "greening" the office. Croxton and Childs added their own goals: to create an environmentally sustainable, human-centered building with off-the-shelf products and existing technology, but without compromising their high design standards.

Recycling the existing 98,000-square-foot building produced the first large savings. This eliminated expensive demolition and preserved the enormous investment of energy and materials already on site. Then the architects determined that the major building systems—heating, cooling, lighting, and ventilation—offered the best opportunities for improvement. The architects upgraded the building's shell and fitted the windows with Heat Mirror™ glass, which possesses the insulating power of a foot-thick brick wall. An efficient gas-fired heater and chiller was chosen for its ability to use both fresh and filtered air virtually free of toxic materials. Using daylight magnificently, the architects designed the interiors to let natural light far into the office core. These design decisions help Audubon save about $100,000 a year on utilities.

Perhaps even more important, the air here is noticeably superior. It actually "breathes" better, partly because all materials used in construction and finishing are free of substances that emit formaldehyde and other VOCs: plywood, glues, and PVC plastic among them. Undyed wool carpets are tacked down rather than glued, floor tiles are made of recycled light bulbs, Homasote subflooring contains 50% recycled newsprint. And—nice surprise—the windows open!

Audubon and Croxton Collaborative have produced a prototype of ecologically sensitive design that serves both the natural world and the built world. They have shown how to reduce the environmental and economic costs of building, over the long and short term, while championing design excellence. This a project that works in New York City, Croxton and Childs point out, and that means it can work anywhere.

Audubon House hosts tours by appointment only. For visitor information, call (212) 979-3000.

B efore this parking garage was built, one of Princeton's most poignant structures stood solitary on its site: a venerable old brick wall with a wrought iron gate by McKim, Mead and White, the 1911 relic of a former playing field. Many architects would have been tempted to topple it, but Machado and Silvetti decided to incorporate it into their design for the five-level garage. The reddish brick wall became a starting point for an intricate layering of colors, textures, and materials. The old wall also prompts Machado and Silvetti's elegant theory that the finished structure is a garden park as well as a car-park.

"This lyrical structure makes poetry out of the most utilitarian kind of building," said the AIA awards jury in 1993. Surely, it is the most carefully thought out parking garage in the country, with the most remarkable design and luxurious materials of any parking garage to date.

Above McKim's wall, and the new brick wall that continues it, a bronze double-lattice screen wraps the top three parking floors. The screen, suspended on steel columns, culminates in a

graceful cornice curved outward toward the treetops. On three sides of the building, the screen is treated to remain dark brown; the fourth side is color-galvanized steel. Copper panels, tinged with a burnished magenta patina, clad the elevator tower and stairwells, where people entering and leaving the garage can best see them.

There's no denying the unromantic nature of the parking structure itself: a 140,000-square-foot, 410-car garage with a galvanized steel frame and poured-in-place concrete slabs.

Even so, Machado and Silvetti's garden-like vision seems plausible. A new garden was created along pretty Prospect Avenue between the old wall and the building. Ivy climbing the lattice trellis is meant to turn the garage into a truly topiary structure.

Rodolfo Machado and Jorge Silvetti are distinguished architectural theorists, and this is their first major built work. They intentionally set a new high standard of a civilized parking garage, which they call "architectural infrastructure." It is also Princeton's first on-campus garage. For this reason, the design had to be especially sensitive to the campus character, which includes the grand old undergraduate eating club mansions across Prospect Avenue, and neighbors on adjacent residential streets.

The Princeton parking garage is entered from a driveway linking Prospect Avenue to the Engineering Quadrangle to the north.

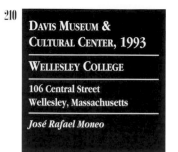

DAVIS MUSEUM & CULTURAL CENTER, 1993

WELLESLEY COLLEGE

106 Central Street
Wellesley, Massachusetts

José Rafael Moneo

A characteristic of 20th century architecture, Paul Rudolph remarked years ago, is that no building is ever truly finished. Change has now come to one of Rudolph's most influential buildings, the 1958 Jewett Art Center at Wellesley. The Davis Museum & Cultural Center, a new five-level structure sits across a plaza from Jewett and is connected to it by an overhead bridge.

The two buildings are connected over time as well as in space. Madrid-based architect Jose Rafael Moneo, in his first U.S. commission, cites the Jewett as an early inspiration in his own architectural career. The Jewett's open plaza, asymmetrical massing, prismatic skylights, and sun screens were frankly modern. And yet, its perfect proportions, vaguely Gothic forms, and mottled salmon brick exterior respected the existing architectural context at a time when standing apart was imperative.

Moneo's stated goal of enhancing Rudolph's masterpiece is most evident in the siting of Davis to frame sympathetic views of Jewett's western facade. Moneo also "completed" Jewett with a

new concrete plaza between the buildings that showcases Rudolph's magnificent fan-shaped outdoor stair and serves to orient Jewett toward its new companion.

In designing the Davis, Moneo faced a constraining site and an extensive program: a 61,000-square-foot museum, with cinema, cafe, administration, and conservation space included. The resulting bulky rectangle looks incongruously urban, and the blank red brick walls reinforce this impression. Only the sawtooth clerestory windows hint at the complexity inside. Enter the lobby, however, and Moneo's brilliant design is revealed. A unique scissor staircase zigzags through the museum, offset to create large and small galleries on each floor. Dim, narrow stairwells lead to bright open landings overlooking the galleries, and the alternation of compression and release provokes an arresting passage through the space. Clerestory windows flood the building with natural light.

The Davis Museum & Cultural Center houses Wellesley's encyclopedic art collection, which spans all periods and cultures. It is open Tuesday to Saturday 11:00 AM to 5:00 PM; Wednesday until 8:00 PM; Sunday 12:00 to 4:00 PM; closed Monday and major holidays. Guided group tours require two weeks notice. Wellesley, the town, is fourteen miles northwest of Boston. For visitor information and commuter rail directions call (781) 283-2051.

A t World War II's end, U.S. soldiers witnessed first-hand the Nazi death camp barbarity and exposed it to full public view. For most Americans, the unspeakable crimes and distant location made it possible to view the Holocaust as real but remote. The Holocaust Museum shatters such complacency. It exhibits the tragedy of six million Jews and other victims of Nazi fanaticism in the heart of our nation's capital.

U.S. HOLOCAUST MEMORIAL MUSEUM, 1993

14th Street near Independence Avenue
Washington, DC

Pei Cobb Freed & Partners

The architectural challenge was daunting: to create a building of beauty and symbolic significance where visitors could experience the unbearable without losing hope. In preparation, James Freed visited Auschwitz-Birkenau in Silesia, Poland, and this museum could only arise from his being there. Freed found that Nazi policy typically called for two separate structures: the concentration barracks and the crematorium, with a field in between. The museum's two buildings and plaza replicate this organization. The most poignant reference is the museum's zigzag roofline, which mimics Nazi watchtowers and conveys the impossibility of either escape or survival.

The main museum building evokes the disorientation of doomed arrivals. Interior walls are raw concrete; halls and stairways cant out at odd angles. A skylight runs the length of the five-story

building, casting light and shadow to haunting effect. The Hall of Witness, the three-level permanent exhibit, begins on the fourth floor and descends. It recounts the Nazi rise to power, the early persecutions, the organization of ghettos, and the "final solution." It also tells of resistance and rescue. This intensely personal exhibit is filled with photographs, documents, audiovisual displays, and eyewitness testament. Visitors proceed to the Hall of Remembrance. The hexagonal skylighted structure recalls the six million Jewish Holocaust victims in its very dimensions: six sides, sixty feet tall, 6,000 square feet in area. Designed for contemplation and remembrance, it feels like both a chapel and a tomb.

An international center for Holocaust studies, the museum also offers a library, archives, learning center, 200-seat theater, and a survivor registry.

The museum is open daily from 10:00 AM to 5:30 PM, closed Christmas and Yom Kippur. Exhibits are suitable for children over eleven, and adults should accompany children throughout. For visitor information call (202) 488-0400.

**APEX PHYSICAL EDUCATION
FACILITY, 1994**

LEHMAN COLLEGE

**250 Bedford Park Boulevard
West
Bronx, New York**

Rafael Viñoly Associates

The modernist belief that architecture can improve the human condition persists, but quietly now, given all the contradictory evidence. So it is still tempting to wonder whether an architecturally inspired sports facility will produce better athletes. The Lehman College Physical Education Facility, also called the Apex, is a good place to find out. The building houses state-of-the-art facilities for swimming, basketball, and racquetball competitions, as well as aerobics, weight training, tennis, and dance.

Rafael Viñoly's design captures the athlete's energy in motion. The building's defining feature—its rounded silver-clad stainless steel roof—is arched like a diver just sprung from the board. This unique curving roof covers a building almost a city block long. It exerts a powerful presence; but its gentle slope helps integrate the new 164,000-square-foot gymnasium into the traditional campus. The building is visually strong in part because it has to be. Located at the extreme north end of the campus, the Apex creates a new campus gateway and draws a visible boundary between the campus and the outside world. Fortunately, it is not a closed world. Viñoly has cleaved the building's below-roof bulk in two, making its main entrance plaza and lobby a pedestrian "through street."

Under the curving roof, visitors enter directly at the level of the spectator seating. The underside of the great roof and its supporting white-painted trusses are completely exposed for the entire 101-foot length of the building. From an interior vantage point, the massive curving roof looks practical and protective. A long row of clerestory windows along one wall fills the gym with light on sunny days.

In contrast to the silver roof that arcs almost to the ground on the campus-facing facade, Apex presents an erect and subdued face to the street. Here the walls are precast concrete to blend with the limestone buildings around it.

The Lehman gym is an early example of Rafael Viñoly's architectural practice, which grew exponentially as he built spectacular convention centers in Pittsburgh, Boston, and Tokyo, Jazz at Lincoln Center, in New York's new Time Warner Building, and restructured the Kennedy Center in Washington. His THINK team's design entry for the World Trade Center competition was the runner-up, although to many it was the emotional favorite.

Lehman College's Physical Education Facility is open Monday to Friday, 7:00 AM to 10:00 PM; Saturday 8:00 AM to 5:00 PM. It is closed Sundays and major holidays. Visitors are welcome; however, photographers and groups require advance permission. Groups should make arrangements in advance. Write to Dr. Martin Zwiren, Director of Athletics. For information, call (718) 960-1117.

E
very summer and into the fall, concertgoers trek to Tanglewood in the Berkshire Mountains to hear a magical combination of world-class music in a farmlike festival setting. Eliel and Eero Saarinen's revered "music shed" here set the precedent for indoor/outdoor concerts. With the opening of Seiji Ozawa Hall, the new summer home of the Boston Symphony Orchestra, the challenge of delivering concert-quality sound to two audiences—inside and out—has been solved in a remarkable way.

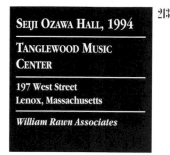

SEIJI OZAWA HALL, 1994

TANGLEWOOD MUSIC CENTER

197 West Street
Lenox, Massachusetts

William Rawn Associates

William Rawn's best-of-both-worlds design starts traditionally, with a shoebox shape with long side walls and a vaulted roof. But the hall's rear wall is ingenious. It consists of a system of five-inch-thick acoustically insulated panels that slide open to create a fifty-foot expanse. With these rear doors open, and its sophisticated exterior sound system turned on, Ozawa Hall delivers the acoustical quality of a symphony hall to its inside audience of 1,200, and to another 2,000 listeners seated on a gently sloping hill behind the hall.

Rawn likens this large, five-story concert hall to a Shaker meeting house, or, even more intimately, "a room for music." Ozawa Hall's Shaker-like slat-back wooden chairs and the wooden grill balcony railings that ring the hall on three sides create an interior space that seems almost communal but a little exotic at the same time. The "community" is genuine: the orchestra and audience occupy the same space, with no proscenium arch between them. Outside, Ozawa Hall's red brick walls are softened with timber side arcades, wood-grilled porches to capture summer breezes. The roof is a simple curved form of lead-coated copper which softens the edge of the building where it meets the sky. In evenings, the lighted building becomes a glowing lantern.

A Performer Support Space, adjacent to the hall, creates a courtyard which becomes the central "greenroom" for the student fellowship program.

Tanglewood is continually open during the concert season (May to mid-October), with building guides on weekends. Off-season, the grounds are open; visitors can see the building's exterior and the beautiful site. For performance schedules, group tour information or directions call Boston Symphony Orchestra at (617) 266-1492; in season call Tanglewood at (413) 637-1600.

WEISMAN ART MUSEUM, 1994

UNIVERSITY OF MINNESOTA

333 East River Road
Minneapolis, Minnesota

Frank O. Gehry

Adventurous new architecture and outspoken criticism go hand in hand. But while most institutions steer clear of controversy, the Weisman Art Museum's benefactors chose to welcome it. A controversial building could be an advantage, they reasoned—a way to interest students and the public in the artwork inside. In commissioning Frank Gehry, university president Nils Hasselmo specifically asked him not to give the campus another bland brick box. Not a chance! Winner of the 1989 Pritzker Prize, Gehry's career as a successful architectural risk taker made him a good choice for a controversial but superb design.

The new 41,000-square-foot museum starts with a can't-miss-it location on a bluff overlooking the Mississippi River. Gehry's flamboyant creation seems like a compressed cityscape collage of stainless steel above the river. All jammed together you see churches and factories, apartment houses and office towers. This tight mini-city seems to rise in unison, even though it appears on the verge of collapse. First-time viewers gasp for comparisons: a medieval castle; a cubist artwork; an exploding silver artichoke. Dynamic, not static, the building continually captivates viewers as they move around it. The structure looks different from every angle and with every change of the light. More modest reddish brick walls on the east and west relate to traditional campus buildings on those sides. Large picture windows on the ground floor open the building to the sidewalk.

Those long familiar with Gehry's work will recognize his aquatic images—a sail-shaped canopy and an ichthys-like "sun scoop"—that mark the main entrance. The computer must also be credited, for it is almost impossible to imagine creating these shapes without one. The builders, however, regressed to using string and rulers to build it.

The Weisman is Frank Gehry's first total museum design. He brought to it a lifetime's experience studying art, and the best ways to exhibit and light it. As a result, as Herbert Muschamp wrote in the *New York Times,* the building contains "five of the most gorgeous galleries on earth." White walls rise to a complex curved ceiling with skylights and white structural trusses that make space and light a vivid inhabiter of these galleries. Galleries occupy the main level of the four-story museum. Parking and storage fill the two lower levels; administrative offices are on top.

The museum is open Tuesday, Wednesday, and Friday from 10:00 AM to 5:00 PM; Thursday until 8:00 PM.; Saturday and Sunday 11:00 AM to 5:00 PM; and is closed Mondays, major holidays, and university holidays. Tours are held on Saturday and Sunday at 1:00 PM. Group tours for fifteen or more require three weeks notice. For visitor information, call (612) 625-9494.

It no longer sounds farfetched to say, as Swiss architect Mario Botta does, that art is the new religion and the museum its place of worship. The museum building of today must be part of the pleasure, and part of the draw. SFMOMA accomplishes all this and more. It's a wonderful place to experience art, and is one of the best works in the collection.

Like a great artwork, SFMOMA first captures attention, then holds it. The outside is shockingly graphic. A boldly striped black and white stone cylinder with a sheared off ocular skylight arises from a sienna-colored brick base, a three-tiered 225,000-square-foot fortress. The interior, in contrast, is coolly elegant and highly refined, careful to balance the architecture of the building with the art on the walls.

Mario Botta's cathedral concept serves him well as a coherent organizing principle for his first U.S. building and first museum. Living in Lugano, Botta understands the cathedral's role as a social center of European cities, and he recreates the piazza in SFMOMA's atrium lobby. This is the heart of the building, a large open space that fairly swirls with activity generated by the cafe, the bookstore, and other public spaces that surround it. Four floors of galleries and related facilities—including a theater, library, and conservation studio—spiral above and beyond the atrium lobby by means of a grand staircase beneath the oculus light.

About the light. Botta orchestrates it like a Gothic cathedral builder, combining light with height to express the spiritual and mystical communion we now seek in art. The giant ocular skylight suddenly makes perfect sense. The higher you go the brighter it gets. (At night the oculus glows in the dark.) A bridge beneath the opening raises visitors to this highest level of most intense luminosity. In the galleries, skylights reminiscent of Louis Kahn's Kimball Museum assure beautiful but controlled illumination.

Fumihiko Maki's Center for the Arts and James Stewart Polshek & Partners' Yerba Buena Theater are across the street. SFMOMA is open daily from 11:00 AM to 6:00 PM, except Wednesday, when the museum is closed; Thursday 11:00 AM to 9:00 PM. Scheduled gallery tours are available. For architectural collectors, the museum sells a snowdome of itself in the gift shop. For visitor information, call (415) 357-4000.

NEUROSCIENCES INSTITUTE, 1995

10640 John Jay Hopkins Drive
La Jolla, California

Tod Williams and Billie Tsien

Architecture always deals with ideas, and the Neurosciences Institute presents an especially big one: discovering how the biological brain gives rise to the mind, with all its thoughts, perceptions, images, values, and sensations. This quest motivates the institute's founder, Nobel Laureate Gerald Edelman, and thirty-two brain scholars in residence. They are joined by visiting scholars in related fields, who come to this scientific crucible in hopes that their intense interactions will spark brain science breakthroughs.

Tod Williams and Billie Tsien saw this need for commingling, for both structured and chance meetings, and based their architecture on it. Commissioned to do a single structure, they pulled the program apart to create a central plaza with three main buildings around it.

The tallest building, the three-story Theory Center, has theorists' offices cantilevered over the lower level, where the dining room, library, and meeting rooms front on the plaza. The long, low Laboratory wing contains two stories tucked into a bermed hillside. Its 200-foot length bends in two places, with angled notches yielding a U-shaped structure. The lab facade is a canted glass wall, half sandblasted, half clear, that extends above the roof. The multiple levels of these "working" buildings are connected by ramps from the plaza to the rooftops, and *on* the rooftops of the lab. The third major structure, an acoustically perfect auditorium, lies across the plaza from the other two. "The design is primarily about promenade, about connective movement," Tod Williams explains. "There is not one route, there are many routes." The odds for chance encounters increase exponentially.

Everyone is on foot here, and both the design and the materials are layered to reward intimate proximity. The architectural forms, like the brain itself, reveal themselves in increments. Design elements appear one way in one place, only to reappear in another relationship somewhere else. The materials, colors, and textures have strong appeal to the senses: the Theory Center's creamy fossil stone, the Laboratory's smooth and sandblasted glass, the rich redwood doors of the auditorium, and the pale green serpentine paving of the plaza.

There's a monastic quality to the work of Williams and Tsien that seems keenly appropriate for NSI, which Dr. Edelman views as a "monastery of science." Despite its nuanced subtlety, the design has the strength necessary to establish a sense of place for the new institute, and to evoke a lively but sheltered atmosphere for its single-minded scientists.

NSI is located within the Scripps Research Institute (Edward Durrell Stone designed the campus) between North Torrey Pines Road and John Jay Hopkins Drive. Parking is very restricted. For visitor and parking information, call (858) 626-6000.

T he early rockers were right. Rock and roll is here to stay. Their art form is newly immortalized in this museum, and it puts on quite a show: 150,000 square feet honoring the singers, the songs, the costumes—all the outrageousness rock is loved and hated for.

The eminent architect I.M. Pei claims never to have heard much rock and roll, but he tried to translate rock's explosive energy into architectural form. Two cantilevered wings clad in white metal panels take off from a square, six-story tower, also covered in white panels. One projection is a trapezoidal box that resembles a giant speaker. The other, a circular form atop a slender column, resembles a turntable and spindle rising out of Lake Erie. These outstretched arms are unified by the glass pyramid facade that soars five stories from the plaza to near the top of the tower. Pei calls the steel-trussed pyramid a tent, and visitors enter into this vast open space. A spectacular mobile of neon- and zebra-striped cars from a U-2 tour hangs from the roof, making it clear that this museum is going to be one wild ride. Dual escalators ascend through the open pyramid to smaller exhibition spaces, and each floor is different in plan.

ROCK & ROLL MUSEUM AND HALL OF FAME, 1995

North Coast Harbor, East 9th Street and Erieside Cleveland, Ohio

Pei Cobb Freed and Partners

The main exhibition area, "Roll Over Beethoven," spreads out underground. Enshrined here are Buddy Holly's high school diploma, parts of Otis Redding's crashed plane, Colonel Parker's $5,000 receipt conveying exclusive rights to Elvis Presley's career, and John Lennon's Sgt. Pepper uniform.

Visitors can explore rock's history through visual displays, recordings, films, a computer data base, a library, and archive. You can trace influences of a particular performer, and the link between cities and sound: Detroit and Motown; San Francisco and psychedelia; New York and punk and rap.

The museum culminates at the top of the tower, where a dimly lit double-spiral staircase leads to the Hall of Fame. In this dark, reverent space, black walls bear the signatures of Hall of Famers like Jerry Lee Louis, B.B. King, the Supremes, Simon and Garfunkle, Marvin Gaye, and over one hundred others.

The museum is open daily from 10:00 AM to 5:30 PM, and until 9:00 PM on Wednesdays; closed Thanksgiving, Christmas, and New Year's Day. Advance tickets are strongly recommended. Reservations are required for groups of twenty or more. For information, call (216) 781-ROCK.

PHOENIX CENTRAL LIBRARY, 1995

1221 North Central Avenue
Phoenix, Arizona

BruderDWLarchitects

The Phoenix Central Library is marker architecture, a galvanizing place-maker for a striving, fast-growing city. Since the place they are making is in the desert, Will Bruder and Wendell Burnette took the desert's light and landscape as natural starting points to be combined with the agricultural and mining past of the people. Further inspired by Monument Valley, they shaped the five-level, 280,000-square-foot building to resemble a manmade mesa of copper walls—curved, corrugated and perforated with a pattern of tiny holes—split by a stunning canyon of stainless steel. Bruder, a self-taught architect trained as a sculptor, also sees the library as a powerful ruin—its copper cladding weathered to a molten purple and bronze patina.

The exotic, almost magical quality of the materials conceals the underlying simplicity of the overall conception: curved copper screens flanking a basic warehouse shape. Because all mechanical equipment is packed into these "saddlebags," the library floors are freed up for an open plan, completely devoted to circulation. Massive glazed walls on the north and south sport lyrical tensioned fabric sails and computer-controlled louvers that let glare-free light into the building.

A cantilevered trellis of stainless steel beams marks the entry. This trellis leads to an "entrance tunnel" of cool air and a wall of diffuse blue light. The tunnel dips down, then rises to propel visitors into a futuristic, five-story "crystal canyon" atrium of glass and sunlight. At the heart of this light well you will find a black reflecting pool, with three glazed elevators and a grand sculptural staircase rising out of it. This atrium is lighted by nine computer-driven, tracking skylights that animate the library with "light art" from dawn to dusk.

The most dramatic space in this dramatic building is the great reading room that fills the highest floor, where the unique "tensigrity" roof is completely exposed to view. The roof is supported by cables strung on columns that rise through the building. These "candle columns" almost touch rooftop skylights, creating a circle of open space where you expect to see solid support. The open feeling is intensified by six-inch-wide skylights along two walls of the ingenious floating roof.

At dusk the building provides high desert theater—its copper, steel and glass start to smolder at dusk, and the mechanical equipment invisible by day appears in a ghostly interior nightlight.

The library is open daily, except major holidays. Tours are hosted by special request. For visitor information, call (602) 262-4636.

A ldo Rossi's first American buildings were also the first of a brand new Disney city, called Celebration, which the company constructed near the Disney World theme park in Orlando.

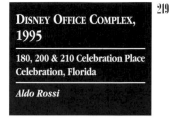

DISNEY OFFICE COMPLEX, 1995

180, 200 & 210 Celebration Place
Celebration, Florida

Aldo Rossi

Rossi certainly got Celebration off to a festive start, with his colorful structures of red and ochre, green and white, and a patina-green-roofed folly. (Anyone familiar with the 1990 Pritzker Prize winner's felicitous beach cabanas and flying pennants will be tempted to paint them into the scene.) But these are not theme buildings; they are serious, meant to be urban focal points for this city-in-the-making.

Rossi envisioned a formal town square arrangement of three buildings fronting a green grass plaza on a site rising two feet above grade. A three-story folly and pylon marker on the grounds enliven the plan's severity and recall the statues and monuments that typically grace city squares. Rows of trees frame the buildings, buffer the parking, and also add life to the plan. The three buildings—a nine-story tower, a four-story lowrise, and a six-story lowrise—will anchor a thirty-acre, 400,000-square-foot complex of offices for themselves and others.

Rossi's indelible mix of classical and industrial motifs—the cathedral and the factory—appear here as well. The tall building's three towers seem churchlike in front, while its gridded green glass curtain walls say factory on the sides. These towers also convey urban density: their windows line up to peer into each other. The four-story building looks less dense. Lower, longer, and more subdued, this building alternates white precast panels with glass curtain wall.

Signature Rossi themes also dominate the public spaces inside the structures. A dramatic domed rotunda is the pulse point of the tall building's interior, which visitors enter via a series of barrel-vaulted passages. Luxurious corridor walls alternate honed red sandstone panels with panels of cherry wood framed by brushed stainless steel. In the four-story building, a lovely light-filled atrium sparks up the interior.

Thanks to Disney president Michael Eisner's appreciation of architecture, Celebration showcases works by distinguished architects like Michael Graves, Cesar Pelli, Cooper Robertson Partners, Moore/Andersson, Graham Gund, William Rawn, Dreamer + Phillips, and Robert A. M. Stern. Sad to say, Rossi's untimely death in 1997 cut short his respected career.

The Disney Office Complex, located south of Highway 192 and I-4, is open during normal weekday office hours. Arata Isozaki's Team Disney headquarters and Michael Graves' Dolphin & Swan Hotel are nearby. For information, call (407) 566-1200.

YANCEY CHAPEL, 1995

Rural Route 17
Greensboro, Alabama

Auburn University's Rural
Studio
Samuel Mockbee, Director

Yancey Chapel is the work of graduate students who are learning architecture in a way that could never be duplicated in school: they are living it. At the Rural Studio, a dilapidated antebellum mansion about three hours from campus, the students resided and worked with Auburn professor Samuel Mockbee, creator of this unique architectural outreach. The architects-to-be put themselves at the service of local residents, many of whom are needy, and most of whom have never seen an architect in their lives. The students assume responsibility for everything. They meet with "clients," design the structures, and construct their designs as best they can, with no money and scavenged materials. In essence, the students are making arresting architecture with their own hands, using junk.

At Yancey Chapel, used automobile tires—over 1,000 of them donated by a man under court order to clear his land—became the building blocks for the little open-air chapel. The tires were filled with earth excavated from the site, stacked like bricks, and coated with cement-based stucco painted light beige. This gives the walls a staggered, bubble effect that is admittedly curious but also remarkably solid. The rough-hewn chapel is also unexpectedly spiritual.

The students' ingenuity in finding and using recycled materials is evident throughout the chapel, which holds about sixty. Heart Pine barn beams a hundred years old frame the ridge beam roof structure reminiscent of Thorncrown. Rustic recycled tin, cut into shingles, covers the roof except for the centerline, which remains open. The lectern and holy water font were cut from a large steel I-beam abandoned by its owner. "We used whatever we could get our hands on," says one of the students. "We had an initial concept in our heads, but it happens as it happens."

"How something built with such crude recyclable materials could be so elegant, that's what stuns me about this," Mockbee remarked.

The magical quality of the hilly pasture site is also treated as a "found object." Visitors approach the chapel by first treading down a slight incline before walking up to the chapel proper, and onto a cantilevered deck high above ground. The design captures a scenic view of the woods at the pasture's edge.

The Rural Studio program continues despite the untimely death of its founder. For visitor information, call Auburn's Architecture School at (334) 844-5426.

An upstart architecture has established its credibility in a major American city. Using metal to build houses rather than warehouses, Cameron Armstrong and others are taking up where Buckminster Fuller's Dymaxion House and Albert Frey's Aluminaire left off. This time, the gleaming silver structures have proven too practical to be deemed experimental, even though they clearly defy residential conventions with their industrial motif.

ARMSTRONG RESIDENCE, 1993

5423 Gibson Street
Houston, Texas

Cameron Armstrong

And yet, Armstrong's metal house does not look like a machine shop for living. "I am not interested in alluding to the esthetic of industrial architecture," says Armstrong, whose fascination with the material dates to his graduate student days at Yale. "I am interested in the values of utility and durability it expresses, and with what I see as metal's extravagant beauty."

Armstrong's house is predicated on a complete rethinking of what constitutes a desirable residence in this subtropical town. In the city's sweltering heat and humidity, traditional building materials fail significantly: brick is hard to cool; stucco grows moldy; wood quickly rots. In contrast, a building constructed with aluminum-coated steel panels, will reflect heat, cool rapidly, and require no maintenance. The architect uses standard metal siding, attached to a wooden frame with screws. An air space and insulation fill the gap between exterior and interior walls, which are gypsum. The practicality of metal construction is enhanced by Armstrong's economical glazing: all the main windows are sliding glass doors.

In Armstrong's eyes, the value of metal's practicality, impressive as it is, lies in design objectives it enables him to achieve. In his 2,450-square-foot house, he created a simple shed shape on the outside that harbors an intriguing two-level interior animated by planes of light and shadow. His plan is a plan of volumes, with large open rooms that spiral around a staircase like a nautilus, creating sensations of expansion and elevation. The downstairs rooms open onto gardens, while the upper-level bedrooms are oriented toward sky views. Pristine white walls present an ideal background for displaying art throughout the house.

About 300 metal houses now exist in Houston. The largest concentration, including Armstrong's house, is in the West End (bounded by Memorial Drive, Washington Avenue, Shepherd/Durham, and Westcott). Because the city lacks zoning, this 100-year-old inner-city neighborhood still retains aged industrial metal structures mixed with bungalows and businesses. The lustrous new metal beacons add a contemporary layer that fits in even as it stands out.

The Armstrong house is a private residence, and visits are permitted by appointment only. For information, call (713) 398-5207.

BANNER BUILDING, 1994

80 Vine Street
Seattle, Washington

Weinstein Copeland

The trend of converting old industrial buildings for residential use reaches its logical conclusion in the Banner Building, where new loft spaces have been constructed to recall those gritty old structures, without the grit. With its combined live-work interiors, the Banner Building also captures a more recent trend, the increasing preference of city dwellers to live and work in the same place.

This condominium residence was conceived by artists for artists. The breakthrough idea, unlikely but effective, was to emulate commercial developers by constructing only raw residential space, with no interior buildout. Costs could be contained, and artists would appreciate having the flexibility to design their own spaces. And although the bare bones interiors might still have seemed a little dispiriting—just glass exterior walls, concrete-slab floors, and gypsum inner walls with electricals and plumbing—the compensations included extravagant Puget Sound views and great light.

To make the artists' lofts commercially viable, Weinstein Copeland organized a three-part solution: a 10-story condominium tower; a retail/commercial base with parking beneath the highrise; and a separate low-rise rental building. The tower, constructed of poured concrete, glass, and steel, offers fourteen studio lofts with 1,800 to 2,400 square feet on two levels. The curved-

roof rental structure, clad in corrugated metal, has six apartments, fully finished. To encourage community, a shared rooftop terrace garden links the buildings and provides a communal gathering space.

"We had to be rigorously economical, designing away the complications and accepting many limitations," Edward Weinstein recalls. Building with inexpensive materials helped control costs and, coincidentally, gives the building an industrial character that suits its Belltown neighborhood north of downtown.

The prospect of future exterior embellishment by the artist/residents was intentionally factored in. Outdoor hallways in the tower residences, called streets in the sky, are eight feet wide, giving artists lots of room to decorate their doorways. At street level, large concrete panels on building's south base are considered a mural-in-waiting.

The Banner Building is named for Bannerworks, an architectural sculpture studio owned by Koryn Rolstad, the project's artistic instigator. The residences are private, and visits are permitted by appointment only. For information, call Koryn Rolstad at (206) 443-1824.

Wendell Burnette visualizes his house as a Band-aid, meant to seal the gash of an abandoned roadbed running through the site. A long, narrow strip of a place, with a small courtyard situated between two living/working areas, the concrete-block design does indeed have a Band-aid's shape. But the effect is not clinical. Its spare elegance is a perfect match for the spareness and drama of the surrounding Sonoran desert. In Burnette's hands,

BURNETTE HOUSE & STUDIO, 1995

9830 North 17th Street
Sunnyslope (Phoenix), Arizona

Wendell Burnette

223

concrete block becomes an inspired residential material, a feat rarely seen since Frank Lloyd Wright's patterned textile blocks in the 1920s.

Like Wright, Burnette is an architectural independent. Just out of high school, he spent three years at Taliesen West, steeping in Frank Lloyd Wright's famously innovative traditions. Then, he traveled extensively to study great architecture first hand. He completed his self-education on the job with Will Bruder, another independent-minded Phoenix architect.

In building this home and studio, Burnette remains very much his own man: architect, client, and contractor. His starting point—a quarter-acre site in a dense neighborhood of ranch-style homes—presented unattractive immediate surroundings but spectacular distant mountain views. Burnette's design focuses on this view, turning the 1,160-square-foot house into a seemingly isolated outpost in the desert. View-mastering begins on arrival, as visitors drive right in to the carport beneath the living area. From there, the progression leads to an internal garden court, open to the sky. A series of layered steel platforms lifts up past a small pool and into the loftlike interiors.

Burnette's Band-aid analogy accurately describes both his plan and his elevation. The long, narrow house (92 x 16 feet) has walls consisting of tall, narrow strips of concrete block alternating with tall, narrow strips of glass. Burnette adjusts the panels' dimensions to frame specific views and modulate the fierce desert sun. They are eight feet wide on the south side, but only four on the north. These interval walls create intriguing light plays throughout the interior. They also make moving through the house an experience in percussion: the mountains appear through the strips of glass, only to vanish from view and then reappear repeatedly.

"I believe in doing a lot with a little," Burnette explains. The interior walls exemplify this philosophy. These panels originated as roof-slab formwork, subsequently overlaid with plywood supported by a cable-stay system. The plywood was burnished to resemble well-tanned leather.

The house is a private residence, and visits are permitted by appointment only. For information, call (602) 395-1091.

MUSEUM OF CONTEMPORARY ART, 1996

220 East Chicago Avenue
Chicago, Illinois

Josef Paul Kleihues

For one of America's liveliest contemporary art museums, German architect Josef Paul Kleihues designed a building based on a cherished classical ideal: he put art back on a pedestal.

The "fall" of art, in case you missed it, occurred in New York City in 1939 at the Museum of Modern Art. The then-new museum's front doors opened brazenly onto the sidewalk—making art easily accessible to anyone. Recapturing the high ground, Kleihues positioned a processional central staircase as a dominant feature of his Chicago design. It gently but unmistakably elevates visitors up to the art. "To have the galleries for art begin on the second floor," the architect said, "that means something."

Kleihues's classical approach honored a magnificent site: a full city block, with Michigan Avenue on one side and Lake Michigan on the other. The site also suggested the building's formal symmetrical organization—a square, four-story structure surrounding a glass-walled atrium at its core. Running from front to back, the atrium supplies what Kleihues called the "missing link" between the city and the water. He aligned the outdoor stair with the atrium, emphasizing the importance of the axial connection. A pair of matching plinths, designed to hold statues, brackets the stairway. A limestone base continues the classical theme. Then, changing to present tense, Kleihues topped the limestone base with a façade of cast aluminum cut into modular panels

affixed with polished steel pins that glisten in the sun.

After the formal, even somber exterior, the transcendent space and light inside come as a welcome surprise. In the main atrium, glass walls soar four stories.

In the galleries, Kleihues respected the art—and the viewers—by offering the privilege of concentration. There are

no bustling ramps or fancy escalators to distract your attention. Circulation and services are tucked to the sides to preserve isolation in the galleries. Temporary exhibitions are mounted on the main level. The permanent collection fills the upper galleries, which are housed in two-level spaces capped by barrel-vaulted ceilings. Throughout the interior, open spaces like the atrium are juxtaposed with cloistered gallery areas to keep architectural interest alive.

"I wanted to come back to the straight and strong image of the Chicago building," Kleihues said. Using an approach that was rational but also poetic, he followed the lead of another German architect, Mies van der Rohe, in recapturing Chicago's modernist spirit. (Incidentally, Mies lived in the apartment house across the street on East Pearson.)

Museum hours are Tuesday 10:00 AM to 8:00 PM; Wednesday to Sunday 10:00 AM to 5:00 PM; closed Mondays, Thanksgiving, Christmas, and New Year's Day. For information, call (312) 280-2660.

N eoclassical architecture is certainly not new in Virginia. In Charlottesville, Thomas Jefferson's white-columned University of Virginia campus offers one of America's great architectural history lessons. Coming full circle, the Darden School of Business Administration brings another classic revival to these grounds. The designer, appropriately, is Robert A. M. Stern, the most prolific proponent of classicism at this time.

DARDEN GRADUATE SCHOOL OF BUSINESS ADMINISTRATION, 1996

University of Virginia
100 Darden Boulevard
Charlottesville, Virginia

Robert A. M. Stern
with Ayers Saint Gross

While much of the New York City architect's historical expertise is expressed in residential work for the out-of-sight rich, the business school is a visible victory in the war against modernism. The modernist challengers (including Stern) have been around for decades, of course. But by the mid-1990s, the classical tradition was on the rise in some academic circles. The Darden School therefore finds itself poised at the intersection of the last Golden Age and a re-emerging one.

The Darden School is designed as a campus within the campus. It follows Jefferson's "academic village" model, mirroring the traditional scale, character, and materials. There are white painted columns, arched porticos of red brick, herringbone brick walkways, even an outdoor clock. Laid out in the classical manner, the school defines an academic quadrangle overlooking a luxuriant green lawn. The main gathering spot, the Commons Building, stands at the center atop a hill on a 20-acre site. It is flanked by a faculty building and a classroom hall. Like Jefferson's buildings, these are separated by small open garden plots and linked by columned arcades.

Stern introduces his 200,000-square-foot campus with a "gatehouse," a 60-room addition to an executive residence that marks the entry and directs the visitor's gaze up the hill toward the Commons Building. Traditional landscaping offers the most natural setting for the design, and Stern employs it. A broad, tree-lined boulevard leads up the hill to a motor court. The driveways, however, are a giveaway. Here, the modern age clearly intrudes upon Jefferson's academic village model. Stern's school is designed to accommodate visitors arriving on four wheels, rather than on foot or on horseback.

The architect's expertise at upscale housing is on exhibit in the fine residential-quality details of the interiors. The color palette in the public rooms of the Commons Building is especially admirable, with mellow yellows, blues, and greens iced with fluorescent white trim.

The Darden School of Business Administration buildings are open, and visitors can tour the public spaces (except faculty offices and classrooms in use). Advance notice is requested for group visits. Those in the mood for modernism can visit the nearby Hereford College (formerly the New College) by Tod Williams and Billie Tsien. For Darden School information, call (434) 924-3900.

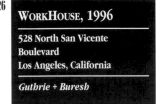

WorkHouse, 1996

528 North San Vicente
Boulevard
Los Angeles, California

Guthrie + Buresh

Its name, WorkHouse, says it all. This studio-residence combines business space for the architects, Danelle Guthrie and Tom Buresh, and a dwelling for their family. At first glance, the townhouse-style scale and massing make the building seem more "house" than "work," especially with its streetside studio windows flung open wide. But the economy of materials and construction call to mind commerce.

The distinction between home and office purposefully overlaps in the WorkHouse, as well as in its surrounding West Hollywood setting, where an unsorted neighborhood allowed the architects to experiment in building a unified live/work world.

The integrated life looks increasingly attractive to many Americans who have the technology and the desire to live and work on their own. But going back to an older tradition—living above the store, so to speak—is easier said than done. The architectural difficulty involves merging polar opposites: the public, productive business environment with the quiet private realm. Guthrie + Buresh's WorkHouse exuberantly shows a way to accommodate commercial realities without leaving home.

Their creative solution (included in the provocative 1999 "Un-Private House" exhibition at the Museum of Modern Art in New York City) is to pull apart the living and working spaces so that they occupy separate volumes arrayed on staggered floors. An autonomous 600-square-foot studio is pushed toward the street on the second level above a carport, with living spaces layered on three levels behind it. A living room and kitchen take up the ground floor, the couple's son's bedroom occupies the second level, and the master bedroom and roof deck fill the top floor. A stairwell, screened with slatted wood, occupies the central space of the 1,800-square-foot interior.

It provides the necessary neutral zone, with home and office facing each other across the open space like friendly relatives. Virtually every interior surface is covered in plywood, and this simplicity of materials lends a soothing neutrality.

"The office feels like an office, and home feels like a home," Danelle Guthrie observed.

Too-close-for-comfort views are veiled with particular ingenuity. Translucent polycarbonate covers the long side walls, letting in light without sacrificing privacy. The extruded hollow-core panels are

mounted in a wood-framed grid resembling shoji screens. Front and rear walls are stucco and glass. In the brilliant L.A. sun, the translucent panels create an astonishing interior illumination, soft yet bright. "The house is like a big lantern, always glowing," Danelle Guthrie said. "In the daytime it glows on the inside, and it glows on the outside at night."

The WorkHouse is private.

The Carlson-Reges House could have easily disappeared into the industrial landscape that surrounds it. There are overhead power lines coursing past its top floor, railway freight cars clanging by at ground level, and a 1915 electric power generating plant as its base. Instead, it is one of Los Angeles' most avant-garde houses and a marker for the newly energized Brewery neighborhood north of downtown. RoTo architects Michael Rotondi and Clark Stevens transformed the industrial esthetic into an architectural landmark.

CARLSON-REGES HOUSE
1996

698 Moulton Avenue
Los Angeles, California

RoTo

The brazen new asymmetrical structure strides across the old, symmetrical power station like plate tectonics in action, wrapping the old building in a protective metal armored shell. The component parts—a combination of new, off-the-shelf materials and recycled industrial items—have been assembled as an abstraction of the industrial site. The most dramatic element of the design—the vertical metal carapace mounted on steel beams—acts as a shield that muffles noises and fumes.

"We wanted to open up to this landscape," Clark Stevens said, "without being exposed." The architects anchored the house to the larger landscape by drawing sight lines that connect it to the tallest downtown office tower, Mount Baldy, and Dodger Stadium.

Because the old power station could bear no more weight, the new work is suspended above and within it. The original 36-foot-tall first-floor power station has been reconfigured, with lower ceilings, as studio space for the owner. A second-story living/dining area and third-level master bedroom have been inserted from above. This new upper volume is created by two extensions of the roof, which drop down into the interior.

The complex geometry that governs this house looks tightly anchored on the outside, but it becomes more expansive indoors. Exposed trusses and pipes draw a series of radiating lines that link the two new interior levels. These interior lines are further extended to define the landings and terraces. A massive fireplace in the living room makes the hearth a solid center of the fluid open space.

The industrial esthetic is surprisingly domestic without going soft. In the master bedroom, for instance, the corrugated metal roof is left exposed, and its fluted underside looks right at home. A lap pool, made of old oil drums, brings the natural enchantment of water to the master bedroom terrace. An especially welcome characteristic of the design is the way light moves through the house; it scales the space as the day progresses.

The Carlson-Reges house is a private residence.

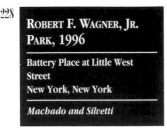

ROBERT F. WAGNER, JR. PARK, 1996

Battery Place at Little West Street
New York, New York

Machado and Silvetti

If in years to come the champions of a vigorous public realm regain the upper hand, Wagner Park may be considered a turning point. This idyllic enclave choreographs an experience of nature to soothe a city dweller's soul: the luxury of wide open space, bountiful gardens, a spectacular water view, and an intriguing set of elevated pavilions from which to appreciate the expansive scene. It is encouraging to see that a public agency, Battery Park City Authority, has brought private-level quality back to the public domain.

The building, landscape, and gardens here are outstanding individually, as well as in their harmonious relationships. The happy confluence springs from a collaboration of acclaimed professionals: Boston-based architects Machado and Silvetti; the landscape architects, Olin Partnership; and garden designer, Lynden B. Miller. A trump card came with the site—reach-out-and-touch-it views of the Statue of Liberty just offshore—and the team made this view the focus of their interlocking design.

The 3.5-acre park resembles an arrowhead aimed offshore. The broad, city-side space along curving Little West Street is the main entry. From here, a pair of allées guide visitors serenely into the park's architectural center, Machado and Silvetti's arresting pavilions. A contemporary rendition of an ancient ruin, this brick bastion consists of two hefty structures spanned by an overhead beam. The resulting breezeway frames the Statue of Liberty at ground level. For elevated views, grand staircases on the city side lead to platforms with benches. These wide staircases also create an informal amphitheater for public performances.

On the water side, the buildings' asymmetrical "eyebrow" arches suggest a human face. They arc over the building's public spaces, a lower-level cafe and restrooms. Reddish Roman brick

clads the concrete structures. Laid in multiple patterns, the brickwork animates the flat walls and arches so they shimmer in the light off the water. Between the pavilions and the water's edge, a sweeping grass-covered terrace ringed with benches offers a serene space to contemplate the historically meaningful view.

Scale was the central problem posed by the site.

"The idea was to make it massive," Rodolpho Machado related in *Architectural Record*. "We had to deal with the monumental scale of the Hudson River and the World Trade Center. The small pavilions had to look bigger than they really are . . . without overpowering people in the park."

The park grounds are open daily. Statue of Liberty tour boats leave just north of the park.

Authenticity is elusive in architecture, but Convent Avenue Studios is one sure place to find it. The four structures, built of rammed earth, are satisfyingly solid; their 18-inch-thick walls offer a visceral experience of mass. This evocative massiveness is balanced by fine-grained sensory details—the crackling of gravel underfoot in the courtyard, the water gurgling in a fountain, the light dappling beneath mesquite trees, the scent of the rammed earth, the cool shade in contrast to overheated streets.

CONVENT AVENUE STUDIOS, 1996

469 South Convent Avenue
Tucson, Arizona

Rick Joy

The studios are located in Barrio Historico, a historic Tucson neighborhood south of downtown. Three new houses have been inserted into a long, narrow site, staggered to allow individual courtyards. An additional casita was created from an abandoned structure on the property. Upholding tradition, the studios are set behind a tall adobe wall, another survivor of earlier days. Now restored and painted white, this freestanding wall is cut with openings that lend an air of mystery by partially hiding the houses from view.

"We decided to build simple and humble structures of earthen materials in much the same way the original settlers built, while also being true to our time," said Joy. The new houses, like the lot, are long and narrow. Their rough, striated walls resemble geologic strata, for they lay bare the process of their construction. A specially blended soil mixture, with red pigment added for color, was poured into standard concrete slip forms in ten-inch lifts, compacted to five inches. The walls were set on spread footings and imbedded with custom structural steel components; openings for doors and windows were inserted between the forms. Roofs of corrugated cold rolled steel are rusting naturally, showing their streaks. Joy acts as his own contractor, and he builds for the ages: each new structure weighs 180 tons.

Despite their massiveness, the studios are designed to provide subtle light modulation in airy, loftlike interiors. "Light is almost a building material here," Joy explained.

Wedge-shaped in plan, the 1,000-square-foot studios have a narrow kitchen that expands to a large living/dining area. A bedroom/bath mezzanine is inserted above the kitchen. The shed-roofed studios also have wedge-shaped elevations, rising to 22 feet on the kitchen/bedroom end, sloping to 14 feet in the living room. Doors, ceilings, and windows are made of rough-sawn Douglas fir. Outside, a chartreuse-painted wall directs visitors through the complex. This wall and rusty corrugated metal fences enclose private courtyards with natural landscaping.

The studios are private residences. Rick Joy's office, a more austere example of his architectural style, is located behind the studios at 400 South Rubio Avenue. For information, call (520) 624-1442.

AITKEN SEA BIRD AVIARY, 1997

Bronx Zoo
Fordham Road at Bronx River Parkway
Bronx, New York

FTL Happold

The progression of architecture from mass to membrane finds FTL Happold at the cutting edge. The gossamer tensile structure they designed for the Aitken Sea Bird Aviary verges on the invisible: fine cable net hung from arcs of steel tubing anchored to a low concrete base. "It's hard to compete with nature," said Nicholas Goldsmith, an FTL Happold founder. "Here the structure is really the sky."

The aviary has a twofold purpose: to contain the zoo's exotic South American sea birds and to protect them from outside predators. The creation of a natural-seeming environment called for an ephemeral space that had to be built on the base of the old aviary. The new structure also had to be strong, for the aviary's predecessor had collapsed under heavy snow.

To achieve strength and lightness in the 30,000-square-foot structure, the architects combined architecture and engineering. They considered the building's shape to be the most likely source of strength, and the shape would be found in the most efficient use of materials. Like Louis Kahn's asking what the brick wants to be, FTL Happold questioned what steel tubing wanted to be in its lightest, strongest incarnation. The answer came from a series of catenary investigations

in which the designers hung weighted chains from forms and inverted the results. These experiments showed that parallel arches would be wasteful in spanning the existing 70-foot-wide base. But by offsetting the arches they could get needed strength with less tubing, thereby reducing the weight.

Seven arches, soaring 90 feet, support the structure. They spring individually from a base on one side and overlap on the other. This offset skews the three-dimensional shape, which is symmetrical in plan but asymmetrical in volume. Hot-galvanized, 12-inch steel tubing is hung with extremely fine (1/25th of an inch) stainless steel strand. Handwoven to the architects' specifications into a seamless one-inch grid, the mesh attaches beneath the tubing on a ring-and-tether system designed by the architects. The net acts in concert with the supporting arches to achieve a rigid structural system. In the end, the architects had designed a new material, a new technique to build with, and a new esthetic in keeping with the technology of their design.

The gauzy aviary allows birds (and humans) to feel free and unfettered in the enclosed garden. The birds must feel very much at home with FTL Happold's work. The population of newborns has surged in the new aviary, giving an especially strong testament to the design's true harmony with nature.

The aviary is located in the zoo's northwest corner. The Bronx Zoo is open 365 days, from 10:00 AM to 5:00 PM weekdays, and to 5:30 PM weekends and holidays, except for November–March, when closing is 4:30 PM all days. The zoo is accessible by car (parking available), bus, subway, and Metro-North trains. For information and directions, call (718) 367-1010.

For artists in every field, the creative process has been likened to a trip through the wilderness that culminates in eventful discovery. The design of the Atlantic Center for the Arts, an artist-in-residence and outreach program, expresses this process perfectly.

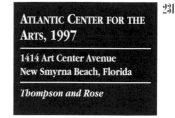

ATLANTIC CENTER FOR THE ARTS, 1997

1414 Art Center Avenue
New Smyrna Beach, Florida

Thompson and Rose

It begins with a dirt road through the Florida brush and leads to an artistic utopia—a sophisticated little village where artists can concentrate on their individual aspirations while benefiting from cross-fertilization with other disciplines. There are five separate studios—theater, dance, sculpture, painting, and music, plus a library—and they are interwoven in the dense landscape of palmetto, scrub oak, and pine. The studios, which are meant to resemble clearings in the jungle, are linked by a raised wooden boardwalk shaped like a slightly twisted arc. The boardwalk itself mimics the artistic process, presenting interludes of mystery alternating with bursts of revelation. The walkway widens in places to provide informal gathering spots where artists can meet.

Artists arriving for their residencies are astounded to find that buildings of such quality and sensitivity have been designed just for them. The painting studio plays to the light, with wood louvers and large light monitors. The music room offers an enclosed cedar-lined space with high ceilings for an uplifting feeling. In the dance workshop, sandblasted windows at the ceiling and clear ones at the floor make dancers feel suspended in space. The sculpture studio sits on a battered concrete base, reflecting sculpture's origins in the earth. The theater is a "black box" that aids the suspension of belief, with a glass lobby that is open and welcoming. The library, set away from the other buildings, affords an island of calm.

The center's structures have a powerful effect in their entirety, even though the individual buildings are strikingly simple. The clean-lined studios are clad in stained cedar, which complements the surroundings; the angled roofs are lead-coated copper. All the buildings on the 67-acre site, except the sculpture studio, are raised on pilings. The strong Florida sun is allowed to filter through the foliage, and into the buildings by means of louvers and glass walls. The design also accommodates occasional environmental assaults, like hurricanes and torrential rains, with special bracing, wind scoops, and linear rain scuppers.

The three-week residency programs pair master artists with those in mid-career. Individual artists may also visit for independent sabbaticals. The center hosts public exhibitions, concerts, and talks. Visitors are welcome (respecting the artists' privacy); tours are available with advance notice. The center is located near Daytona off U.S. 1; turn north on Art Center Avenue about 1 1/2 miles north of the airport. For information, call (386) 427-6975.

Avisit to the galleries of Atlanta's High Museum, where Scogin Elam and Bray designed the installation for the permanent collection, conveys how it feels to be in this house—all movement so effortlessly choreographed it's like gliding. The rooms of the house dissolve into a series of spaces that Mack Scogin refers to as "situations." The few interior walls exist as pure planes, as in the museum displays. The furnishings underscore the exhibit-like quality. In the almost-bare interiors, practically every piece of furniture is a work of art.

From the street, the Wakefield house also resembles a gallery. Its main façade consists of a concrete shell inset with large glass panels. The clear glass on the first floor reveals the interior with astonishing candor, since the residence sits near the street, across from a busy but beautiful neighborhood park. (Its inspired transparency was also displayed in the "Un-Private House" exhibition at the Museum of Modern Art in New York City in 1999.) The upper level is more private. A low balcony wall of opaque glass spans the front of the house; it shields the bedroom, the lap pool beside it, and an outdoor terrace.

The pool desired by the owners became the design's organizing principle. The new house had to follow the outline of their former dwelling, which was damaged by hurricane, so the architects decided to raise the pool to the second story. This inspired innovation not only solved the spatial dilemma but also allowed the architects to design the pool as yet another art object in a gallery-like house. The long, narrow pool seems to float between the clear-glass-walled bedroom and the frosted-glass balcony wall. Perched in the treetops, the bedroom and pool levitate together in a leafy paradise.

The see-through house is a bold exception in Brookwood, an idyllic enclave of traditional brick houses, gently winding streets, and luxuriant trees. Even though the house is constructed of

industrial materials—glass, concrete, and steel—it is surprisingly compatible. The new house respects the setbacks and scale of the neighborhood, and grand old trees lining the street go a long way toward establishing continuity.

Behind the 3,600–square-foot house, the property is bounded by a studio and a guesthouse. These structures make a triangular courtyard of the old backyard, which springs to life every summer as the owners' personal watermelon patch.

The Brookwood section of Atlanta is located in "midtown," off Peachtree Road and Brighton, about two miles from Richard Meier's High Museum. The house is a private residence, and visits are by appointment only. For information, call (404) 525-6869.

The Getty Center gives new meaning to the term "art world." Richard Meier's travertine-clad art acropolis resembles a self-contained city-state glowing on a mountaintop. Even from the freeway far below, it looks immense, and half the space is buried underground.

THE GETTY CENTER, 1997

1200 Getty Center Drive
Los Angeles, California

Richard Meier

The Getty's artistic universe includes all facets of art exhibition: museum, conservation, research, education, grants, and management. Each entity is housed in a separate structure. Almost a million square feet of buildings are spread across 110 acres. It's an awesome experience of scale—big scale—an experience further heightened by the cinemascopic views of the city and the sea. Conversely, this is also a place to see a great variety of design and detail. As a museum official wryly notes, "no thousand square feet are the same as any other thousand square feet." In all its grandeur, after 13 years and a billion-dollar budget, The Getty Center is a monumental public place.

Richard Meier mastered this enormous commission by dividing and conquering. He breaks the center into its six component parts and arranges the individual buildings around a central

entrance court. The museum proper consists of two-story pavilions separated by gardens. It's a pleasure to move between the gallery and garden spaces, relieving impending museum fatigue.

Meier achieves continuity with the exterior cladding, an off-white travertine, left rough cut, that covers most of the buildings. The architect was prohibited by contract from creating one of his signature all-white metal buildings; nevertheless, he clad some walls in enameled aluminum panels, but in off-white.

Meier has designed extremely elegant galleries: rooms rather than open-plan exhibition spaces, illuminated with natural light coming in from above. There is, however, a jarring disruption of Meier's crisp purity in the picture galleries. They are decorated in 18th-century French style by the architect Thierry Despont, who asserts that his style is more compatible with the traditional art.

Given the Getty's formidable mass and aloof siting, it could easily have appeared impenetrable and forbidding. Meier's complex geometry redeems it, as does artist Robert Irwin's vividly colored garden.

A visit to the Getty requires advance planning, for this "billion dollar art theme park" has been overwhelmed by crowds. You must have parking reservations (which may take months) or get dropped off at the tram that runs up the hill. Los Angeles Bus #515 and Santa Monica's "Big Blue Bus" #14 will take you there. The museum is open Tuesday to Thursday, 10:00 AM to 6:00 PM; Friday and Saturday 10:00 AM to 9:00 PM; and Sunday 10:00 AM to 6:00 PM; closed Mondays and major holidays. For reservations and information, call (310) 440-7300.

PATTERSON RESIDENCE, 1997

**1196 Sandpiper Point
Counce, Tennessee**

Mockbee Coker

Two southern architects, Samuel Mockbee and Coleman Coker, designed this house that is rooted in the land. The lively mysteries of their native culture—the presence of the past, the myth-making tradition, the freighted relation to the "outside" world—influenced them as much as the physical factors. Architectural relics such as tin roofs and noble chimneys often appear as poignant links in their cultural chain. But the architects were clearly not New Urbanists reworking recognizable features in a nostalgic vein. As the Patterson house shows, these nationally recognized architects were investing the south's time-honored forms with new twists.

A sense of place grounds the house from the outside. In fact, the design seems integral with the site as it steps down the bank toward the Tennessee River 120 feet below. At the carport entry, a cluster of red-brown sculptural steel beams mimics an armful of branches gathered from

nearby woods. Exterior brickwork also connects the house with the land. Earth-colored long bond is laid with short ends projecting randomly; this creates an irregular surface pattern that blends so naturally it could almost be camouflage. The galvalume roof and sculpted chimney stand out above all, the most obvious southern architectural touchstones in contemporary guise.

The rooted sense of place is nicely balanced by forces of movement. On the outside, the carport roof soars like a bird's wing away from the river; the house's roofline skips along in the other direction, at first horizontal and shedlike, then dipping down like a ship's prow above the water.

Inside, the 3,200-square-foot vacation retreat starts low and ends high. Paradoxically, the lowest part of the house occupies the highest part of the property. The entry is a 60-foot-long corridor that doubles as a gallery for the owners, who are art collectors. At the door, the ceiling height is seven feet, rising to 30 feet in the main living area overlooking the river. In a process the owners describe as "unfolding," the gallery descends in stages toward the living areas. Splayed walls break up the long linear gallery space, which has exposed crossed beams overhead; these splayed spaces also allow separated areas for displaying artwork. Among the interior levels, bedrooms occupy the first floor, the living/dining area is on the second floor, and a study sits on top.

The house captures a magical light, especially in the living/dining area. Tall and open, it overlooks the water with a two-story window wall divided by Mondrian-like frames. Conversely, an adjacent low-ceiling inglenook with fireplace affords cozy seclusion.

The Patterson house is located just east of Shiloh National Park, where Tennessee, Mississippi, and Alabama converge. The house is a private residence, and visits are permitted by appointment only. For information, call Dr. James Patterson or Dr. Rushton Patterson at (901) 452-6152.

E very building tells a story and this one turns on international intrigue. It began in the late 1980s, when thieves pried two Byzantine religious frescoes from a tiny 13th-century church in Lysi, Cyprus. They cut the curved wall paintings—a dome and an apse—into thirty-eight fragments to sell off in pieces. Renowned Houston art patron Dominique de Menil learned about the frescoes, and, attracted by their rarity and quality, she worked out an innovative compromise to save them. Mrs. de Menil ransomed and restored the frescoes, vesting ownership in the Church of Cyprus, while creating a permanent repository in Houston. An accomplished builder of both chapels and museums (the Menil Museum, the adjacent Cy Twombly Museum, and the Rothko Chapel), she merged these two building types into a new setting for consecrated art, a chapel museum.

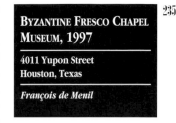

BYZANTINE FRESCO CHAPEL MUSEUM, 1997

4011 Yupon Street
Houston, Texas

François de Menil

New York City architect François de Menil gave form to his mother's idea. Designing sacred space posed a challenge in a secular world, as did the difficulty of transporting Byzantium to a modern American city. The architect considered replicating the ancient chapel, a shallow Greek-cross shape with barrel vaults.

Instead, he abstracted it as a ghostly apparition and set it within a darkly protective outer shell. The old chapel's gentle geometry is recreated with curved panels of opaque laminated glass. The frescoes, beautifully restored, are mounted into the new glass dome and apse, regaining their rightful orientation.

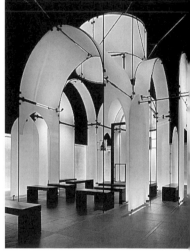

"Here, unlike conventional museums, you walk into the art," de Menil observed. The building and its reflection pool and garden are all designed to prepare you for this artistic and spiritual encounter.

The architect viewed the building as a reliquary box protecting treasured relics. Asserting this protective quality, he clad the 4,500-square-foot structure with rough-cut limestone and precast concrete. Inside, the plan unfolds in a "decompression promenade" in which the light steps down in stages. Visitors enter a naturally bright lobby overlooking a meditative garden and tranquil reflection pool. An antechamber follows, lighted by a clerestory, providing a transition zone and a chance to notice the pool's light reflecting on the inner chapel doors.

Within the chapel proper, the lighting culminates in a powerful effect. The little Lysi chapel recreation is illuminated so its pale green glass panels glow ethereally in a well of deep shadow. This inner chapel appears freestanding; the darkness obscures a tungsten-welded steel space frame tethering it to the outer shell. (The glass panels are held by metal clips to recall the frescoes' fragile past.) Charcoal slate floors and an inner shell of black steel plates serve to intensify the glass chapel's reverse silhouette. Perimeter skylights illuminate the upper walls with a halo of light that seems to radiate from another dimension.

Located one block from the Menil Museum, the Byzantine Fresco Chapel Museum is open Friday through Sunday from 11:00 AM to 6:00 PM. For information, call (713) 521-3990.

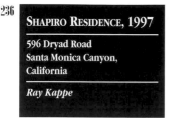

The timeline of modern architecture in Los Angeles runs through Ray Kappe's residential work from one end to the other. His earliest houses, in the mid-1950s, continue the groundedness of Frank Lloyd Wright's textile block constructions, leavened with the lightness of Neutra. Over the next four-plus decades, Kappe created an unwavering succession of modern houses. (He was also a founder of SCI-Arc, the innovative Los Angeles architecture school, in the 1960s). The Shapiro residence is the latest in his long career. Like the other houses, its cutting-edge quality is smoothed by an aura of timelessness. Still, the timing is fortuitous. The Shapiro house coincides with the emergence of a larger trend—the resurgence of interest in modern architecture, and in Los Angeles-style mid-century modernism in particular.

The Shapiro house, with its elegant, exposed steel frame and airy interlocking volumes, looks even more modern than most Kappe designs, which are built of wood. Here, the choice of minimal materials—steel, concrete, and glass—was dictated by the site. The property consists of a narrow slice of a steep hill that required stabilization. Kappe designed the steel-frame system to span the precipitous 43-foot slope in three giant steps; the poured concrete walls provide the required rigidity. By hanging the house on an overhead frame, the architect was able to create open interiors with treetop views. He further extended the interior space with outdoor terraces

that capitalize on Los Angeles's temperate paradise. The ocean-like colors—sandy white concrete walls, painted steel, and blue-green glass—also connect the house to its place.

The inside-out atmosphere of the 3,900-square-foot interior is a Kappe trademark. The interiors step snugly up the hill, and throughout the house the unadorned concrete walls and floors seem perfectly balanced with the warm light that filters

in through the glass. The sequence of walking through the spaces is designed to enhance this inside-out effect, and a series of stairs rises up through the house. A glass door at the sidewalk opens to the first set of stairs that leads to an entry court on the first level, which also includes a small bedroom and study. More stairs lead to the loftlike living/dining/kitchen area. Here, glass walls provide an almost invisible separation from a deck just outside; a formidable concrete wall on the other side has slender horizontal and vertical slit windows to control views and modulate the sun. The house culminates in a master bedroom suite with its own deck on the third level. A separate pool pavilion and garden occupies the site's highest point.

The Shapiro house is a private residence. In the neighborhood are 10 houses by Ray Kappe, including his own residence, completed in 1967, which is located at 715 Brooktree Road in Pacific Palisades.

The Chapel of St. Ignatius is a small Roman Catholic church with the emotional and architectural impact of a Gothic cathedral. This condensed intensity results from what Steven Holl called his urgent mission: using architecture to put essence back into life. He designs buildings that appeal to all five senses. In the chapel, he also incorporates "archaic echoes" of ancient religious structures that resonate mystically through this fascinating new kind of sacred space.

CHAPEL OF ST. IGNATIUS, 1997

**Seattle University
near 12th Avenue and Marion Street
Seattle, Washington**

Steven Holl

The visual sense is Holl's primary concern, and light becomes the design's central theme; the chapel's patron saint experienced God as light from above. Holl translates Ignatius's belief into seven "bottles of light." These quixotic little rooftop towers infuse the chapel's interior spaces with a profusion of colors. And yet, the exterior gives scant indication of the kaleidoscope waiting inside.

The entry is a transition zone of natural illumination. From there, haloes of clear light draw you in toward mysterious pools of red, blue, green, and gold light that define the interior spaces. Tinted lenses set in the rooftop tower "bottles," technically light monitors, produce the rainbow effects. The light is further enhanced by the monitors' inner surfaces, painted with the complementary color of each tower's skylight lens.

In contrast, a brilliant shard of white light illuminates the main altar and silhouettes a modern crucifix on an adjacent wall. By day, the interior colors have a velvety softness; the light monitors glow like cheerful beacons in the night.

Catholic churches have changed since Gothic times, and the chapel's 6,000-square-foot interior recognizes the liturgical advances of Vatican II. The altar, tabernacle, and sanctuary occupy separate spaces. The ambro, where scriptures are read, is located beside the altar. The choir loft also adjoins the altar, incorporating music and musicians into the Mass.

Holl's practical dexterity is impressive here, for he achieved his intricate, symbolic design with tilt-walled construction. Twenty-one concrete panels were poured into molds, hardened, and erected by crane, with windows formed in the interlocking spaces. The walls went up in a day.

Because this is a small building, Holl has said, "we could do every detail as you would in a home." Among these high-quality custom details: glass panels depicting St. Ignatius's life, a narthex rug designed by Holl, and handblown glass lanterns, also Holl-designed.

A serene lawn and reflection pool ease visitors into the spiritual realm; wild grasses and stones placed in the pool lend Zenlike tranquility. Still, the chapel's intense spirituality is countered by its uplifting contemporary appeal.

The chapel is open Monday to Thursday, 7:00 AM to 10:00 PM; Friday 10:00 AM to 7:00 PM; Saturday 9:00 AM to 5:00 PM; and Sunday 9:00 AM to 10:00 PM. For information, call (202) 296-6075.

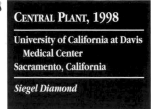

CENTRAL PLANT, 1998

**University of California at Davis
Medical Center
Sacramento, California**

Siegel Diamond

The energy processes that power our buildings are usually rendered invisible by design, but the Central Plant brings energy-making capacity into full view. As this power house shows, the massive equipment and extensive processes that produce electricity and supply heated and chilled water inspire considerable awe. It's been a long time since architects sought to express the wonders of industrial technology (Albert Kahn's Ford Glass Plant and Ohio Steel Foundry come to mind), and it is heartening to see this renewed respect.

The plant produces energy via an "energy cascade": a succession of steps in which high-pressure gas is forced through a series of massive jet turbine engines to produce electricity and superheated steam. The building's function is the basis of its form. The design not only facilitates the industrial processes; it showcases key pieces of equipment as beautiful objects within glazed "jewelry cases."

"We are creating and using energy all the time," says Kate Diamond, a firm principal. "People should be aware of what it takes to make this energy." To help evoke this awareness, the architects created a virtually transparent structure. Large expanses of glass form most walls of the two-story, 58,000-square-foot plant. In daylight, these walls look opaque. At night their translucent glow brilliantly acknowledges the energy being produced. The structural cross-bracing is dramatically backlighted behind the glass, reinforcing the jewel-box effect in the evening.

The interior is also designed to encourage viewing. Every major component—chillers, boilers, and cogeneration units—is on full display. In the lobby, the architects cut a hole in the floor to expose the three-foot-diameter water pipes below. The lobby's steel staircase with wire banisters leads to a second-floor mezzanine. This elevated platform lets visitors "walk through" all stages of the process taking place on the plant floor, from a safe distance.

Siegel Diamond's design respects its industrial predecessors. It draws, too, from the history of the site, a former state fairground filled with agricultural structures. "Barns and old sheds and industrial buildings; I like that combination," says Diamond.

The familiar materials of industrial and agricultural construction—glass, concrete block, and corrugated metal siding—are used with contemporary architectural sophistication. But the architects also include unexpected elements in their design. Flying buttresses arrayed along one outer wall recall Notre Dame. Clad in corrugated metal, the buttresses perform the structural task of transferring the heavy equipment loads. The plant's clock tower also lends an unexpected image. While it recalls the symbolism of old town squares, it too has an important structural purpose: releasing the last remaining vapors at the end of the energy stream.

Plant tours can be scheduled by request. For information, call (916) 734-8685.

C arlos Zapata has changed the face of an American supermarket with a space-age design. His gleaming façade—an angular aluminum pennant exploding from a rounded glass atrium—greets Miami Beach grocery shoppers with a pizzazz you won't find anywhere else.

The Zeppelin-like façade is more than just a compelling presentation. Its form derives logically from its function. The see-through bullnose-shaped atrium is actually a clever circulation system that encloses a vertical grand promenade: three stories of stairs and moving ramps that transport shoppers between the ground-floor market and the two parking levels above it. Seen from outside, the stream of shoppers further animates an already lively design. On the inside, the shoppers are traversing an elliptical course whose turning point opens up sweeping views.

The circulation system also presents a creative solution to a vexing problem. A supermarket's economic success requires a sizable store area served by generous parking—a tall order for this restrictive 1.92-acre site. Zapata met these basic requirements by stacking the parking levels on top of a 47,000-square-foot store and pulling his circulation system away from the building. The parking ramps atop the building are curved to complement the curving façade.

PUBLIX SUPERMARKET, 1998

1920 West Avenue
Miami Beach, Florida

Carlos Zapata
Wood & Zapata

While Zapata successfully changed the supermarket façade, he was not allowed to change any more. The architectural interest, sad to say, stops short of the store itself. Other, more traditional architects laid out the interiors in accordance with Publix's predictable parallel-aisle formula.

It is also unfortunate that Zapata's innovative design is unlikely to be repeated. The new façade proved a costly experiment, despite construction economies like on-site prefabrication of the tubular steel structure that supports the skin. Exciting architecture may be an acceptable loss leader in a design-conscious city like Miami Beach, but it seems executives of the Publix chain are not taking this show on the road. They consider the store to be a flagship design, not a prototype.

Publix Supermarket is located just a few blocks from Morris Lapidus's new Lincoln Road promenade. Store hours are 7:00 AM to 11:00 PM daily; the phone number is (305) 535-4268.

SANTA FE OPERA THEATER, 1998

Highway 84-285
Santa Fe, New Mexico

Polshek Partnership

Out in the high desert, surrounded by the colorful Sangre de Cristo Mountains, Santa Fe presents one of its strongest attractions—world-class, open-air opera. In the company's original theater, which was only partially roofed, performances were occasionally drenched by spur-of-the-moment cloudbursts (the seats had drain holes!). In the mid-1990s, the opera decided to improve the facilities, despite the fact that their combination of culture and inconvenience had been cheerfully incorporated into Santa Fe's "City Different" mythology. Still, no one wanted to forgo the exhilaration of watching great opera against the backdrop of a Santa Fe sunset, with summer lightning flashing through the evening air.

The new 75,000-square-foot structure marries open-air freedom with technical sophistication. Because the site lies beyond the city's restrictive historic core, the architects were not required to build with adobe. Nevertheless, local architectural tradition was taken into account. The architects anchored the theater on an adobe base, which grounds the dynamic superstructure rising above it.

Seen from afar, this superstructure looks like a modern counterpoint to the ancient mountain landscape. A sweeping two-part roof seems to float above the base, upheld by a series of white-painted cable stays arrayed in peaked formations. The steel-ribbed roof sections—one high, one low—arc gently toward one another. The larger, lower roof begins at the stage, where it is supported by four concrete columns remaining from the old theater. The smaller roof advances from the rear; its slope culminates just above the companion structure. A diaphanous vertical clerestory truss joins these two roof sections, emphasizing their separation and recalling the old theater's legendary gap. Overhanging on two sides, the roofs protect against wind-driven rain. A row of vertical baffles mounted beside the orchestra seats also helps block the elements.

Polshek Partnership, widely heralded for restoring Carnegie Hall, a musical landmark in New York City, where the firm is based, has taken care to heighten the concert-going experience in the diffuse open-air environment. By curving the ceilings, which are clad on their undersides with wood, they have created giant acoustical reflectors that enhance sound quality. A state-of-the-art electronic libretto system displays illuminated text strips on the seat backs.

Besides the opera, Santa Fe offers other contemporary architectural sights: a new arts complex, the Santa Fe Art Institute and Visual Arts Center by Ricardo Legorreta, and the Georgia O'Keeffe Museum, with Richard Gluckman interiors.

The Santa Fe Opera, in season July through August, is located seven miles north of Santa Fe on Highway 84-285. Backstage tours are held in season Monday through Saturday at 1:00 pm. Tickets required. For information, call (505) 986-5900.

I t's a shock, at first, to see the Dominus Winery walls. They look like rubble barely controlled. Natural basalt stones, in colors shading from black to green, press against the thin restraint of gridded wire. The "will-it-hold?" effect is intensified by the two-story stacking. Small rocks, densely packed, compose the base; larger ones are piled loosely on top, with light shining through. Europeans respect

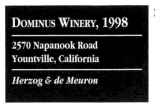

DOMINUS WINERY, 1998

2570 Napanook Road
Yountville, California

Herzog & de Meuron

the strength of these caged-rock structures, called gabions, which are commonplace in road building and river engineering. Swiss architects (and Pritzker Prize winners) Jacques Herzog and Pierre de Meuron bring a double-edged quality of art and architecture to this utilitarian construction.

These avant-garde practitioners say they have created a new architectural element based on nothing more than a simple wall of stones. These "simple walls" blend naturally with the agrarian vineyard setting, for the basalt was quarried near the Napa Valley site. The siting is also the soul

of simplicity. The winery sits long and low on the land, surrounded by the regimented arbor grid and backed by the undulating Macayama foothills. Two perfect rectangular portals splice through the dark structure, opening vistas and emphasizing the building's connection to the earth. By marrying a rustic construction with a sharp-edged linear design, the architects show their grasp of more than one kind of simplicity.

As you might expect, all this simplicity is not so simple after all. The startling gabion exterior is actually a freestanding two-story outer shell, an evocative wrapper for an inner concrete-walled structure of 50,000 square feet. A cutaway in the east wall reveals the structural duplicity. In plan, the long, linear space (over 300 feet long and 82 feet wide) is crystal clear. Large rooms are laid out like dominoes to mimic the three steps of wine-making: fermentation, aging, and storage. Two outdoor portals separate these functional zones. Inside, as outside, clarity is coupled with dramatic tension. The dimly lighted fermentation and storage rooms rise two stories. Glass-walled catwalks upstairs offer heightened views into the lofty, cave-light spaces. They also reveal the perforated portion of the gabion. Crackles of light filter through the fissures, so the minimalistic interiors sparkle. The architects' ability to enliven monastic spaces with light can be appreciated (along with the wine) in the tasting room off the main portal.

Herzog and de Meuron credit Napa Valley hot days and cold nights for inspiring their use of a traditional material to create an advanced design. Rather than automatically relying on air-conditioning, the architects "activated the walls" with gabions to moderate the extremes. "We wanted to design a structure that would take advantage of these conditions."

Dominus Winery is located 50 miles north of San Francisco, a quarter mile off Highway 29, Napa Valley's main road. Dominus hosts architectural tours once a month. Reservations are required. Otherwise, the winery is private. For tour dates and information, call (707) 944-8954.

KLINE HOUSE, 1998

26645 Latigo Shore Drive
Malibu, California

Lorcan O'Herlihy

Lorcan O'Herlihy is a fortunate architect: he is presented with spectacular sites to build on. The Kline house enjoys a prized perch overlooking the Pacific Ocean, and the architect takes it as his inspiration—not just the land but the entire panorama of sun, sand, and sea.

The Kline house seems visibly alert to its dramatic site. The front of the house, which faces both the street and the ocean, presents a series of glass volumes, framed in steel, that step back up the hill. These glass volumes ascend from a concrete base that elevates the living areas so all you see from inside is the view. The architect describes this fragmented design as a "layering of trays," and the layering conforms to the steep vertical topography. The series of glass volumes culminates at the top of the hill with an elliptical guesthouse solidly coated in troweled plaster.

Variations in transparency add architectural interest and solve critical design problems. O'Herlihy installs clear glass when he wants to open the house to the view. But on selected side walls, he installs a special structural channel glass that requires no mullions. This ribbed glass is translucent and lets in an ethereal light and gauzy landscape views while affording privacy. In the main rooms, pivoting glass walls merge inside and out; operable windows mounted above the large fixed panes also heighten the inside-out atmosphere. Garage doors of die-punched metal contribute yet another see-through effect.

In contrast to the open front façade, the rear of the house, with its elliptical plaster-coated guesthouse, is more closed and firmly grounded in the terrain.

Inside the 6,200-square-foot interior, expansive volumes flow smoothly. A wide entrance leads to the living/dining area overlooking the ocean. Two small rear

bedrooms complete this floor. The upper-level master bedroom, aimed at the ocean, is paired with a rear studio. Warm wood floors extend to outdoor decks on both the two main levels.

O'Herlihy is a painter as well as an architect, and he prefers a warm palette of colors and materials. Sensitive to the site, he picks up surrounding natural tones—a natural colored concrete base; glass walls reflecting colors of the light; rusty red canvas canopies and a soft bluish green plaster for the guesthouse.

A dyed-in-the-wool modernist, O'Herlihy finds himself in synch with the times now that modern architecture looks new again. "I attended architecture school from 1976 to 1981, so I escaped the postmodern period in my practice," he says. "My heroes were always Mies van der Rohe and Louis Kahn, even though they were not so popular in my student days. It's interesting to see architecture coming full circle, back to where I started."

The house is a private residence.

L os Angeles, the capital of the moving image, has tackled its people-moving problems with a new subway system in hopes of prying Angelenos from their cars. But there was no guarantee that the transit system would have the desired "build it and they will come" effect. To attract riders to the stations, the Metropolitan Transit Authority allowed more architectural creativity than we generally find in the public realm. Specially constituted architect/artist teams received a challenging brief: create a station that presents a unique image that is also meaningful to the neighborhood. The Metro Red Line Station at Santa Monica and Vermont, at Hollywood's edge, is the most architecturally adventurous thus far.

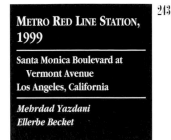

METRO RED LINE STATION, 1999

Santa Monica Boulevard at
   Vermont Avenue
Los Angeles, California

Mehrdad Yazdani
Ellerbe Becket

Because this station is located in a culturally diverse neighborhood, the architect Mehrdad Yazdani and his artist-collaborator Robert Millar sought a strong image that would cross cultural boundaries, and tap residual images, familiar and strange, ancient and modern. "We also wanted something that would evolve over time, helping to draw much-needed commercial and residential development to the area," says Yazdani.

An elliptical steel-and-glass canopy, projecting over a plaza, was their solution, and it became an instantly recognizable, attention-getting icon. "This is a billboard city; that's how we communicate here," Yazdani explains. "We had to have that kind of visibility."

The canopy has an overwhelmingly playful appeal. It is often compared to a fish leaping out of water (the Pacific Ocean is near), about to be caught by "fishing poles"—the tensile red light standards that illuminate the station's brick and glass-block plaza.

Despite this lighthearted character, the design is architecturally rigorous. The stainless steel and glass canopy, which is lighted from within, is 30 feet long and cantilevers 30 feet into the air above a 20,000-square-foot street-level plaza. Its metal sides are perforated to emit pinpoints of light in a grid design. The plaza is inset with glass blocks that filter light to the subterranean structure. An elevator tower on the plaza is sheathed in glass that exposes a steel-tubed frame.

The canopy shades an escalator and staircase leading down to the platform, an inspired design. The walls are ribbed concrete, and they have been treated as the artist's canvas. Using white paint on the concrete surface, Millar has painted ten thousand questions that take up universal themes, one of which is the station's design process itself. A steel stair rail lends a jazzy glint; perforated aluminum ceiling baffles add crisp light; stainless steel platform walls gleam with reflections; and colored fluorescent lights give the whole platform the aura of an art installation.

To visit the station via subway, take the Red Line Train to the Vermont/Santa Monica City College stop. Tickets are sold in vending machines located in the stations.

WINTER SOLSTICE BUILDING, 1999

Sinte Gleska University
1 Spotted Trail Drive
Antelope, South Dakota

RoTo

The adventurous intellectual architecture of RoTo's Michael Rotondi and Clark Stevens in Los Angeles might seem far removed from Antelope, North Dakota, where land is more prevalent than buildings. But these architects believe in generating buildings from the place and the people. In the Sinte Gleska Winter Solstice Building, a science and technology center at the country's oldest Native American university, they sought to capture a distant landscape and heritage without resorting to facile image making or condescending nostalgia. Consequently, RoTo breaks new ground in a vastly neglected architectural arena: rural design.

This land holds crucial meaning for the Sicangu Lakota Indians, whose elders support the school. To them the land is intimately connected to the sun, moon, and stars. It is the source of the tribe's place memory and cultural memory. Storytelling relates the land to the cosmos and to the people: it is through stories that the tribe keeps its ancient heritage alive in the modern age. "Our goal was to design buildings that support the telling of stories," says Clark Stevens. "And

our point is that finding a deeper meaning is an appropriate way to generate a building's design."

A work of architectural allegory, the Winter Solstice Building evolved from a five-year effort to understand the tribal cosmology as relayed in its tales. The siting along the winter solstice axis turns the building into a big calendar, framed by the earth and sky and ignited by the solstice.

An old forked path and a circle on the ground established the geometry of the building, which combines four reclaimed industrial units with a new central structure.

The industrial buildings were mounted in pairs on raised foundations in a formation that relates to two buttes in the Black Hills landscape, linking them sequentially to sun and sky. RoTo's new central space, which contains the student center and the Pipe, bridges the pairs with an asymmetrical timber frame structure clad with galvalume.

The Pipe is the most vibrant and meaningful design, and it lies at the heart of the structure and its stories. An "observatory" shaped like an inverted cone, the Pipe is made of an acrylic resembling rice paper wrapped inside a timber frame. Named for the Pipe Constellation, it lights up at solstice time, mirroring the students' understanding of their cosmology. Other facilities include classrooms and laboratories for life- and physical sciences and information technology; a distance learning broadcasting facility, and faculty offices. The architects literally incorporate the landscape in the buildings by using locally logged timber, assembled with joinery.

Perhaps most important, outsiders gain understanding too—you don't need to know the stories to feel their power coursing through the design. Sinte Gleska University is about two hours south of Pierre by car. For information, call (605) 856-8100.

Glass is all around us, and yet we seldom consciously take note of it. The goal of Henry Smith-Miller and Laurie Hawkinson's design is to make glass more visible—as a building material, light conductor, container, and art object. At Corning, the architects designed a stunning glass-walled entrance pavilion as the centerpiece—and showpiece—of a larger design that incorporates preexisting buildings. Together, the newly configured structures create an expanded home for the company's great cultural resource, the Corning Museum of Glass.

CORNING MUSEUM OF GLASS, 1999

1 Corning Glass Center
Corning, New York

Smith-Miller+Hawkinson

Smith-Miller+Hawkinson's entrance pavilion is a Crystal Palace for the twenty-first century, and it sets the stage for the museum experience. Within the pavilion's glass-walled shell, the architects have installed more glass—soaring sheets of it, tilted and layered like transparent ship's sails hung on delicate, exposed steel supports. Arriving visitors walk through these layers as if they were see-through sculptures, experiencing first-hand the most remarkable properties of this material: its strength, its fragility, and its clarity.

The stellar entrance addition leads to the museum galleries, which feature outstanding exhibits designed by Ralph Appelbaum. In the Glass Innovation Center, occupying the former Visitors Center, Corning presents the world's most comprehensive survey of glass art and technology. The Glass Sculpture Gallery, housed in another existing structure, displays pieces from the company's vast collection, and some of these artworks are amazingly large. Glass-blowing is showcased in an old Bauhaus-style factory, with ongoing demonstrations. The museum complex also includes a theater with an intriguing glass panel screen, a museum shop, and a bridge connecting the buildings.

For all the visibility of the new 117,400–square-foot museum, one of the design's most ingenious aspects is not obvious to newcomers. It is the architects' skillful rethinking of the dysfunctional relationships of the older buildings. They have tied together a disparate lot: the modernist Visitors Center designed by Wallace Harrison in 1951; the amoeba-shaped Gunnar Birkert structure from 1972; and the former factory, another Harrison design. To unify the mismatched architecture, and to rectify the ungainly circulation patterns, Smith-Miller+Hawkinson designed a spectacular glass connection. Known as the West Bridge, this structure solved the problems while adding a dynamic elevated viewing platform that further enhances the visibility of glass.

The museum is open daily from 9:00 AM to 5:00 PM (8:00 PM in July and August). Corning's corporate campus includes a new headquarters building by Kevin Roche, John Dinkeloo and Associates and a day-care center by Scogin, Elam and Bray. The company's all-encompassing glass library is also open to the public. For information, call (607) 937-5371.

VONTZ CENTER FOR MOLECULAR STUDIES, 1999

University of Cincinnati Medical Campus
Martin Luther King Drive at Eden Avenue
Cincinnati, Ohio

Frank O. Gehry

From the moment his Guggenheim Museum opened in Bilbao, Spain, Frank Gehry has enjoyed international super-celebrity. It is a mixed blessing, he says, for he is now constantly confronted with the panic-inducing question: "What will you do for an encore?" But luckily for Gehry's creative process, architecture's near-glacial pace provides a saving grace. By the time Bilbao captivated the world, his "encores," like the Vontz Center, were well underway.

The Vontz Center shows Gehry remaining true to himself: the man who tossed out the T-square in favor of the computer, creating brave new worlds of architectural possibility.

The Vontz Center appears to be freeform, yet these forms are created in the service of highly specific architectural goals. Most obviously, the eccentrically curving, twisting, colliding shapes give the strong identity the building needs to mark a main campus entrance. At the same time, the low-rise surroundings argued against too-great monumentality. Gehry's clustered shapes—a cruciform arrangement three stories tall—break down the scale to fit the context. The exterior design also yields exciting interior spaces. Every office and laboratory is different, although all have high ceilings, and lively light. As Gehry says, "Each space is an episode in itself."

Gehry considers architecture an emotional process with emotional goals as well as physical ones. His unique forms are meant to engage the viewers. Here, he draws you in with a sweep of movement that seems to course through the building like an architectural jet stream.

For all his innovations, Gehry never forgets traditional architectural caretaking. His feeling for materials comes through in the warm brick cladding and the fine steel edging that defines the curved exterior corners. In a telling evoca-

tion of his design process, Gehry says it took a year to choose the brick color. He lavished considerable attention on the windows: no two of them look alike. Some stretch up toward the roofline. Others veer off at odd angles. Many project at an angle from the flat wall surface; others recede from it. Some windows seem to accomplish all of the above.

Perhaps only the iconoclastic Frank Gehry would describe the Vontz Center as simple. "It's just a box," he says, "cracked open with offices running through." In fact, the offices arrayed on the cross's short arm divide the laboratories into two parts. Researchers are seeking cures for cancer and neurological diseases, and Gehry's open-design spaces are meant encourage spontaneous interaction among them.

The campus is open; the building interior is not accessible to the public. For information, call (513) 558-4553.

Come to the Brasserie restaurant to see and be seen, for this building is also watching you. Voyeurism is the design theme, and the architects have a fine time playing with different points of view.

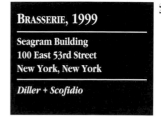

BRASSERIE, 1999

Seagram Building
100 East 53rd Street
New York, New York

Diller + Scofidio

The action starts outside. A hidden camera catches the passing scene and relays it to a plasma monitor behind the hostess's station. This monitor becomes a picture window providing the outside view the basement restaurant lacks. A second camera snaps photos of patrons entering the revolving door and displays them inside like a high-tech receiving line on a "video beam" of fifteen LCD monitors above the bar.

Reaching a table involves further exposure. Diller + Scofidio stage-manage your entry with a long ramplike stairway of green translucent glass steps. But don't be intimidated. It is the sophisticated architecture that steals this show.

The entrance to the 220-seat restaurant opens to a pair of exquisite molded pearwood walls. Pearwood also wraps the dining room's walls and ceiling in a continuous sweep. The bar area on the right, with the video monitor lineup, is the most visually active space. The bar's broad wall of translucent glass doubles as a striking piece of graphic design: behind it the wine bottles lie sideways in regimental rows, with just their ghostly images showing through. Opposite the bar, booths are separated by tall upholstered walls that veer back at a precipitous angle. Tabletops of thick green resin slabs are great to touch as well as see.

In the restrooms, the architects show a playfully subversive streak. They separate the men's and women's rooms with a honeycomb-glass-paneled wall that seems transparent but is actually (and modestly) opaque. The two sexes share a single sink—a sleek burnt-orange resin trough—that spans the spaces though a slot cut in the common wall.

Interest in Elizabeth Diller and Ricardo Scofidio soared in 1999, when the New York City team became the only architects to receive a MacArthur Fellowship (the so-called genius grant). Best known for museum installations and media-savvy theories, they had little built work to show. The Brasserie offers a timely opportunity to experience their high-concept work.

Diller + Scofidio's Brasserie completely replaces Philip Johnson's original scheme. In redesigning this legendary haunt, the architects relished the irony of a windowless basement level space in America's premier glass tower, embarking upon what they described as "a series of contemplations about glass and vision."

The Brasserie is an architectural hotspot in a prime architectural neighborhood (including Lever House, the Museum of Modern Art, and Grand Central Terminal). The restaurant opens daily from 7:00 AM to 1:00 AM. For information and reservations, call (212) 751-4840.

LVMH Tower, 1999

19 East 57th Street
New York, New York

Christian de Portzamparc
with The Hillier Group

In a space barely wider than a townhouse, Christian de Portzamparc has interjected a corporate skyscraper that breathes new life into our stuffiest building type. His light, lilting structure rises 23 stories and has a prismatic façade that draws your eye upward and changes virtually every step of the way.

The tower is the American headquarters of LVMH, the French fashion conglomerate. Portzamparc's intricate design has a stylish, recognizable look, but he successfully avoids the "building as logo" syndrome that seems to strip all the life out of the identity it purports to represent. The façade for LVMH is so lively, in fact, the architect has compared his design to a flower.

The focal point is a blue crystal pyramid located midway up the façade's western side. From there, the "flower petals" unfold. Below the crystal flower, an asymmetrical base segments into two angled volumes that advance toward the street; one is 9 stories, the other, 10. A setback cur-

tain wall rises from this base. On its eastern side, above the base, another faceted origami-like projection bursts out on the diagonal, creating a long zigzag stroke that energizes the entire façade. A light show enlivens the building at night. White lights placed beneath the concrete floors create ghostly outlines visible from the street. And in an especially grand gesture, a diagonal light trough 300 feet tall washes the walls in mutating colors.

The tower's exterior attracts your attention and then pays it off with finely wrought architectural details. The curtain wall, for example, offers considerable variation—a subtle mosaic juxtaposing opalescent, clear, and green-tinted glass in a special nonreflective finish. Refined wedge-shaped panels are sandblasted into the white panes of glass; these panes are further defined with etched horizontal lines that catch the nighttime lights.

Portzamparc, the youngest Pritzker Prize winner to date, has been called a high-wire artist with a sure footing. Perhaps it is this quality that allowed him to produce a significant building under stringent constraints. Not only hemmed in by a sliver site, the architect was also confronted with New York City's setback regulations, notorious for turning city buildings into bulky graph-paper cutouts. Other constraints arose from the design itself and from the client's requirements. Portzamparc's staggered, asymmetrical profile means that every floor has a different footprint. Each of LVMH's corporate entities has its own floor, also complicating the interior designs.

LVMH's corporate offices are private; the lobby and Christian Dior retail store (by Peter Marino) are open to the public. The tower is located near Madison Avenue. As a tantalizing side trip, you might continue up Madison to the Whitney Museum at 74th Street, where Marcel Breuer's jutting "artist's eye" windows will seem like premonitions of LVMH's projecting prism.

When MoMA Design Store opened in 1966, it was the place, that is, the only place, to buy modern design works like Alvar Aalto's fluted crystal vase or Le Corbusier's pony-skin chaise. The shop was located inside the Museum of Modern Art, itself a design mecca: the first museum to display contemporary design objects alongside fine art. But by the 1990s, the shop had lost its luster and its exclusivity. Relocated across the street to a nondescript bank building, it was almost invisible, and once-mesmerizing merchandise no longer seemed special.

MoMA Design Store, 1999

44 West 53rd Street
New York, New York

1100 Architect

1100 Architect put the design back in MoMA's Design Store. The key to the new design is its interactive quality, a give-and-take rhythm that works from inside out. From the street, newly enlarged display windows allow the interior light and action to project outward like an interesting invitation.

Inside, the architects' interactive design makes visitors both spectators and participants in an architectural theater. An undulating wall greets you and lures you subtly into the space. Its frosted Plexiglas shelves embedded with thin horizontal neon bands are bathed in a pure, crisp light that seems to signal your entry into a sort of design heaven. Objects on display are few—some delicate glass bowls and elegant vases— which heightens appreciation of each individual item.

The interactive star is the "virtual mezzanine," a perforated metal screen that advances into the space like a three-dimensional billboard with products wall-mounted behind it. Made of stainless steel weave, the screen pulses with computer-controlled lights that change its surface from transparent to opaque. During the transparent phase, design icons like George Nelson's bubble lamps are illuminated through the scrim. In the opaque phase, images can be projected onto the screen's perforated face.

The virtual mezzanine solves critical problems besides showcasing merchandise, says 1100 Architect's principal Juergen Riehm. By dropping ceiling heights along the side and back walls, it creates a residential scale within the commercial expanse. The poured epoxy floor, an eye-catching "Yves Klein blue," grounds the 5,000-square-foot shop with texture and color.

Juergen Riehm and his partner, David Piscuskas, practice "second glance" design. "The experience of the space should not hit you all at once," Riehm believes. "It should evolve as you spend time there. The MoMA Design Store has a layering and a complexity—this is not an architectural one-liner."

Indeed, the design's strong initial impact almost assures that many details—the intricate lighting balance, the floor's mosaic of blues, the tailored beech rear wall—will come to mind only later.

MoMA Design Store is open daily (including Wednesdays, when the museum is closed); closed on major holidays. Hours are 10:00 AM to 6:30 PM, and until 8:00 PM on Friday. For information, call (212) 767-1050.

U.S. ARMED FORCES RECRUITING STATION, 1999

Times Square
43rd Street between Broadway
and 7th Avenue
New York, New York

Architecture Research Office

The "Americanization" of Times Square is one of the country's most remarkable urban transformations. The burlesque-show atmosphere of decades past has been swept away, replaced by a new, if distinctly corporate, wholesomeness. The area still blazes, but these days, building regulations promote the expected glitz by requiring high-voltage signs—the bigger, the better.

In this gigantic fireworks show, the U.S. Armed Forces Recruiting Station seems like a small jewel. Stephen Cassell and Adam Yarinsky, ARO's principals, countered the intensity with pure simplicity: a rectangular stainless steel and glass structure whose two main façades sport neon American flags. The tiny new building replaces a tiny old building that was known as recruiting central. Generations of young Americans signed up in this spot. The station's large purpose is contradicted by its small site: a triangular traffic median above a subway grate, bounded on all sides by frantic traffic and throbbing neon lights.

"We knew we were creating an icon within an icon, like the clock at Grand Central," Cassell explained. "The American flag design may seem like a one-liner, but in this case it actually makes sense." The design's clarity produces an impact far beyond the building's diminutive size (it's just 520 square feet). Still, neon is the context. "Lights always seemed like the solution," said Cassell.

ARO's Old Glories span the building's two broad sides like illuminated billboards, 33 feet long and 14 feet tall. The flags are created with standard fluorescent lights in a running-bond pattern set in frames attached to the outer glass walls. Reflective gels make the colors.

To "pop out" the flags, the architects downplayed the narrow front and rear elevations. The main entry is a simple glass wall. Metal louvers clad the south side, which houses mechanical equipment (and the fiberoptics to drop the ball on New Year's Eve). The roof is painted camouflage.

The architects impart a subtle sense of motion by slightly staggering the fluorescent lights. Interior bays, which accommodate individual desks for Air Force, Army, Navy, and Marine recruiters, are staggered too. The ceiling introduces a curve into the rectangular space. Even so, indoors most movement comes from the street: cars and people are visible through the clear glass strips between the neon lights.

The U.S. Armed Forces Recruiting Station is open from noon to 7:00 PM, Monday through Friday. For information, call (212) 575-0080. The building's miniscule triangular plaza, defined by reflective bollards painted red, white, and blue ("our landscaping," said Cassell), is a beehive of activity—a band, a speech, a party, something is always going on. See it at night for best results.

Thom Mayne's Diamond Ranch High School is a startling sight. The jagged, corrugated metal buildings seem like bolts of lightening, a far cry from the static, traditional buildings where most Americans spend crucial, formative years. But this is exactly Mayne's point. His innovative design speculates that a challenging, creative environment encourages students to break old molds and forge new paths.

DIAMOND RANCH HIGH SCHOOL, 2000

100 Diamond Ranch Drive
Pomona, California

Thom Mayne, Morphosis

The avant-garde design expresses another simple notion: the school is a community, and interaction between students, teachers, and administrators is beneficial to all. To facilitate camaraderie, the architect organized two-story structures into small clusters arrayed around central courtyards. The clusters are laid out in two long rows, flanking a pedestrian walkway that cuts through the campus. Individual buildings are canted inward toward a central spine in a gesture of outreach, while elevated structures cantilever toward one another like outstretched arms across the open space. The architecture symbolizes the intermingling it seeks to foster, but the lunging forms also create a spatial experience that is visceral.

Mayne has integrated these clustered metal buildings organically into the landscape. This architectural feat is especially impressive because the site is a steep 72-acre hillside considered so unbuildable that it sold for $1. Mayne's angled rooftops echo the San Bernardino Mountains in the distance, and the resemblance between the school and the slopes is uncanny.

In a challenging environment, and on a restricted budget, the architect conceived a new prototype school for California. The 150,000-square-foot campus for 1,200 students includes 50 classrooms, a gymnasium, cafeteria, administrative offices, parking, and athletic playing fields. The soccer field is tucked into the base of the hill and the football field is on top, a design that integrates the playing fields into the school community as well as the site. A monumental concrete stairway, a conduit between the school buildings and the football field doubles as an amphitheater carved out of the hillside.

This is not the first time Thom Mayne has re-envisioned education. As a young architect in 1972, he co-founded the Southern California Institute for Architecture (SCI-Arc) in Los Angeles to combine innovative architectural training with social consciousness. Diamond Ranch also marked a breakthrough in Mayne's career: a transition from forward-thinking houses and interiors to large-scale public projects, including the Caltrans Building in Los Angeles (2004) and New York City's proposed 2012 Olympic Village. After three decades, Mayne's iconoclastic architecture is suddenly becoming mainstream.

Diamond Ranch High School, in Pomona, about 40 miles east of Los Angeles. For visitor information, call the school at (909) 397-4715.

MILWAUKEE ART MUSEUM, 2001

700 North Art Museum Drive
Milwaukee, Wisconsin

Santiago Calatrava

Santiago Calatrava's Milwaukee Art Museum is architecture in action. At noon every day, weather permitting, an enormous birdlike plume on the roof opens as if poised to fly out to sea. This soaring structure is actually an imaginative *brise soleil*—rising 12 stories high with a 217-foot wingspan—and its 72 movable, steel-louvered fins control light and temperature inside the building. Still, it's something to see an apparently stationary building prepare for takeoff.

Calatrava's buildings are unlike any others: they transcend traditional categories. Part architecture, part engineering, part sculpture, these structures recall the dramatic bridges he constructed early in his career in his native Spain. Like the Milwaukee Art Museum, his first building completed in the U.S., his designs are always inspired by nature.

The Lake Michigan siting seems tailor-made for Calatrava's visions. "I have worked to infuse the building with a certain sensitivity to the culture of the lake—the boats, the sails, and the always-changing landscape," he said. Like sails, the museum's buildings are pure white, and they stand out all the more against the blue water.

In this water-oriented design, the Quadracci Pavilion is the anchoring structure. A white concrete parabola, it supports the bird-like *brise soleil* rising from its roof, as well as an angled mast of cables 200 feet high that counterbalances the gigantic mobile sculpture, which weighs 90 tons.

A white suspension bridge links the museum to downtown Minneapolis and provides a suitably dramatic entrance to this extraordinarily dramatic building. The bridge leads visitors into the Quadracci Pavilion, where a grand entrance hall with tall glass windows overlooks the lake. A 90-foot skylight floods the main hall with light and frames a breathtaking view of the *brise soleil* from below.

The Quadracci reception hall leads to galleries in a wavelike structure by Calatrava, and to two older, adjacent buildings. One gallery building is by Eero Saarinen, and its partially elevated design with projecting rectangular galleries from 1957 still looks fresh. In the galleries, a particularly strong Jasper Johns collection is stunningly displayed.

Outdoors, Dan Kiley laid out a series of lawns separated by 10-foot-high hedges. A lighted

water wall connects visually to the lake.

The museum is open daily, 10:00 AM to 5:00 PM, Thursdays until 8:00 PM. Closed Thanksgiving and Christmas. Parking is located in a Calatrava-designed garage so beautiful it could be another gallery. For information, call (414) 224-3220.

For the American Folk Art Museum, Tod Williams and Billie Tsien designed a building that is cool, austere, and moodily lighted—it would seem to offer a barren backdrop for the lively works folk artists create. But what a surprise: the "unsophisticated" homemade objects—quilts, furniture, sculpture, paintings, ceramics, and beadwork—are revealed as immensely sophisticated in this modern setting of concrete, glass, and green cast-resin fiberglass. Pairing cerebral architecture with naive art was a risky strategy, but an inspired one; in 2001, World Architecture magazine named the museum the "Best New Building in the World."

AMERICAN FOLK ART MUSEUM, 2001

45 West 53rd Street
New York, New York

Tod Williams Billie Tsien

For visitors, Williams and Tsien envisioned the museum as an architectural journey, which starts with the façade. Molten-looking white-bronze panels are folded and faceted into a twisted shape that rise up the tall, narrow structure. These panels are manufactured products, but their contrasting textures seem hand-cleaved. The architects achieved this illusion by casting some panels on concrete and others on stone, then juxtaposing the panels to create an abstract, quilt-like pattern akin to the handmade quality of the museum's collection. The architects left open seams between panels to expose a solid wall—the metallic façade is revealed to be a hanging shield, not part of the structure.

Sliver windows on the narrow, 40-foot façade pique the visitor's desire to see what's inside. The entry is angled to encourage visitors to move gracefully through the front door.

Inside, the architects let light be a guide. In the two-story atrium lobby, moody dimness quiets the city's noise and heightens expectations. Intensified by the dimness, lights draw you upward through the four-level atrium, where galleries flank a central open space. Along the way, spotlights help create memorable landmarks, highlighting important pieces of the museum's collection—a weathervane, a Native American statue—displayed at critical junctures. A top-floor skylight offers a suffused inner glow.

The journey theme is underscored by staircases that change in size and positioning. A grand central staircase connects two gallery floors. Other staircases are very narrow, almost residential, and pushed against the walls. The atrium also shape-shifts from floor to floor, and ceiling heights rise and fall. As a result, the 30,000-square-foot space feels different on each of its eight levels.

By carefully integrating folk art with modern architecture, Williams and Tsien emphasize the humane qualities of both. The architects' cherry wood benches and handrails invite the visitors' touch.

The museum is open Tuesday through Sunday from 10:30 AM to 5:30 PM, and Friday until 7:30 PM; closed Monday and holidays. For information, call (212) 977-7170.

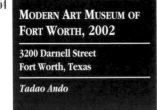

MODERN ART MUSEUM OF FORT WORTH, 2002

3200 Darnell Street
Fort Worth, Texas

Tadao Ando

The site of Fort Worth's new Modern Art Museum was important long before the building appeared. Situated across the street from the Kimbell Museum, Louis Kahn's beloved American masterwork, the site posed a high-stakes challenge for anyone who would build there. Fittingly, in a competition, the museum selected Tadao Ando, the 1995 Pritzker Prize laureate who taught himself architecture by visiting great monuments around the world.

Ando's museum is a powerful work composed of simple elements: concrete, glass, water, and light. It is one of the few American examples of the Japanese architect's signature style, which fuses stark international modernism with an Eastern appreciation of nature, basic materials, and superior craftsmanship.

A spiraling, rust-colored Richard Serra sculpture marks the entrance. Otherwise, viewed from outside, the museum's main façade seems deceptively corporate—a low-slung two-story structure with transparent glass walls framed in metal. But inside, the airy double-height lobby offers an architectural revelation. This huge glass-walled space explodes with natural light and a breathtaking view of an elliptical reflecting pool strewn with stones. Three gallery pavilions extend into the water, which rises so high the buildings appear to be floating. Mammoth Y-shaped pillars 40 feet tall terminate each gallery pavilion and support the roofs. Like Atlas with arms outstretched, the pillars convey Ando's vision of architecture rooted in the earth but reaching for the sky, even as their reflections dissolve into ripples.

The museum is beautifully tailored to its art (the country's second largest contemporary art collection) and to the circulation paths that lead you through it. Ando organized the structure's 153,000 square feet into a logical series of rectangles interspersed with elliptical interludes. Five rectangular pavilions—two long and three short—are laid out parallel with spaces between them. The long bays, in front, contain the lobby, auditorium, museum shop, and an elliptical cafe (with an outdoor terrace beside the reflecting pool). The shorter bays house galleries. The pavilions are double walled, with concrete inner cores surrounded by glass. The separation expresses the Japanese concept engawa, the distinction between inside and out. Occasional glimpses outside to light, water, and an outdoor sculpture court refresh the viewing experience and help prevent museum fatigue.

In the galleries, a sophisticated system of skylights and clerestory windows yields indirect natural light that is sympathetic to the art, but protects the pictures from damaging rays. The building's materials are exquisitely wrought. In Ando's hands, the concrete walls seem like fine silk, a texture achieved by putting ice and chilled water into the concrete mix. Aluminum window frames are bead-blasted and anodized to jewel-like perfection.

The museum is open Tuesday, Wednesday, Thursday, and Saturday 10:00 AM to 5:00 PM; Friday 10:00 AM to 8:00 PM; Sunday 11:00 AM to 5:00 PM; closed Mondays and holidays. For information, call (817) 738-9215.

T he Starlight Theatre, for decades little more than a platform beside a pond, has been transformed into an origami-like building that enacts a performance of its own. On pleasant evenings, the theater's new roof springs into action. With the click of a mouse, its six triangular panels open, one after the other, like the petals of a flower. The slow-motion sequence unfolds quietly (it takes about 12 minutes). Fully opened, the pointed panels frame the sky and

STARLIGHT THEATRE, 2003

Rock Valley College
3301 North Mulford Road
Rockford, Illinois

Studio Gang/O'Donnell

the theater becomes an observatory as well. Closed, the peaked roof panels form the points of a star, reinforcing the theater's long-established name and lending new interest to the concept of theater under the stars.

A light-hearted "constellation wall" supports the ingenious roof. Punched with holes and backlighted, this curved concrete structure has a constellation-like twinkle that greets patrons ascending the wide entrance stairs that run beside it. The 18-foot-tall "wall" actually houses a new box office and restrooms. Open space between the wall and the roof helps retain the old theater's open-air feeling.

"It was like building a bird's nest," said Jeanne Gang, of Studio Gang/O'Donnell (now Studio Gang), a young Chicago architect who worked with Rem Koolhaas in Rotterdam. "We put it together piece by piece."

Because of the theater's summer performance schedule—and Illinois winters—the design was constructed in stages over three years. The renovation increased seating capacity from 600 to over 1,000. The architects also upgraded theater production capabilities with a new rectangular 50-foot-high fly tower clad in copper. As Ms. Gang said, "Out of mundane criteria, we tried to build something beautiful."

The stainless steel roof panels—twenty-six triangles in eleven sizes—are elegant in design as well as appearance. Only six panels open and close; seemingly light as feathers, they weigh 15 tons each and have smooth undersides that hide the screw jacks from view. On the outside, their stainless cladding is a terrific contrast to the fly tower's copper, which has acquired a rusty Cor-Ten-like patina.

Theater-going is a social event, Ms. Gang noted, and Starlight engages its hillside with a variety of levels that encourage personal interaction. Visitors ascend a wide, shallow staircase to enter—a perfect promenade. Terraces and built-in seating extend the mix-and-mingling activities into the surrounding landscape.

Starlight Theatre's season runs from May to October. To see the roof in action (weather permitting), visit in early evening before a performance and stay through the first act. The theater is located an hour west of Chicago's O'Hare Airport. For ticket information, call (815) 921-2160.

ROSENTHAL CENTER FOR CONTEMPORARY ART, 2003

44 East Sixth Street at Walnut Street
Cincinnati, Ohio

Zaha Hadid

Zaha Hadid, the first female Pritzker Prize winner, seemed destined to be a "paper architect." For over twenty-five years, her precedent-shattering designs—often resembling geometric galaxies exploding in space—were confined to paper, paint, and computer screens. With an avant-garde following, imposing personal presence, and penchant for public outbursts, she gained a reputation as the design-world's "diva." Then, in the 1990s, the Baghdad-born, London-based architect finally began to build.

The Rosenthal Center for Contemporary Art is Hadid's first American building. Winning honors from the Royal Institute of British Architects (RIBA) and from WIRED magazine's Rave competition, she successfully penetrated the mainstream without shearing too much off her avant-garde edge.

Here, Hadid's long-proposed ideas of motion and landscape finally come to life. On a corner site, the building is a collage of boxes, some concrete, others blackened aluminum. They zoom in and out, creating an irregular, sculptural façade. The heavy-looking boxes loom over a fragile glass base. Hadid designed the boxes to mimic the neighborhood's street grid, transforming the grid into a three-dimensional shape. (The center's Web site animates this arresting exercise in architectural acrobatics.)

Central to the design is Hadid's "urban carpet," a series of structural devices drawing visitors into and around the building. Starting at the corner of Sixth Street and Walnut, the sidewalk curves slowly upward. On the façade facing Walnut Street, the museum's back wall curves like a skateboard ramp to frame the blocky structure. Inside, the urban carpet becomes a monolithic stair-ramp seemingly suspended in space. It zig-zags up through the building, propelling visitors to the five upper gallery levels of the 85,000-square-foot center, peaking curiosity with each new twist of perspective.

Gallery spaces are torqued in response to the exterior's explosive appearance. No two levels are alike, no two galleries are alike, and it's often difficult to get your bearings. The erratic procession culminates with another explosion on the top floor—this time it's light. Along the way, concrete walls alternate with glass walls that funnel in light and connect with the outdoors.

Hadid believes the building's controlled creative outburst truly represents the needs of the museum, which has no permanent collection and presents only temporary exhibitions. As Hadid said, "The museum conceived as a neutral space is an oxymoron. No space is neutral."

For the museum's director, Charles Desmarais, "Being inside a Zaha Hadid building has a physical effect on your body. It speeds up the pace of your heart and probably elevates your temperature too. It's an exhilarating experience."

The museum is open Monday from 10:00 AM to 9:00 PM; Wednesday through Friday 10:00 AM to 6:00 PM; and Saturday and Sunday 11:00 AM to 6:00 PM. Closed Tuesday and holidays. For group tours, call (513) 345-8420. For information, call (513) 345-8400.

The Walt Disney Concert Hall was a most eagerly anticipated architectural event. Fifteen years in the making, the project teetered from one disaster to another, including cost overruns, urban violence, and an earthquake. Also, much was expected of it. Besides showcasing Los Angeles's Philharmonic Orchestra, the concert hall was meant to invigorate the city's underwhelming downtown scene. Also befitting L.A.'s civic pride, it was high time to celebrate the local architectural hero, whose star turns were turning up almost everywhere but here.

WALT DISNEY CONCERT HALL, 2003

111 South Grand Avenue at First Street
Los Angeles, California

Frank O. Gehry

Contrary to appearances, Disney is not a sequel to Gehry's 1997 masterwork in Bilbao. In 1988, the architect won the competition for the concert hall, to be funded with $50 million by Lillian Disney in honor of her late husband's love of classical music. (The final design dates to 1993.)

A new kind of concert hall, it literally bursts out of its block-sized site: a sculptural interweaving of swooping stainless steel walls on a limestone base. Conceived as a garden in a park, its shape looks different from every angle, and it shimmers a little differently with each subtle variation of the light.

Three entrances exist, each designed to make visitors feel drawn into a work of conceptual art. Especially intriguing is the entrance at the corner of First and Grand, where a grand stairway reminiscent of New York's Metropolitan Museum leads to the high-ceiling lobby walled in glass with spectacular views.

In the concert hall, the exterior's sleek metallic quality turns warmer. Douglas fir clads the walls, which are straight, and the ceiling, which is curved. Gehry's pipe organ, the focal point behind center stage, looks like an artful bundle of kindling. His computer-designed floral carpets and flower-patterned seat fabrics honor Mrs. Disney's appreciation of flowers. Thirty-six foot rear windows and skylights give daytime concerts a special luminance.

Acoustics by the Japanese specialists Nagata retain the superb sound of a traditional "shoebox" hall while allowing Gehry's design flexibility. Seats radiate from the stage in vineyard style: concert-goers can hear everything, and easily see everyone as well.

The concert hall is certainly its own destination; however, within blocks you'll also find Arata Isozaki's Museum of Contemporary Art, Rafael Moneo's Cathedral of Our Lady of the Angels, and Morphosis's Caltrans Building.

The concert hall's lobby, gift shop, and cafe are open daily, even when no concerts are scheduled. For information and concert tickets, call (213) 972-7211.

DIA: BEACON, 2003

3 Beekman Street
Beacon, New York

OpenOffice Architects,
Robert Irwin and others

Dia: Beacon is an architecture traveler's ideal: both the journey and the destination are superb. The museum sits beside the Hudson River in a renovated 1929 Nabisco box printing factory and its rail shed, 60 miles north of New York City. Leaving Grand Central, trains glide along the water, past leafy river towns, providing an atmospheric prelude to the Dia: Beacon experience.

One of the world's largest contemporary arts centers (it's bigger than Bilbao), Dia: Beacon seems more like an enormous working artist's studio. This roll-up-your-shirtsleeves quality reflects the Dia Foundation's unconventional approach to art and to architecture. For decades, the Chelsea-based organization, with its deMenil family connections, generously supported favored artists. Primarily 1960s and '70s groundbreakers like Donald Judd and Walter de Maria, Dia artists created works too big and unorthodox for traditional museums.

Rather than display its rarely seen collection in a famous architect's monument that might outshine the art, the foundation bought the box factory and launched a unique design initiative. Each of Dia's twenty-four artists received his or her own space, and living artists were invited to participate in its design. The artists teamed with OpenOffice, a young artistically-minded New York City architectural firm, with the intention of fitting the art and the architecture to each other.

OpenOffice seems to have barely touched the old buildings, and that's the beauty of the museum. The old red-brick factory was almost mystically sympathetic to the art as it was. The high ceilings, broad spans between columns, ninety north-light skylights, and wooden floors resembled SoHo lofts, where much Dia art actually originated.

The architects' subtle achievement is creating visceral spatial experiences throughout the museum's 300,000 square feet. Richard Serra's towering rusty Torqued Ellipses feel intimate in their tall narrow confines, while vast exhibits like Michael Heizner's huge sunken geometric voids produce vertiginous frissons. The old gridded factory windows also catch your eye; clear and sandblasted panes are juxtaposed to blur inside and out. As OpenOffice's Linda Taalman said, "The architecture is not a neutral presence, it is an active presence—but it is a stealth active presence."

Robert Irwin, an artist and garden designer (of Getty Museum garden fame) choreographed the site. Visitors descend a hill to a regimental orchard of flowering trees, followed by a "grass-crete" forecourt with grass popping out of a concrete grid. The entrance, a curious intermingling of ticket counter, bookstore, and cafe, is downplayed, emphasizing the big spaces and big art to come. A casual atmosphere prevails. Visitors feel free to wander in Dia: Beacon's generous space and natural light, appreciating the wonderful way in which the art and the architecture bond together.

From April 15 to October 14, museum hours are Thursday through Monday, 11:00 AM to 6:00 PM; from October 15 to April 14, museum hours are Friday thorough Monday, 11:00 AM to 4:00 PM. MTA/Metro-North trains run frequently from Grand Central (grab a left-side seat going out to catch a view of the river). For information, call (845) 440-0100.

"In my own mind, I am as much a writer as an architect," said Rem Koolhaas, the Dutch-born Pritzker Prize laureate whose books—*Delirious New York* and *S, M, L and XL*—are cult favorites. And so, the visionary writer/architect has created a building to dazzle readers and architects alike. In his first major U.S. work, Koolhaas makes learning look cool.

SEATTLE CENTRAL LIBRARY, 2004

1000 Fourth Avenue
Seattle, Washington

Rem Koolhaas, Office of Metropolitan Architecture

The Seattle Central Library resembles an off-kilter icecap that fills a city block. Wrapped in a dynamic lattice of blue-painted steel and glass, it would cover five football fields if laid flat. But flat it is not. The 11 stories fold and lunge, with asymmetrical angles and top-heavy projections unique on each side.

The unconventional exterior heralds a library for the information age. There are four hundred computers and wireless technology, yet books are still the heart of the new structure. Koolhaas's core idea—and the building's physical core—is called "The Book Spiral": four levels of continuous shelving connected by ramps, like a parking garage. This endless-shelf configuration frees librarians from having to break up the Dewey Decimal category when linear shelves become full. For readers, the spiral structure encourages browsing and serendipitous discoveries. (The spiral structure is easiest to see at night, when it's illuminated.)

With gridded glass walls, the library is open and translucent, and its inner liveliness is visible from the street. Visitors entering on Fifth Street encounter the greenhouse-like Reading Room, a soaring light-filled atrium with a garden-patterned carpet by Petra Blaisse, a large indoor planter of grasses and ferns, and chairs upholstered in purple and pink.

From the main floor, a fluorescent chartreuse escalator ascends to "The Mixing Chamber," Koolhaas's version of the reference/circulation area, where librarians and computers offer assistance. This area prepares visitors for the Book Spiral platforms located just above. Atop the Book Spiral, on the 10th level, another magnificent reading room awaits, this one with water views. The uppermost floor houses administration. In some areas, slanted, glass-gridded walls mutate into "floors" you can see through. Throughout the building, all vertical circulation is color-coded chartreuse, except one stairway that is lipstick red.

Koolhaas has integrated practical considerations into the architectural effects. The steel lattice provides seismic bracing for earthquake protection; glass panes contain metal-filtered sunscreens to help safeguard books and conserve energy.

The Seattle Central Library is open Monday through Wednesday, 10:00 AM to 8:00 PM, Thursday to Saturday, 10:00 AM to 6:00 PM, and Sundays 1:00 to 5:00 PM; closed holidays. Parking is located on the lower level. For information, call (206) 386-4636.

"SOLAR UMBRELLA" RESIDENCE, 2004

616 Boccaccio Avenue
Venice, California

Angela Brooks and Lawrence Scarpa

Los Angeles is famous for its innovative houses, especially the ones architects design for themselves. With "Solar Umbrella," Angela Brooks and Lawrence Scarpa helped launch a new generation of architectural innovation, one that embraces solar power as an integral element of sophisticated modern design. Casting off frumpy hippie-era perceptions, the husband-and-wife team shows that a house can be energy efficient and look good, too.

In designing the two-story, 2,200-square-foot addition to their 1930s bungalow, the architects recalled Paul Rudolph's "Umbrella House" in Florida, where tomato stakes shade the roof. Brooks and Scarpa mounted solar panels in rusted steel beams to protect the roof and create a crisp modernist frame for the façade. Framed photovoltaic panels

hang from a side wall like a vertical shield.

The façade is a work of abstract art. A vertical concrete slab, impressed with ghost images of eucalyptus leaves, rises on the left. It is offset by a hanging screen of industrial broom bristles tied to a rusted steel frame and by the large, recessed glass living room wall. In the California tradition, the distinction between inside and out virtually disappears.

Visitors enter an enclosed front courtyard through a rusted steel gate. A large, square green lawn ringed with gravel is inset with a small square swimming pool. A rectangular reflecting pool near the door reinvents the welcome mat; stepping stones give the sensation of walking on water.

The main living space overlooks the courtyard, and the inside/out atmosphere fills the open interior. The lofty space has concrete walls and floors and cherry built-ins. A perforated metal staircase floats up to the master bedroom, which overlooks the garden and a private terrace. Clerestory windows and a central skylight bring extra light.

"The technology is all there, people just don't know how to use it," said Scarpa, a partner with his wife in Pugh+Scarpa Architects, a 2003 World Habitat Award finalist. "We simply took standard materials and recycled materials and repositioned them as design elements."

A photovoltaic solar system powers the house. It generates electricity that flows to the utility company's grid, which returns it as needed. In-floor radiant heating and high-efficiency appliances also help. The monthly energy bill is zero.

The architects also utilized passive energy conservation strategies, including proper siting, insulation, and tight construction. Recycled materials predominate. Studs are recycled steel; some floors are concrete, other are covered with oriented strand board. Kitchen walls and cabinets are homosote, recycled newspaper sanded to silkiness. Outside, drought-tolerant plants are ecologically appropriate and are starkly compatible with the modern design.

At night, the "Solar Umbrella" is spectacular. A strip of gas fire blazes along the front courtyard fence; the living room fireplace crackles; light shines through the perforated staircase creating Sigmar Polke-style graphic effects; the skylight glows purple. You'd never guess this fascinating house is a paragon of energy efficiency. The house is a private residence.

Not since the mid-century Case Study Houses in Los Angeles has there been such an orchestrated attempt to bring modern architecture to modern houses. On the eastern tip of Long Island, known as the Hamptons, the developer Harry J. "Coco" Brown has conjured a real-life design laboratory in the guise of a 100-acre subdivision of speculative vacation homes. With his friend Richard Meier, he selected an "all-starchitect" cast of thirty innovative practitioners. Each architect was assigned an individual lot and told to let their imagination run free. Brown's utopian enclave, in a rather less desirable part of a celebrity-encrusted locale, quickly came to be called "Sagatopia."

The houses are small by Hamptons' standards—just 2,000 to 4,500 square feet on lots of one-and-a-half to three acres—but that is partly the point. Brown views the residences as livable, eco-friendly antidotes to Hamptons McMansions, where supersizing Shingle-style replicas is a local sport.

The first five "unHampton" houses were begun in 2004, with real architecture as promised. Gisue and Mojgan Hariri's residence, the first completed structure, featured a sleek L-shaped swath of cedar and glass. I. M. Pei partner Henry Cobb completed his first house, a Buddhist-like structure with individual pavilions and 108 louvered doors. Shigeru Ban, Japan's "Best Young Architect" in 1997, designed a house supported by cabinets and bookcases and surrounded by stands of bamboo. Annabelle Selldorf's design has outdoor rooms merged with a garden. And Stan Allen, Princeton's Dean of Architecture, produced an all-white horizontal house with prominent light scoops protruding above the roof (pictured here).

In the next phase of the project, new house designs will come from international talents like Sir Richard Rogers and Zaha Hadid of London and Antonio Cittero of Milan. The hefty East Coast contingent will include Peter Eisenman, Charles Gwathmey, James Inigo Freed, Tsao & McKown, Jacquelin T. Robertson, Smith-Miller + Hawkinson, Deborah Berke, Richard Gluckman, and Steven Holl. Young New York architects including Reiser & Umemoto and Lindy Roy are expected to produce exceptionally innovative designs. Richard Meier may build his own house.

West Coast architects Mark Mack, Eric Owen Moss, Hodgetts + Fung, Stephen Kanner, and Michael Rotondi, along with Houston's Carlos Jimenez and Phoenix-based architect Marwan Al-Sayed, have also agreed to design new houses.

The development is north of Montauk Highway (Route 27), midway between Southampton and East Hampton. Driving east on Route 27, past Bridgehampton and immediately past Poxchogue Golf Course, turn left onto Wainscott Harbor Road. The new houses, interspersed with preexisting ones, are found on Wainscott Harbor Road, East Woods Path, and Forest Crossing. All are private residences. For information, call The Brown Companies at (212) 683-4400.

GREENWICH STREET [PROJECT], 2004

497 Greenwich Street
New York, New York

*Winka Dubbeldam,
Archi-Tectonics*

Winka Dubbeldam's Greenwich Street [Project] is a freeze-frame presentation of a lower Manhattan neighborhood's transformation from an industrial waterfront warehouse district to a high-end residential zone, where the water view is an expensive amenity.

Dubbeldam's 11-story condominium in the far West Village has a crystalline glass façade that resembles artfully crumpled paper. Each floor slab is defined by a protruding, horizontal silver fin. This futuristic design could only have been created on the computer, yet it is joined to an old red brick warehouse erected a hundred years ago.

It must have been tempting to demolish the industrial relic, which filled roughly a third of the building site. Instead, Dubbeldam chose to work with the old structure, incorporating it into her new design. The warehouse floors were converted to loft-like apartments with the structural timbers left exposed—chalk marks and all. Above the warehouse, the architect added a four-story extension, superimposing her glass and steel construction across the top of the old roof. The juncture between the two buildings is marked with a vertical "crease" of small cantilevered balconies—just right, the architect said, for champagne for two.

While Dubbeldam designs in cyberspace, it's interesting to see that in real life her serpentine blue-green glass façade seems intuitively linked to the Hudson River three blocks away. After sloping backward at ground level, the 10,000-square-foot curtain-wall façade undulates upward. (Its curvatures were carefully planned to meet city setback requirements.) The glass is mounted on free-standing steel columns. From inside, the curves of the glass act like lenses, creating gentle distortions of the view. Rooftop terraces are wrapped in transparent glass to express ephemeral glass volumes, rather than a parapet's solidity.

In this, her first major public building, Dubbeldam sought out new materials and methods from around the world. The window frames come from Norway, the glass was bent in Barcelona, the aluminum fins were extruded in Hong Kong, and the pieces were assembled in Brooklyn. Side walls and the lobby wall are constructed of Anchor, a new high-density concrete block manufactured in New Jersey.

A New York-based architect, Dubbeldam was born near Rotterdam and is part of the Dutch explosion of innovative modern architects whose primary design tool is the computer. In 2004, she participated in the Venice Architecture Biennale. She has also worked with some of the profession's most cerebral practitioners, including Rem Koolhaas, Steven Holl, and Peter Eisenman. Her adventurous spirit is evident in the building's lobby, which resembles an art gallery, displaying the interactive artworks Dubbeldam has picked for the walls.

The neighborhood pops with new, architecturally significant residential buildings, including Richard Meier's Perry Street apartment towers and an apartment building by Philip Johnson at Spring and Washington Streets.

The Greenwich Street [Project] lobby is accessible to visitors. A commercial art gallery is planned for the ground floor retail space. For information, call (212) 334-8080.

At Millennium Park, architecture finally comes out to play. Frank Gehry has designed a jubilant setting for outdoor summer concerts at the Pritzker Pavilion, a bandshell crowned with billowing stainless steel streamers, overlooking a cheerful green lawn spanned by a domed trellis. Gehry's joyful spirit is contagious, animating a new kind of park—an urban space where the art, architecture, and landscape invite you to participate and to take pleasure in the artistic interaction.

MILLENNIUM PARK, 2004

Michigan Avenue, between
    Randolph and Crown Streets
Chicago, Illinois

Frank O. Gehry and others

Millennium Park is like Bilbao, but better. Overlooking Lake Michigan in downtown Chicago, the 25-acre park replaced old rail yards and parking lots with a spectacular civic attraction that includes original artwork. Besides Gehry's amphitheater, the high points include a silvery bean-shaped sculpture by British artist Anish Kapoor, a pair of glass-block tower fountains that display video portraits, by Barcelona artist Jaume Plensa, and a Kathryn Gustafson garden.

Gehry's outdoor amphitheater is his first Chicago building, and it's clearly a signature piece, with swirling stainless steel forms 120 feet tall. The billows seem solid, like the Walt Disney Concert Hall, but they're actually shells whose structure is exposed in plain sight around the back. The amphitheater is home to the Grant Park Symphony, seating 4,000 people and accommodating 7,000 sprawlers on the vast lawn. Thanks to Gehry's innovative steel pipe trellis, which supports a speaker system with high-quality sound, the lawn doesn't feel like Siberia.

A pedestrian bridge with stainless steel walls meanders alongside the park and across Columbus Drive. An elevated platform from which to gain different perspectives of Gehry's larger design, its 925-foot length is also an impromptu mezzanine where people gather during concerts (without the enhanced acoustics).

The curvaceous silver theme continues in Anish Kapoor's Cloud Gate sculpture, which weights 110 tons but seems to dissolve into thin air as you approach it. Blurring art and architecture, the gigantic sculpture touches down at two points, with an arch in the middle that you can walk through. With every step, the highly polished curved surface catches your reflection like a funhouse mirror, along with Chicago's vintage skyscrapers on the park's periphery. While it's among the largest sculptures in the world—66 feet long and 33 feet high—Chicagoans simply called it "Da Bean."

Juame Plensa's Crown Fountain also blends art and architecture with a playful spirit. On two huge video screens, which are inset into a pair of glass-block towers flanking a reflecting pond, Plensa displays a succession of faces belonging to Chicago residents. At the end of each video sequence, a jet of water pours gargoyle-style from the person's mouth into the central pool.

The park is open daily from 6:00 AM to 11:00 PM. The Chicago Architecture Foundation, across the street at 224 South Michigan, conducts tours twice weekly from May to mid-December. For tour information, call (312) 922-3432.

INDEX OF ARCHITECTS

INDEX OF LOCATIONS AND WEB SITES

MAPS

The maps will help you in organizing architectural tours of specific areas. The map of the United States has been divided into nine parts, each of which shows the approximate geographical location of all the projects featured in this book. Numbers on the map refer to the buildings' page numbers. Names of cities and towns, as well as interstate, U.S., and state highways, are also provided. Keep in mind that these maps are not substitutes for local road atlases. Once you've located the area(s) you'd like to visit, refer to a more detailed map for accurate driving instructions.

LEGEND

00 Page number of building

(00) Interstate highway

(00) U.S. or state highway

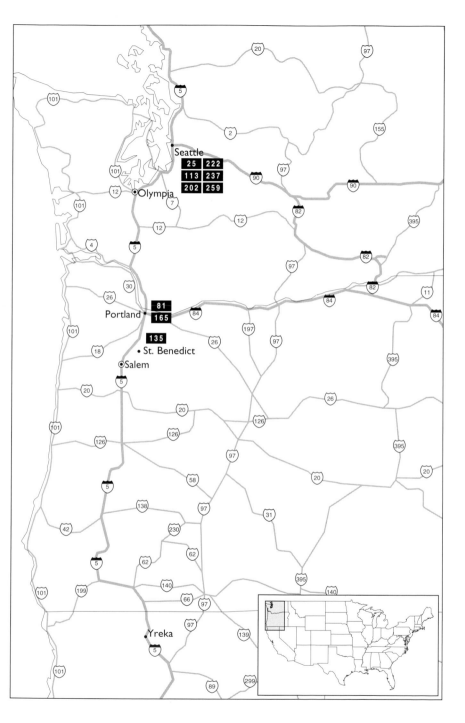

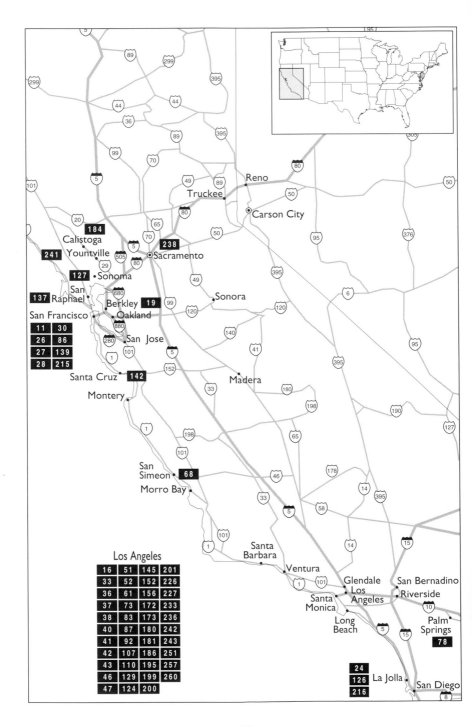

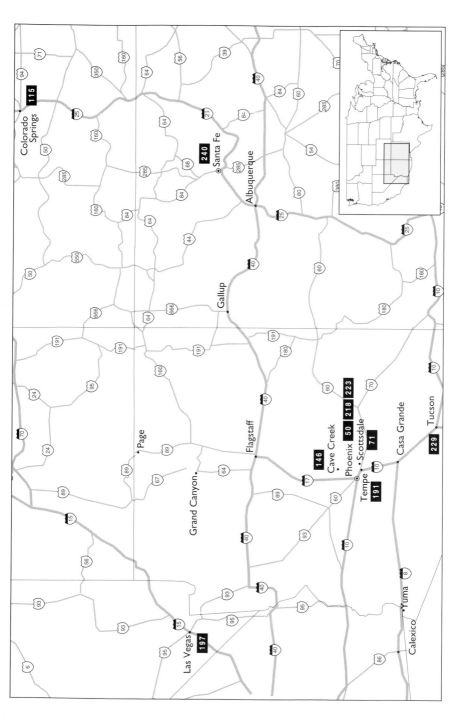

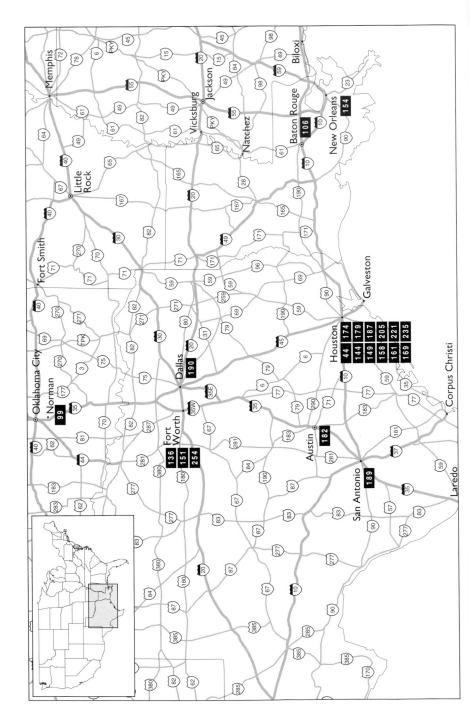

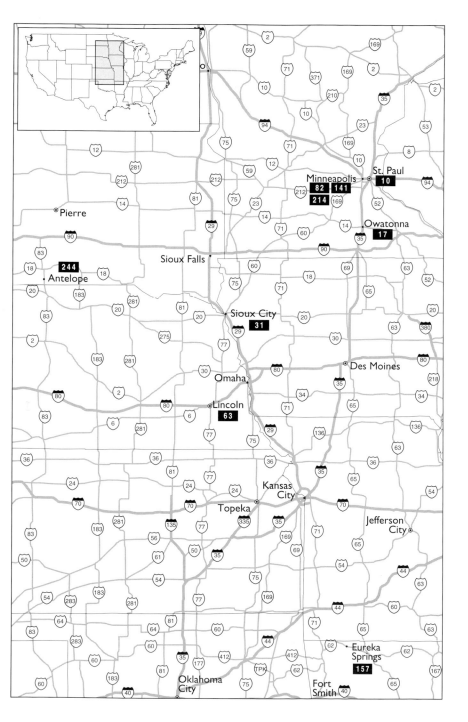

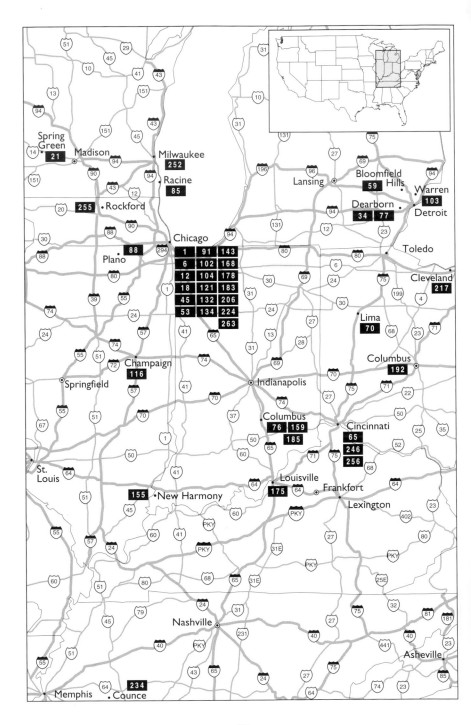

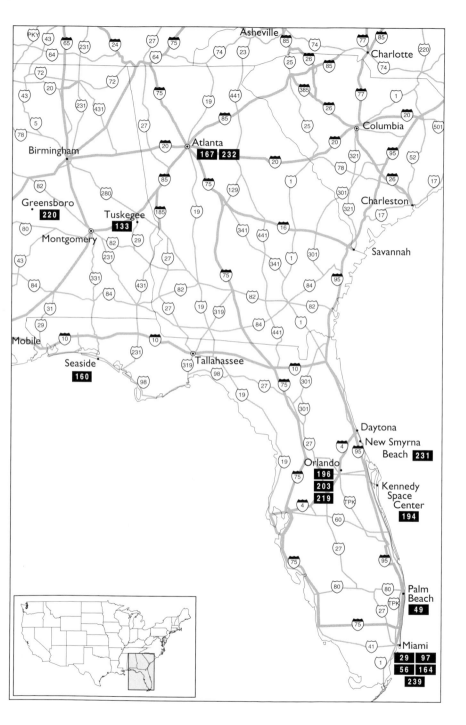

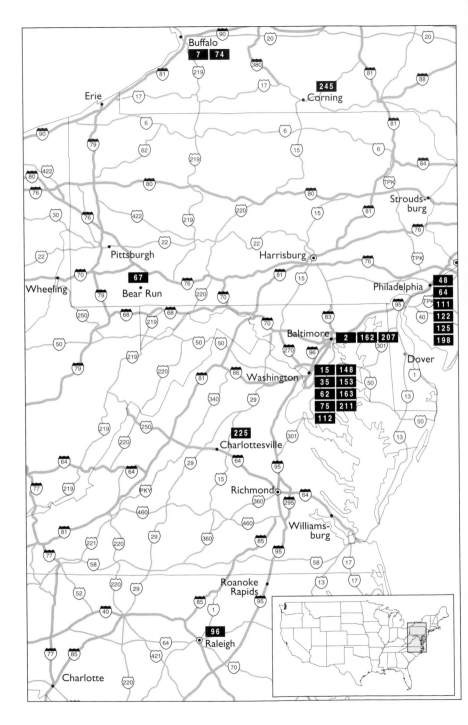

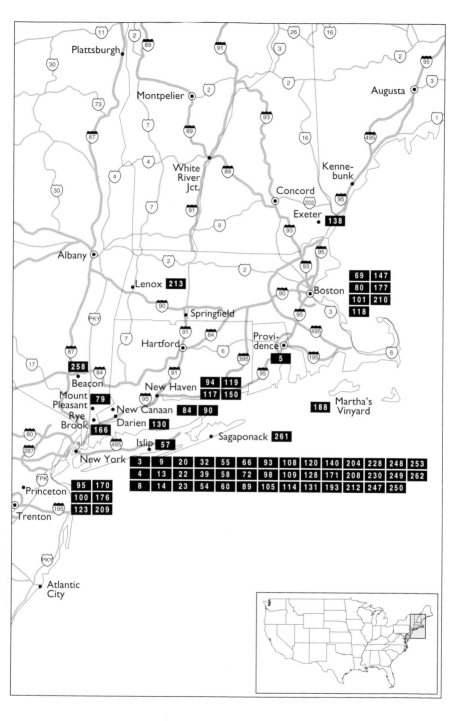

ART AND PHOTOGRAPHY CREDITS

The photographs on the pages listed below appear courtesy of the following photographers, foundations, museums, and organizations.

1 Photo by Don Kalec, courtesy of Frank Lloyd Wright Home and Studio Foundation

3 Metropolitan Museum of Art

5 Photo by Alec Tavares

6 Library of Congress, Prints and Photographs Division, HABS Collection

7 Buffalo and Erie County Historical Society

8 Library of Congress, Prints and Photographs Division

10 Library of Congress, Prints and Photographs Division

11 Fairmont Hotel

12 Frank Lloyd Wright Home and Studio Foundation

15 LaSalle Partners

16 Photo by Tavo Olmos, courtesy of Gamble House

17 © Edward S. Cunningham Photography, Owatonna, Minnesota. Courtesy of Norwest Bank

18 Library of Congress, Prints and Photographs Division, HABS Collection

19 Photo by Julius Shulman

20 Casey Cronin © 1990

21 © 1988 Frank Lloyd Wright Foundation

22 Grand Central Partnership

23 Woolworth Corporation

24 La Jolla Historical Society

25 Museum of History and Industry, Seattle, Washington

29 Vizcaya Museum & Gardens

31 Photo courtesy of Woodbury County; drawing courtesy of Wetherell-Ericsson Architects (retracing of original from 1916)

34 Albert Kahn Associates

35 Library of Congress, Prints and Photographs Division

36 Photo by Julius Shulman

40 Photo by Julius Shulman © 1982

41 Photo by Julius Shulman

42 Photos by Foaad Farah, courtesy of Hardy Holzman Pfeiffer Associates

43 Photo by Julius Shulman

44 Photo by Rick Gardner, courtesy of Museum of Fine Arts, Houston

45 The Chicago Tribune

46 Mann Theaters

47 Library of Congress, Prints and Photographs Division

48 Philadelphia Museum of Art

49 K.U.K.Y.

50 Arizona Biltmore Hotel

51 Photo by Julius Shulman

52 Photo by Julius Shulman

53 Chicago Board of Trade

54 Cooke Properties Inc. and William A. Bassett, Jr.

55 New Jersey Institute of Technology

56 Top: Miami Design Preservation League
Bottom: K.U.K.Y.

57 Photo by Michael Schwarting, New York Institute of Technology

58 Howard J. Rubenstein Associates, Inc.

59 Cranbrook Academy of Art

62 Photo by Julie Ainsworth, courtesy of Folger Shakespeare Library

63 Photo by Jim Holm, courtesy of State of Nebraska

64 Philadelphia Savings Fund Society

65 Cincinnati Historical Society

66 Chicago Board of Trade

67 Photo by Harold Corsini, courtesy of Western Pennsylvania Conservancy

68 Photo by Ken Raveill, courtesy of Hearst San Simeon State Historical Monument

69 Photo by J. David Bohl, courtesy of the Society for the Preservation of New England Antiquities

70 Photo by Hedrich-Blessing, courtesy of Albert Kahn Associates, Architects & Engineers; Detroit, Michigan

71 Frank Lloyd Wright Foundation

72 Top: Edward Durrell Stone Associates PC
Bottom: Timothy Hursley

74 Kleinhans Music Hall

75 Library of Congress, Prints and Photographs Division

76 Balthazar Korab Limited, courtesy of the Columbus Visitors Center

77 © 1960 The Estate of Buckminster Fuller. Courtesy of Buckminster Fuller Institute, Los Angeles

78 Photo by Julius Shulman

79 Photo by Pedro E. Guerrero

80 MIT News Office

81 Far West Federal

82 Christ Church Lutheran

83 Photo by Julius Shulman

84 Photo by Ezra Stoller, courtesy of Philip Johnson

85 Library of Congress, Prints and Photographs Division, HABS Collection

88 Jon Miller, Hedrich Blessing, courtesy of Landmarks Preservation Council of Illinois

89 UN photo. 103 905 Y. Nagata/ARA. Courtesy of United Nations

90 Photo by Nick Wheeler. Original House (1951): Marcel Breuer, architect. Renovations and additions (1979 and 1981): Herbert Beckhard, architect. Courtesy of Herbert Beckhard

91 New Jersey Institute of Technology

92 Wayfarer's Chapel, Rev. Harvey A. Tafel

93 Photo by Julius Shulman

94 Courtesy of Yale University Art Gallery, New Haven, Conn.

95 Lawrence Tarantino AIA

96 Eduardo Catalano

97 Morris Lapidus, architect

98 Photo by Michael DiVito, courtesy of Chemical Banking Corporation

99 Photo by E.J. Deighton, courtesy of the Fred Jones Jr. Museum of Art, University of Oklahoma

101 MIT News Office

102 Illinois Institute of Technology

103 General Motors Corporation

104 Inland Steel Industries Inc.

105 Seagram Building, 1956-58. Architects: Ludwig Mies van der Rohe and Philip Johnson. Photo by Ezra Stoller, 1958. Lent by Joseph E. Seagram & Sons, Inc.

106 © 1960 The Estate of Buckminster Fuller. Courtesy of Buckminster Fuller Institute, Los Angeles

107 Photo by Julius Shulman

109 Ezra Stoller Associates

110 Photo by Julius Shulman

112 New Jersey Institute of Technology

113 John Graham Associates/DLR Group

114 TWA

115 United States Air Force Academy

116 Assembly Hall, University of Illinois

117 Beinecke Library. Ezra Stoller/Esto

118 Andrés Batista

119 Photo by Roberto de Alba

120 Edward Durrell Stone Associates PC

121 Photo by Hedrich-Blessing, courtesy of Bertrand Goldberg Associates Inc.

122 Photo by Rollin LaFrance, courtesy of Venturi Scott Brown and Associates Inc.

126 The Salk Institute

127 Charles W. Moore Archives

128 The Whitney Museum

129 Photo by Julius Shulman, courtesy of J. Paul Getty Trust

130 Ezra Stoller/Esto, courtesy of Richard Meier & Partners

132 Photo by Tony Soluri

133 Paul Rudolph

134 Photo by Hedrich-Blessing, courtesy of U.S. Equities Realty Inc.

135 Exterior photo by Vincent Zollner, courtesy of Mt. Angel Abbey

136 Photo by Michael Bodycomb, courtesy of Kimbell Art Museum

137 Photo by Roberto de Alba

138 Herndon Associates, courtesy of The Library, Phillips Exeter Academy

139 Photo by Julius Shulman

140 Lower Manhattan Development Corporation

141 Top: New Jersey Institute of Technology
Bottom: Federal Reserve Bank of Minneapolis

143 Sears Roebuck and Company

144 SITE Projects, Inc.

145 Photo by Tom Bonner, courtesy of Pacific Design Center

146 The Cosanti Foundation

147 Gorchev & Gorchev, courtesy of John Hancock

148 National Air and Space Museum

149 Richard Payne, AIA, courtesy of Philip Johnson and John Burgee

150 Photo by Thomas A. Brown, courtesy of Yale Center for British Art

151 Paul Rudolph

152 Photo by Tom Marble

153 National Air and Space Museum

155 Photo by Ezra Stoller/Esto, courtesy of Richard Meier & Partners

156 Photo by Richard Payne, courtesy of Philip Johnson and John Burgee

157 E. Fay Jones

159 Balthazar Korab Limited, courtesy of the Columbus Visitors Center

160 © Steven Brooke, courtesy of Seaside

161 Taft Architects

162 George Grall

163 Peter Aaron/Esto

164 © 1982 Norman McGrath

165 Photo by Paschall/Taylor, courtesy of Michael Graves, Architect

166 Philip Morris

167 Photo by Ezra Stoller/Esto, courtesy of Richard Meier & Partners

168 Photo by Barbara Karant, courtesy of Kohn Pederson Fox

169 Photo © Richard Payne, courtesy of Philip Johnson and John Burgee

171 Photo © Richard Payne, courtesy of Philip Johnson and John Burgee

172 California Museum of Science and Industry

173 Loyola Law School

175 Photo by Paschall/Taylor, courtesy of Michael Graves, Architect

176 PA consulting group

177 Andrés Batista

178 Murphy/Jahn

181 Top: Photo by Kurt Gunther, courtesy of Paladino & Associates Bottom: Photo by Tom Marble

183 Photo by Timothy Hursley, courtesy of Murphy/Jahn

184 Photo by Paschall/Taylor, courtesy of Michael Graves, Architect

185 Photo by Timothy Hursley, courtesy of Susanna Torre

186 Koning Eizenberg Architecture

187 Hickey & Robertson, Houston, courtesy the Menil Collection

188 Photo by Paul Warchol, courtesy of Steven Holl

189 San Antonio Botanical Center

190 Photo © Richard Payne, courtesy of Pei, Cobb, Freed & Partners

191 Photo by Lin Waldron, courtesy of Nelson Fine Arts Center

192 Kevin Fitzsimons/Wexner Center for the Arts

193 Photo by Wolfgang Hoyt, courtesy of Olympia & York Companies (U.S.A.)

194 Photo courtesy of The Astronauts Memorial Foundation

195 Timothy Hursley

196 Courtesy of Tishman Realty & Construction Co., Inc.

197 Antoine Predock Architect FAIA

198 Photo by Peter Olson, courtesy of Mandell Futures Center

199 Photo © M. Robert Markovich

200 Photo by Donatella Brun, courtesy of Chiat/Day

201 Drawing courtesy of Eric Owen Moss Architects Photo by Todd Conversano © 1990, courtesy of Eric Owen Moss Architects

202 Photo by Matt Wargo, courtesy of Venturi, Scott Brown and Associates Inc.

203 © The Walt Disney Company, photo by Susan E. Mitchell

204 Drawing by Gregory Ihnatowicz

206 Photo courtesy of Hammond Beeby and Babka, Inc.

207 Jeff Goldberg/Esto

208 Photo by J. Goltz, courtesy of The National Audubon Society

209 Chuck Choi

210 Scott Frances/Esto

212 Jeff Goldberg/Esto

213 Photos by Steve Rosenthal, courtesy of William Rawn Associates

214 Chris Faust

215 ©SFMOMA/Richard Barnes

216 Bill Timmerman

217 Bill Schuemann Architectural Photography

218 Timothy Hursley

219 Photo by Susan Mitchell, ©Walt Disney Co.

220 Timothy Hursley

221 Photo by Hickey-Robertson

222 © J. F. Housel

223 Bill Timmerman

224 Photo by Steve Hall, © Hedrich Blessing

225 Courtesy of Darden Graduate School of Business Administration, photo by Jack Mellott

226 Photo by Tom Bonner

227 Courtesy of RoTo Architects

228 Peter Aaron/Esto

229 Bill Timmerman

230 Photo by Michael Lent

231 Photo by Chuck Choi

232 Timothy Hursley

233 © J. Paul Getty Trust

234 Timothy Hursley

235 Photo by Paul Warchol

236 Photo by Michael Webb

237 Courtesy of Seattle University

238 © Antonio Garbasso

239 Jeff Goldberg/Esto

240 Photo by Robert Reck

241 Timothy Hursley

242 Conrad Johnson

243 Timothy Hursley

244 Benny Chan/Fotoworks

245 Scott Frances/Esto

246 Courtesy of University of Cincinnati Medical Center Public Relations and Communications